PASSING THE BUCK

Coleman Francis and Other Cinematic Metaphysicians

James J. O'Meara

978-0-6487660-9-4
Passing the Buck: Coleman Francis and Other Cinematic Metaphysicians.
James J. O'Meara.

Cover image: William Holman Hunt, *The Scapegoat*, 1854, oil on canvas.

Thema Classification: ATF (Film & Cinema), QTDJ (Metaphysics)

MANTICORE PRESS
WWW.MANTICORE.PRESS

Contents

"A Christian cannot pass the buck and blame another. Christianity is built upon the foundation that all are one. That man is forever drawing conformation of what he is doing within himself. That your world bears witness to what you are doing to yourself. This is difficult to accept, yet it is Christianity."

– Neville Goddard, *"The Secret of Prayer"*

"Naturally all men desire to pass the buck."

– Ezra Pound, *ABC of Economics*, Ch. II

""Not to be a good man, but to become a god – this is the aim."

– Plotinus, *Enneads* 1.2.4,7

"Virtuous and devout men go to 'heaven' – but a different path is taken by the Awakened Ones."

– *Dhammapada* 126

Preface

THIS COMPILATION REPACKAGES a series of essays on films, famous and unknown, that appeared over several years on the Counter-Currents website, in order to bring them to a broader audience. Constant Readers may be assured that they have been gone through with a fine-tooth comb, updated, corrected in the unlikely event an error has been found, and on occasion modified to reflect later, even better thoughts.

I call these "essays" rather than "reviews" because in each case the film, although always center stage, is mostly a jumping off point. The films were selected — or rather, demanded to be addressed — not for their merits, which are various and disputed, but for two metaphysical themes they reveal and exemplify: first, repetition, which is both a theme and the means — compulsive re-watching — whereby such themes were brought to the surface; and second, what I have chosen to call *Passing the Buck*: rising to a higher level of existence through the disposal of their karma, mainly by dumping it on some other poor sucker.[1]

I recall with pleasure a sake-fueled dining experience with Collin Cleary in New York's East Village, where we discussed the question of whether such themes can be found in any work of art, being part of its structure and only requiring the talent and diligence to unveil them. For example, although the great mid-century transatlantic mystic Neville Goddard used

---

[1]   Passing the Buck resembles the idea, proposed by French critics Eric Rohmer and Claude Chabrol in their *Hitchcock* (Paris: Éditions Universitaires, 1957), that Hitchcock's films often feature "the transfer of guilt." However, in the latter case the other party is tainted as well, the crime serving to manifest or manifest a secret desire; thus, in *Strangers on a Train*, the tennis player Guy secretly wants to kill his wife already before meeting the sociopathic Bruno. In Passing the Buck, the second party is usually a patsy and in any event his or her secret guilt is irrelevant.

Bible stories to convey his teaching, he also, on one occasion, did so using *The Count of Monte Cristo*.[2] Could he, or someone else, to illustrate the same teaching use, say, *Beowulf* or the *Iliad*? To my surprise, the normally sternly reserved rune-master upheld what I called the "idealist" position: every work of art contains these metaphysical themes, ready to be used for our spiritual benefit, awaiting only the "tact," as Spengler would say,[3] of the right interpreter.

With a characteristic combination of audacity and diffidence, I offer these essays to the public, so that they may decide for themselves how well they succeed at that task.

Stars Hollow, Conn., 2020

Sources

All these essays were originally published at Counter-Currents.

---

[2] Of course, one might argue that Dumas' novel is obviously part of the culture of Christendom, and hence likely to be "contaminated" by Biblical themes.

[3] *The Decline of the West,* English edition, Vol. I, p. 100.

Acknowledgements

I wish to thank Dr. Gregory R. Johnson for publishing these essays and for his encouragement in their writing, publishing and now re-publishing; and Mr. John B. Morgan IV for selflessly undertaking their initial editing … especially the rather delirious and profligate footnotes. I must especially thank Spencer Quinn for giving the manuscript a through and badly needed going over, although all remaining errors are, of course, on me.

I also thank the writers, readers, commenters, and supporters who make Counter-Currents possible.

The Babysitting Bachelor as Avatar

Clifton Webb in Sitting Pretty

Mister City Policeman *sitting/Pretty* little policemen in a row ... /
Elementary penguin singing Hare Krishna. ...

– "*I Am the Walrus*," Lennon/McCartney

FOR A TRADITIONALIST living in the Kali Yuga, there's no better example of 'riding the tiger' than making use of this fancy new "moving-pictures" technology. By providing a sort-of living image of the past, they provide solace, instruction in how things went wrong, and even, perhaps, inspiration for the future.[4]

Of course, not just any old film will do. You want to avoid anything where some smart-ass director or screenwriter tries to inject his phony, notions of "uplift" – you know, that whole "Barton Fink feeling."[5]

---

[4] Even grumpy old Harry Haller, the eponymous Steppenwolf, admits that the bourgeoisie's new toy, radio, is based on "a fact which every thinker has always known [though] put to better use than in this recent and very imperfect development." and at the end is sentenced by Mozart "to learn to listen to the cursed radio music of life and to reverence the spirit behind it and to laugh at its distortions." As for inspiration, in "Mad Männerbund?" — reprinted in *The Homo & the Negro: Masculinist Meditations on Politics & Popular Culture*; Second, Embiggened Edition, edited by Greg Johnson (San Francisco: Counter-Currents, 2017) — I pointed out how even the modern actors themselves felt that period correct costumes helped create not only postures but attitudes appropriate to 60s characters. The example of the revolution in classical music brought about by "period performance" styles — overthrowing decades of hysterical, subjectivist "virtuosity" — which was decisively influenced in the beginning by Traditionalist Marco Pallis, and mentioned already by Hesse in the mock-historical Introduction to *The Glass Bead Game*, is too familiar to need discussion here. Needless to say, this has nothing to do with prancing around in nerdy "Mediaeval Times" get-ups, which de Benoist rightly dismisses in *On Being a Pagan*, trans. Jon Graham, ed. Greg Johnson (Atlanta: Ultra, 2004).

[5] Of course, one has to use discretion here. Even the blacklisted stooges did work that's

11

Usually, you want a "B" picture, where the director had neither the time, nor the money, nor the talent or interest, to impose any kind of "vision." You don't want some Hollywood schmuck's outdated and stupid "vision," you want a window onto a better time, probably just what the "message" guy wanted to screw up, and in many ways has succeeded in doing so. Forget elaborate sets or FX; these guys didn't even use the studio back lot![6]

But don't worry; I'm not going to force you to slog through some forgotten B movie "gem" like some French cineaste or ironic hipster. The movie I caught a few weeks back on the aptly named Turner Classic Movies was somewhere in the middle, a modest but respectable little picture, based on a bestselling novel, and starring name actors, including one who would receive a Best Actor nomination to add to his two Best Supporting Actor nods. It's *Sitting Pretty*, starring Robert Young and Maureen O'Hara, and featuring Clifton Webb.

You've probably never seen or heard of it, and Clifton Webb is probably unknown as well, though you might immediately recognize him, or his

---

useful at least for their location shots and retro-tech: Sam Fuller's *Pickup on South Street*, for example — where Manhattan is still so underdeveloped that Richard Widmark lives in a shack on a rickety pier projecting out onto the river! — or Abraham Polonsky's *Force of Evil*, one of the last great noirs, where John Garfield wears great suits, and you know he's mobbed up because he has a secret telephone ... in his desk drawer!

[6] A good example is *The Dead Talk Back*, a 1953 production so bad that no one bothered to pick it up at the lab, where it sat on a shelf until 1993, when it was released at the peak of the so-bad-it's-good wave and became the first film to actually have its debut on MST3K the next year. Anyway, about midway through there's a chase scene that apart from its inherent goofiness — imagine Lurch chasing Arnold Stang — was obviously filmed on the street without permits and gives us several minutes of live Hollywood Boulevard circa 60 years ago. For our purposes, the most interesting feature is that the whole plot revolves around the apparent fact that in the '50s, aspiring DJ's and models, as well as scientific cranks, came to LA and lived in boarding houses with kindly grandmothers cooking dinners, rather than today's tiny little individual rat-infested cells; how do you think that influences the "art" produced therein?

Speaking of D. W. Griffith and history, Woodrow Wilson was perhaps the Worst President Ever, since he's served as the template for every Imperial President since: "idealistic" wars and meddling overseas, "progressive" legislation at home, such as imposing the Federal Reserve and the Income Tax, all bolstered by a vigorous program of domestic repression. He's the model for Barack Obama, who I'm sure wishes he could someday put Ron Paul in jail, just like Wilson did Eugene Debs. (In the understanding of "democracy" there can be no "loyal opposition," only cranks and stooges, so in the "progressive" state one is governed by judges, Ivy League grads and other "experts.")

voice (he was the inspiration for Mr. Peabody on the Rocky and Bullwinkle Show, kids), in a "oh, that guy" way. But the picture was a hit, Webb already a big Hollywood star and would continue to be until his death in the early '60s, and that suggests it illustrates some interesting changes in our culture. Plus, there are some rather rarified Traditionalist themes in it that add a special layer of interest.

As an example of cultural distance, consider this viewer's reaction, on the Internet Movie Data Base:

> I had never seen this movie before and was curious about it. What a disappointment — there is nothing to like about it — especially Clifton Webb's annoying portrayal of an arrogant know-it-all jerk. There is nothing funny or humorous, all it had me thinking was why he didn't get his ass kicked and thrown out. The way he treats the kids is mean and awful and the way the whole plot is written out is nothing more than showing how mean spirited and arrogant people can be in using and hurting others. From the rat faced neighbor to the snooty boss and secretaries - this movie is just plain mean and unpleasant. And then they made that awful sitcom with the equally annoying Christopher Hewett playing the 1980s version of Mr. Belvedere. 1/10

Well, admittedly he has a point about the sitcom. Still, it's entirely possible this guy finds himself entertained, even edified, by the likes of *Django* or *Basterds* or *Saw* or *Hostel*. And yet the feel-good hit of 1948 nauseates him like he's undergoing the Ludovico treatment from *Clockwork Orange*.

And then, I remembered an incident from literally 40 years ago, when I was in grad school in Canada. I was sitting around one afternoon with a very "progressive" folk-singing friend when *Cheaper by the Dozen* came on screen. And yes, that had starred Clifton Webb too! This being years before most people had cable, we tended to watch whatever came on – itself an indication of an entirely different mode of culture-formation back then. In fact, if we hadn't been in Windsor, with access to Detroit stations, there would only have been one, the CBC – and this was indeed a bit of American TV slipping over the border. Again, having vaguely heard of the film, or at least the phrase, we watched. Many minutes of silence passed as we beheld this "vintage comedy." As the lovingly, sentimentally portrayed father once more began to verbally abuse one of his many adoring children, my friend turned to me, sneered "Is this supposed to be funny?" and switched channels in disgust at this bourgeois American filth.[7]

Same reaction, same actor, equally popular film, and even largely the same character.

Why such vastly different reactions, then and now – or even then and 30 years ago? I think it lies in almost equal parts with the movie as a token of the Way Things Were, the actor as embodying a unique kind of masculinity, and the underlying traditional themes of the character and plot. The movie is an affront to liberal notions of marriage and parenting, liberal notions of the proper way to be "gay," and liberal notions that spirituality and especially religion are subjective whimsies and probably bunkum anyway. And thus it also demonstrates how liberalism functions as a pseudo-opposition to modernity, offering false alternatives while distracting from the One Thing Needful.

The Movie: Mr. Belvedere

Tacey King: Mr. Belvedere, is there anything you haven't been?
Lynn Belvedere: Yes, Mrs. King – I've never been an idler or a parasite.

The action takes place in (or on?) Hummingbird Hill, and though there's enough budget to shoot on a studio set, we are meant no doubt to see it as reflecting, humorously, on the problems of a newly prosperous post-War generation moving into the expanding suburbs. The opposite, then, of today, with a flat housing market and college graduates moving back to live with their parents.

These suburbs, at least at first, were not today's empty concrete wastelands but more like the British pre-War suburb,[8] or the planned or 'garden' suburbs promoted by Lewis Mumford, such as Forest Hills or Sunnyside in Queens, or older, quasi-cities like Grosse Pointe. Relatively large, two storey, detached houses, some on actual hills, winding roads

---

[7] Much later the same evil Americans remade the film with the very different Steve Martin, which I can't imagine viewing, though it must have been pretty well sanitized to be acceptable today, even as what my friend would still think of a propaganda for middle class values. Even so, bothering to remake it at all is a way another indication of how popular Webb's original character had been.

[8] See "How Britain built Arcadia: The growth of the suburbs in the Thirties brought a better life to millions" by Juliet Gardiner, *Daily Mail*, 29 January 2010.

and plenty of space for gardening (the movie opens with a lost cab driver asking directions of a gardening denizen – who will later play a pivotal role in the plot).

We zero in on our main protagonists: Henry King (Robert Young), his wife Tacey (Maureen O'Hara), and their three children. In this prosperous and patriarchal era, Harry is an up and coming lawyer, and can not only afford his house and car, but has no need to, and wouldn't dream of, sending his wife out to work. And she apparently is just fine with being a "homemaker." (Teeth are already starting to grind in the TV audience.) Except: she's unable to handle the kids. Fortunately, Harry can also afford to hire some help.

Why she can't handle them, since they seem to be perfectly normal, has puzzled viewers, but it's the implausibility that is needed to set the plot in motion.

The cab, it transpires, was called by the maid or nanny, who also can't stand living with the children any longer. A series of teenage babysitters have also given up, except for one with an obvious crush on Harry, which he tolerates with amusement, as well as his wife's not entirely amused jealousy. Here again we see a different era; today, this would start a movie starring Drew Barrymore or Alicia Silverstone, in which she insinuates herself into the family and kills them all, or else, if on Lifetime, Tacey would start kickboxing classes and take out the kid or husband, or both, with much shattered glass. In real life, Harry too would be setting himself up for a long stay at the Crowbar Hotel. In any event, the babysitter throws a "wild" dance party, which is reported to Harry and Tacey by ... hey, it's that gardening guy again! Back to square one.

Tacey suggests hiring a responsible, older, live-in babysitter, and thinks the way to do this is to put an ad in the *Saturday Review*. Remember that bastion of middlebrow taste? And did they really take ads for nannies? Anyway, Harry is justifiably skeptical, but lo and behold, a letter arrives, announcing the imminent arrival — presumptuous, much? — of one Lynn Belvedere.

And now the fun starts! Here's the IMDB summary:

Tacey and Harry King are a suburban couple with three sons and a serious need of a babysitter. Tacey puts an ad in the paper [sic] for a live-in babysitter, and the ad is answered by Lynn Belvedere. But when she arrives, she turns out to be a man. And not just any man, but a most eccentric, outrageously forthright genius with seemingly a million careers and experiences behind him. Mr. Belvedere works miracles with the children and the house but the Kings have no idea just what he's doing with his evenings off. And when Harry has to go out of town on a business trip, a nosy parker starts a few ugly rumors. But everything comes out all right in the end thanks to Mr. Belvedere.

I've emphasized a few phrases that seem a little significant, and we'll get to that in a bit. For now, go over to YouTube and watch how Mr. Belvedere proves to the Kings that despite his gender, and self-confessed hatred of children, he's just the man for the job.[9]

This is the sort of thing that delighted audiences in 1948 and disgusted my folk-singing friend just a generation later. Today, it's impossible to imagine this in a Hollywood film, and in real life the parents, rather than chuckling and deciding to hire the guy, would have called the police.

The Actor: Clifton Webb

"I have destroyed the formula completely. I'm not young. I don't get the girl in the end and I don't swallow her tonsils, but I have become a national figure." – Clifton Webb

I called Tacey's inability to handle the children the implausibility needed to start the plot. But as John Braine told William F. Buckley, when the latter sought advice on novel-writing, a work of fiction must have at least one implausibility, but no more. The other potential implausibility is Mr. Belvedere himself; why did audiences not consider him at least to be an insufferable jerkass, and on the contrary, demanded two more sequels (until Webb, like Sean Connery, put his foot down to prevent typecasting,

---

9   One of the ironic advantages of the pursuit of such unpopular material is that it's cheap! Although it's a cultural disgrace that there's no DVD release of our film, it's easy to find a copy burned from the VHS release online (mine was $5.00) and indeed, since no one bothered to renew the copyright, the whole film is available for viewing on YouTube. Additionally, some maniac has posted an almost shot by shot synopsis of the movie here: http://www.san.beck.org/MM/1948/SittingPretty.html.

only, like Connery, to be sucked into at least a couple of similar roles, such as *Mr. Scoutmaster* and *Dreamboat* – in the latter he's a college professor whose old movies turn up on the new medium of TV, like old porn roles haunting a politician today, and concludes with him watching that same breakfast clip from *Sitting Pretty*).

One crucial reason is that Belvedere is not bragging or overcompensating. He is what he says he is. He says he can handle the children, and does so immediately. When he accidentally meets Tacey one night and invites her to dance, he doesn't just say "I taught Arthur Murray" he proceeds, as Tacey exclaims, to "dance divinely."

And that scene, at least, wouldn't work unless the actor could indeed dance divinely. Indeed, the whole performance, portraying a man of Western rectitude and modest pride in real accomplishments, itself succeeds because it is barely a performance at all. Clifton Webb may not have raised anyone's children, including any of his own (he lived with his mother, throwing legendary Hollywood parties, until her death in the early '60s) but he was a divine dancer, and he embodied the virtues of the Western Man.[10]

In fact, Webb had already had one career, an accomplished dancer and performer on Broadway (he introduced "I've Got a Crush on You" and also "Easter Parade," thus unknowingly launching the Judaic assault on Christian holidays) long before he came to Hollywood at the age of 54. (There were some screen tests in the '30s; he may not have actually taught Arthur Murray but the studios thought he could replace Fred Astaire). He was brought to Hollywood by Otto Preminger to play Waldo Lydecker in *Laura* precisely because Webb reminded him of the real life model for Waldo, New York theatre critic Alexander Woollcott. No need to "act" but a good enough performance to get a Best Supporting Actor nomination.

---

[10] Emblematic of the decline of interest in Webb is that there is only one biography, published just last year, entitled, inevitably, *Sitting Pretty: The Life and times of Clifton Webb*, and published by relatively *déclassé* University Press of Mississippi. The first six chapters are actually written by Webb himself, part of an abortive autobiography begun at the behest of his friend Bennett Cerf of Random House. A few years ago, David L. Smith obtained the notes from the estate, and added on a standard "star" bio, for which we owe him much thanks. Webb's own work only covers the period before his Hollywood days; the project was abandoned due to a combination of WASP modesty and politeness; to go further would have involved talking about one's friends and contemporaries: "Truth is a desirable quality in an autobiography," he said, "though obviously not indispensable, and candor, I have found, compels me to put certain persons and events in a revealing, rather than a flattering light."

At this point, similarities with Humphrey Bogart begin to arise, along the lines I explored in my review of the Bogie bio *Tough Without a Gun: The Life and Extraordinary Afterlife of Humphrey Bogart* by Stefan Kanfer.[11]

Both were born in the late 19th century, providing them with a sense of being from an earlier, better, era. Both were raised in the New York of Edith Wharton — Webb remembers it being "completely settled only as far north as 72nd St." — with artistic mothers; both came to prominence on Broadway before being brought to Hollywood relatively late in life by the demand of a director. There the similarity stalls a bit; Bogart was brought over to recreate his role as Duke Mantee for the film version of *The Petrified Forest*, not for his physical resemblance to a fussy critic. It's interesting to note, though, that even then his co-workers remarked on how, while playing a vicious killer, his personal behavior continued to be polite, even courtly, especially to women. No "method" acting for Bogart. Bogart as a person was of Webb's type, but also able to act against type. Indeed, his early career floundered as he played butlers and playboys (he is supposed to have been the first to utter on stage the phrase "Tennis, anyone?" – Bogart!) until the role of Mantee gave him the chance to show another side of himself.

Of course, this is why Bogart was the "better" actor, or rather, a major actor rather than a minor one, in the sense Colin Wilson gives the words in describing major and minor composers. Major composers, like Mozart, have more to say, but that doesn't prevent a minor composer, like Delius, from being one's favorite.[12]

As Kanfer notes, the key to Bogart's appeal was that his WASP background (or, as I would prefer to say, his Western nature) gave an interesting, straight from the headlines dimension to his villains; rather than the immigrant gangsters of *Little Caesar* or *Scarface*, Bogart suggested the new, angry middle class of Americans produced by the Depression, like Pretty Boy Floyd or Clyde Barrow. And yet, being average guys, the audience could assume they must be fundamentally honest, fundamentally Nice Guys. Thus, he was able to take unlikable characters, both murderous

---

[11] Now reprinted in *The Homo & the Negro: Masculinist Meditations on Politics & Popular Culture*; Second, Embiggened Edition, edited by Greg Johnson (San Francisco: Counter-Currents, 2017).

[12] *Chords and Discords* (New York: Crown, 1966), p. 132. The 3-disc DVD of *The Maltese Falcon* includes "Becoming Attractions: The Trailers of Humphrey Bogart," hosted by TCM's Robert Osborne, which documents the changing ways Warners packaged Bogart, from gangster and outlaw to romantic lead and accomplished actor, illustrating his range but also, unintentionally, his evolving style of masculinity.

thugs and wise-cracking detectives, and make the audience root for them, as well as make it believable that that sophisticated women played by Mary Astor and Lauren Bacall would fall for them – in the latter case, even off screen.[13]

And there was in fact some skilled acting involved in those roles of Webb's. He was able to make audiences actually root for a manipulative psychopath like Waldo rather than the plodding detective and believe that Gene Tierney would — almost — love him too. And he could make audiences take to the imperious Mr. Belvedere, and even believe that the children would come to love him, and that the neighbors would suspect Tacey was having an affair with him. That was the quality that Ayn Rand perceived even before Webb came to Hollywood, which led her to insist — unsuccessfully — that Webb play the role of Ellsworth Toohey in *The Fountainhead*. The actor they used, she said later, "was too obviously evil." Not subtle enough for Ayn Rand!

The studio overruled Rand, and almost overruled Preminger, for the same reason modern audiences probably don't believe Webb in those roles: Western men are all evil jerks, right? And isn't he obviously, well, gay? The fact that creative artists as different as Rand and Preminger actually fought for him in those roles, while today's audiences think like 1940s studio heads, suggests that moderns aren't as "smart" or "progressive" as they think they are, that Hollywood studios have indeed shaped our culture, and that "gay liberation" has been a disaster for homosexuals themselves – as I argue throughout my book.[14]

Bogart forged a new, different kind of masculinity, "his own brand of masculinity" whose outstanding characteristics, Kanfer says, are "integrity,

---

[13] For an example of a private dick deliberately rendered as an unlikable jerkass, consider Ralph Meeker's take on Mike Hammer in *Kiss Me Deadly*, where director Robert Aldrich wanted to make some point about fascism or something. No one likes him even in the film, and it's hard to believe any woman would fall for his greasy smarm. And as for "who needs acting," Mickey Spillane was so angered by the performance that he actually played the character himself in *The Girl Hunters*; while it's another film priceless for its New York location shots, Hammer comes across, ironically, as even less likeable, despite everyone telling him what a great pal he is, and almost getting Shirley Eaton, right before her *Goldfinger* role.

[14] "Constant Readers" (Waldo Lydecker, Alexander Woollcott, Dorothy Parker, get it?) will recall my discussion of Preminger's further, less successful involvement with cinematic homosexuality in "Mad Men Jumps the Gefilte Fish," — reprinted in my *End of an Era: Mad Men and the Ordeal of Civility* (San Francisco: Counter-Currents, 2016) — where the making of *Advise and Consent* re-unites him with Gene Tierney but not, alas, Clifton Webb, who would have made a far better President than that jerkass Franchot Tone.

stoicism, a sexual charisma accompanied by a cool indifference to women"
(p. xi), "aloof, proud, unwilling to accede to the demands of fashion"
(p. 234) and, describing Sam Spade, "wounded, cynical, romantic and
incorrodible (sic) as a zinc bar" (p. 69). All of which are exemplified by Mr.
Belvedere, and Clifton Webb.[15]

Neither actor is a traditional Hollywood beefcake. Both seem slight of
frame (Bogart would hardly do better than Webb in that famous bathtub
scene with Dana Andrews), they share what Tom Shone has called Bogart's
"stiff, slightly old-fashioned patrician bearing," and it's Webb that's clearly
the handsomer, what with Bogie's battered, scarred face — and it's Bogart
who has the lisp.

It's when Kanfer contrasts Bogart's masculine appeal to that of
Hollywood's crop of youthful stars like Johnny Depp, Tom Cruise, and
Tobey Maguire that their real similarity and appeal comes into focus.
Both, in their different ways, are real men, middle-aged and with lives and
accomplishments already behind them, not boys. That's why Belvedere
can excite gossip as a rival to Robert Young, a misnamed "King" who's
really just a struggling young husband under the thumb of a boorish boss.
Belvedere, we recall, hates children – and that's why then come to love him.

---

[15]   Anyone who finds such effortless effeminate multitasking implausible would do well to
"contemplate" the career of Neil Munro ("Bunny") Roger (1911–1997), who was an English
couturier (he ran the department at Fortnum, invested in House of Amies, and invented
Capri pants), dandy (bought up to fifteen bespoke suits a year and four pairs of bespoke
shoes or boots to go with each) and ... war hero in the Italian and North African theatres.
Nicky Haslam claims to have witnessed a kilted Bunny beating his men up a Highland
hill, pausing at the summit to adjust his makeup using a compact hidden in his sporran
(*Redeeming Features* [New York: Knopf, 2009], p. 79).
He also shared Webb's way with an ad lib:

> Roger, like all proper dandies, rivaled Oscar Wilde in the one-liner department. When
> a gobby cab driver yelled from his window, "Watch out, you've dropped your diamond
> necklace, love," Roger replied, in a flash, "Diamonds with tweed? Never!" ["All mouth
> and trousers" by Simon Mills; *The Guardian,* Friday 16 June 2006]

Once, when his sergeant asked him what should be done about the advancing enemy troops,
Roger, who liked to wear rouge even with his khakis, replied, "When in doubt, powder heavily."
When he ran into an old friend in the hellish, bombed-out monastery of Monte Cassino in
Italy he responded to his pal's incredulous "What on earth are you doing here?" greeting with
one word: "Shopping" [BUNNY ROGER | BRITISH STYLE ICON YOU'VE PROBABLY
NEVER HEARD OF; The Selvedge Yard, January 28, 2010, here: https://selvedgeyard.
com/2010/01/28/bunny-roger-english-style-icon-youve-probably-never-heard-of/
Belvedere is actually a shade less violent, as fitting his Krishna-like role; his war experience
was setting bones in Pershing's army.

Webb, as I said before about Bogart, embodies the Western character as delineated by Baron Evola:

The sober, austere, active style, free from exhibitionism, measured, endowed with a calm awareness of one's dignity. To have the sense of what one is and of one's value independently of any external reference, loving distance as well as actions and expressions reduced to the essential, devoid of any exhibition and cheap showmanship – all these are fundamental elements for the eventual formation of a superior type.[16]

On a personal level, Bogart and Webb had known each other in their Broadway days, and kept in touch; Webb was even a charter member of Bogart's original Rat Pack, that index of heterosexual cool (Kanfer, pp. 201-2). As I outlined in my essay on Bogie, Webb was the sort of homosexual Bogart could like and even admire, like Truman Capote (who impressed Bogart with his work ethic — doing re-writes for *Beat the Devil* from a hospital — and his arm wrestling) or, fictionally, dignified, erudite, but devilishly clever Casper Gutman. Not in your face flamboyant, but ironic and quietly competent – like Bogart, like the Roman ideal.

Gutman: [Pouring a stiff drink; Spade lets him pour] We begin well, sir. I distrust a man who says 'when.' If he's got to be careful not to drink too much it's because he's not to be trusted when he does. Well, sir, here's to plain speaking and clear understanding. (They drink.) You're a close-mouthed man.

Spade: No, I like to talk.

Gutman: Better and better. I distrust a close-mouthed man. He generally picks the wrong time to talk and says the wrong things. Talking's something you can't do judiciously unless you keep in practice. Now, sir, we'll talk if you like. I'll tell you right out I'm a man who likes talking to a man who likes to talk.[17]

---

[16]   *Men Among the Ruins* (Rochester, Vt: Inner Traditions, 2002), p. 261.

[17]   Gutman would be even more impressed when Belvedere downs a whole tumbler of gin; we know the boys are using the bottle to hold cold water, but Belvedere succeeds in horrifying Clarence the snoop. By the way, Gutman's openly effeminate associate, Joel Cairo, who impresses Spade with his determination if not his competence, announces several times he is staying at the Hotel Belvedere.

As wonderful example of how Webb's Western professionalism and imperturbability underlie the Belvedere character, take another look at the breakfast table scene. After Belvedere delivers his line about how horrible the children are, the baby sneezes, and Webb, without missing a beat, adds "Gesundheit." Needless to say, you can't get a baby to sneeze on cue; this was entirely an accident, but Webb was able to improvise a perfect response, saving the scene and even stealing it back from the kid.

Speaking of styles of homosexuality, another reason the film succeeds in presenting an agreeable Belvedere is the nosy neighboring gardener, Clarence, played by Richard Haydn. He serves not only as a plot foil for Belvedere but also as a kind of Doppelganger, presenting a different, more hateful image of effeminacy. By contrast, Belvedere seems, as the cliché goes, crusty but benign, or a jerk with a heart of gold.

In fact, when I first watched the film, I began from the first scene thinking Haydn was Webb, especially as he began snooping around the Kings during the whole babysitter fiasco, figuring that's how he'd get hired, but wondering why they would take in such an obvious creep.

Note the almost split-screen effect, Haydn's self-hugging suggesting weakness and narcissism while Webb carries what we will learn is a present for the family, and the subtle way light and dark characters are suggested in black and white film. In the next section, we'll see how the Clarence/ Belvedere couplet works on a higher, spiritual level.

I also thought Haydn's performance, in looks and sound, closely resembled Michael Redgrave's Crocker-Harris in the far classier vehicle *The Browning Version* (Rattigan's play premiered in 1948 as well, but was not filmed with Redgrave until 1951, so perhaps the influence went the other way). Stiff upper lip, meek wispy voice, etc. Crocker-Harris's tragedy (apart from being a closeted homosexual with an unfaithful wife and a bad heart) is that rather than succeeding as a teacher, his prissy and haughty demeanor has made him hated and despised; the discovery that his pupils refer to him as "the Himmler of the upper fifth" precipitates his agonizing reappraisal of his failed life.

Sitting Pretty effectively splits the archetype of the bitchy, closeted homosexual, assigning Haydn the role of "Himmler" that Harris wandered into and to Webb the beloved pedagogue the boys all cheer for at the end: "Hooray for the Old Croc!"

Needless to say, some viewers implicitly run to Clarence's defense, crying "homophobia" against the film makers. How dare they suggest "there's something wrong with that" (to paraphrase *Seinfeld*) in living with your mother, obsessing about cross-pollinating orchids and amusing yourself by opening other people's letters and going through their trash cans in search of gossip. How camp! Why, it's positively divine![18]

The Myth: Mr. Belvedere as Krishna

Whenever there is a decline of righteousness, and the rise of unrighteousness, then I re-incarnate myself to teach *dharma*.
Bhagavad Gita, Chapter IV, Verse 7

Tacey King: Mr. Belvedere, you dance divinely!
Lynn Belvedere: Yes, I do.

Over and above all this, there are still some other, even stranger things going on in this movie. I think its original, and ongoing appeal, such as it is, also arises from the no doubt unconscious, but therefore all the more interesting, echoes of Traditionalist themes, especially from the *Bhagavad*

---

[18] Just as modern audiences react differently to Belvedere than did his contemporaries, they may find an additional, unintentional level of creepiness in Haydn's Appleton – a strong resemblance to Anthony Perkins' Norman Bates. In that opening scene, we find Appleton lives with his mother in a gingerbread Victorian house on a hill. We soon learn that he's a snoop, just as Norman Bates has a peephole to spy on guests. Belvedere will suggest sending a flock of bees to "ruin his irises" referring to his flowers but also suggesting his visual fetish. Appleton's obsession with cross-pollinating orchids suggests unhealthily artificial relation to sexuality, like Norman's stuffed birds. Above all, the scene where Appleton finds his mother in her chair, having fainted from reading Belvedere's tell-all book, is shot almost exactly like the famous "reveal" at the climax of *Psycho*. Ironically, in "real life" it was Webb who lived with his mother until her death at age 91; he died a few years later, almost to the day. (His protracted grieving led his friend Noel Coward to comment, "It must be terrible to be orphaned at 71." His grief was similar when paying his last visit to the dying Bogart, when he collapsed into Lauren Bacall's arms (Kanfer, p. 225); "he was definitely more of a problem than Bogie ever was:" (Smith, p. 218). But unlike the scene in which Belvedere dances divinely with Tacey while Appleton, wheeling his crippled mother around, looks on censoriously, Webb's mother, always known as Maybelle, was an uninhibited "Auntie Mame" type who helped him host some of the most decorously wild parties in Hollywood history. However, according to Myrna Loy, she did look exactly like Clifton, sans moustache, in drag, which brings us back to Tony Perkins.

Gita. As we finally get around to going through the storyline in some detail, I'll point out some features not commonly associated with 1940s screwball comedies, and with any luck you'll come to see the comparison is not that far-fetched.[19]

There are two reasons to think Belvedere is Krishna: what he is, and what he does. Let's go back to the movie and see how these play out in the storyline.

The King Family — that is, the King's Family — is in disorder! Henry King is, as we've already noted, a king in name only; his children run wild, his dog jumps on his back, and he is forced to all but kowtow to his boss, including taking his wife to his boring bridge evenings, necessitating the hiring of a babysitter.[20]

The first clue that Belvedere is their Avatar, or Redeemer, after his announcement that he is a "genius," is that his imperious instructions about room and board include the information that he is a vegetarian, and that the rooms will be acceptable, once he "removes some items." The next morning, the hallway is filled with the comfy furniture and knick-knacks that Tacey brought in to make expected babysitter feel at home.

The room is now an ascetic cell, and when the couple enters after hearing no reply to their knock, Belvedere is discovered to be standing on his head. He apologizes for ignoring them; when practicing *yoga*, he is "completely out of this world; I neither see nor hear a thing." (We recall his earlier comment that Harry's absence when he arrives is "a matter of complete indifference to me.") Harry concludes he is "weird."

The audience would likely agree. In 1948, *yoga* was still the province of side-shows and *fakirs* at best, con men and sex-cults at worst.[21] While,

---

[19]   Trevor Lynch has criticized *The Hobbit's* "one-damn-thing-after-another feel;" I hope to show that *Sitting Pretty* exhibits a tightly structured whole that develops a coherent spiritual lesson. See his review: https://counter-currents.com/2012/12/the-hobbit-an-unexpected-journey/

[20]   In the suburban utopia proclaimed by pipe-smoking Sub-Genius prophet J. R. "Bob" Dobbs, endless amounts of Holy Slack replace work, and the motto is "Every child and dog a slave."

[21]   "The story of yoga in America" is told in Stephanie Syman's *The Subtle Body* (New York: FSG, 2010) but more relevant to our movie is Robert Love's *The Great Oom: The Improbable Birth of Yoga in America* (New York: Viking, 2010) whose subject, Pierre Bernard (of Iowa) was, despite constant harassment by cops and tabloids (whence the sobriquet "The Great Oom"), still operating at the time of the film and would have been the most immediate image 'yoga' would call to mind.

as we've said, modern audiences are horrified by the breakfast scene that follows, but find "*yoga* for kids" wonderful and "progressive," contemporary audiences would have been more concerned by what follows it: Belvedere begins to instruct the children in *yoga*, the post-War equivalent of being recruited into the Manson Family, or at least Scientology.

There follows the breakfast table scene we've already looked at, which convinces the Kings to keep on Belvedere (or "give him a whirl" as Henry thinks). After instructing the children to chew their food exactly 28 times (another popular "health food" gimmick) the baby throws cereal on him. Belvedere dumps the bowl on his head, and announces to the parents:

"I have taught him an object lesson, and as you can see, he doesn't like it. I guarantee he will never throw cereal at me or anyone else again. Ever!"

And Harry is convinced Belvedere is just what they need, since "He's done that to me too."

Belvedere is the first one, though, to have had the gumption to reply in kind. He's taught the boy, and the onlookers, a lesson about *karma*, the inevitable linkage of cause and effect, action and appropriate reaction,[22] just as, earlier in the scene, he insisted Harry had no choice but to keep him on, once he responded to Tacey's ad: "I am perfectly willing to carry out my end of our agreement; I see no reason you should default on yours."

The scene is book-ended by two remarkably explicit exchanges, first:

Lynn Belvedere: I am, in my way, a philosopher.
Harry King: Oh, I see, you just sit and think.
Lynn Belvedere: Mr. King, if more people just sat and thought, the world might not be in the stinking mess that it is.

Then:

Harry King: You've got something.
Lynn Belvedere: I couldn't agree with you more, Mr. King. You might even say I have ... everything.

---

[22] "The most important of all perceptions is the continual perception of cause and effect – in other words, the perception of the continuous development of the universe .... When one has thoroughly got imbued into one's head the leading truth that nothing happens without a cause, one grows not only large-minded, but large-hearted." – Arnold Bennett, *How to Live on 24 Hours a Day*.

What we see, in short, is that Belvedere is a philosopher who, by "just sitting," has acquired everything.[23] The furious activity of the world leaves it in a stinking mess, whilst the frantic King Family truly possesses nothing – it's the American Nightmare of "work hard to afford to buy a commodified form of what you gave up and can never have the time to enjoy."

While Harry ignorantly thinks he'll give Belvedere "a whirl," Belvedere will bring order to the King Family, by teaching them to stop whirling around "doing" things and instead just sit and think.[24] He begins with the children; in the next scene, Harry arrives home and finds them not running around carousing in the driveway, but in the garage, practicing "yogi" headstands.

Inside the house, everything is "under control," the children "good as gold" (the Platonic ruling caste and the alchemical goal),[25] appliances fixed,

---

[23]   Due to the American habit of identifying people with their professions, Belvedere, by doing all, is, like Krishna, all. "What haven't you been?" Tacey asks, in wonderment. Or rather, like Krishna, he is the best in all things, the essence of them; see *Bhagavad Gita*, 10.17-10.40.

[24]   In this he presents a contrast with the real *American Psycho*, Patrick Bateman. The latter, despite his *yoga* and "rigorous exercise routine" (Belvedere is content with an evening walk) works a boring job he doesn't need, because he "wants to fit in." Bateman is all about fitting in and above all being seen to fit in. The emphasis on "being seen" links him to Clarence, thus another *Psycho* connection. While today's audiences likely think Belvedere is a sadist and Clarence merely 'camp', they likely nod their head when Bateman, the true sadist, mouths his list of approved causes and upbraids his colleagues, appealing to the "community standards" enforced by Clarence's gossiping.

By contrast, Belvedere resembles Rory Gilmore, as conceived by *Gilmore Girls* creator, Amy Sherman Palladino:

> What to me had not been done was a girl who wasn't fucking around at 14. A girl who was not interested in boys, not because of an aversion to boys, but who was academically goal-oriented and really that's what made her tick. And a girl who was very comfortable in her skin. Didn't need to be popular, wasn't popular, but didn't care. – "The Best of Friends" by Susan LaTempa, http://www.gilmoregirls.org/news/211.html.

All of which could account for *The Gilmore Girls* having a Belvedere level of (un)popularity when it was programmed against *American Idol*.

[25]   The relationship between Belvedere and the boys reminds one of how the young Fritz Peters saw Gurdieff who served as much as his father figure as his guru: "strong, honest, direct, uncomplicated – an entirely 'non-nonsense' individual." See Peters, *Boyhood with Gurdjieff* (London: Victor Gollanz, 1964; Fairfax, CA: Arête Communications, 2006).

and dog fully trained (Belvedere "had a talk with him" like many popular "dog whisperers" today). We also notice for the first time, since the name is repeatedly used, that the dog is named Henry. Who names a dog after himself? Anyway, this Henry is trained – the other one, and his wife, are next.

We've seen that Belvedere is an ascetic philosopher — really, a gymnosophist, as the Greeks called the Indian holy men — who practices *yoga* and teaches it as a technique to induce harmonious relations with children and animals. As the movie goes on, and shifts to the adults, we get a more detailed idea of how Belvedere's *yoga* works its magic, which makes my identification of him as Krishna more plausible.

In the *Bhagavad-Gita* Krishna describes and praises many forms of Yoga, but reserves his undivided endorsement, of course, to that form in which the devotee abandons concern with the fruits of action and concentrates their attention on Him alone (*mat-manāh,* 'always-me-thoughted' as the Sanskrit language delightfully puts it). Concern for results, and for impressing others, falls away.

While traditionally such teaching addresses situations of grave spiritual crisis, such as Arjuna's despair at the apparent conflict between his warrior's duty and his filial piety, this movie does not try to present an updated version in modern Manhattan, as Salinger would a few years later in *Franny and Zooey.*[26] As Alan Watts pointed out, such "metaphysical" notions are really "rockily practical,"[27] and the movie wisely stays on the level of domestic disorder.

For paradoxically, action undertaken without concern for results becomes more, not less, effective, for:

Yogah karmasu kaushalam, Krishna uvacha.
Yoga is skill in action, Krishna says.[28]

Like Krishna, Belvedere has answered the call and arrived to restore order, through his *yoga* of non-action ("just sitting," like the Taoist *wu-wei*),

---

[26] The twee pretentiousness of which has lasted to our own day, best exemplified by the named by Salinger-fan parents of Zooey Claire Deschanel.

[27] Alan Watts, *In My Own Way* (Pantheon, 1972), p3.

[28] "The verses 47-51 of the second chapter of the *Bhagavad Gita* constitute indeed a capsule version of the entire *karma yoga* of the *Gita.*" See the discussion at http://www.krishnamurthys.com/kvforp/ng/yoga_as_skill_in_action.html.

activated by capturing the attention of the family through his imperious charisma, distracting them from goals and the expectations of others.[29]

Another paradox: just as action is easier, more successful, when unconcerned with results, so the object of devotion grows more attractive the less he responds, as writers from Aristotle (the unmoved mover) to Baron Evola (the resolute, upright individual who attracts rather than pursues spiritual influences) to the theorists of "game" in today's "Manosphere" have observed.

If all this sounds a little "furrin," then it should be noted that the same, or largely similar, doctrine can be found in the West, specifically the great Neoplatonist, Plotinus.

As Brian Hines notes, Plotinus:

[T]urns upside down one of the most widely accepted tenets of modern culture: that action is the key to success in life. [Kindle loc. 2197]

We think the answer is to concentrate more and more on ourselves, our desires, our clever plans, rather than on the One who knows all and is all and thus really does all; instead, Plotinus suggests otherwise:

[Shun] the role most people long to play, albeit unconsciously, but are terribly unqualified for: Master of the Universe. ... [W]e do our best to be mini-masters of our mini-universes, an exhausting, frustrating, unfulfilling and ultimately impossible task. We try to create order in our lives but messiness always seeps in around the edges of the little personal islands of peace and harmony we keep trying to construct in the midst of a larger cruel world. [loc. 2126]

Belvedere will concern himself with these "little islands of peace and harmony" that the Kings have tried to set up, without success. As with Krishna, what's needed is, ironically, to stop acting, to step back, step away, and ... just contemplate the One:

---

[29] Transcending action oriented to results, as well as mere inaction ("I've never been an idler"), this Yoga also partakes of both the male characteristic of impassivity as well as the feminine method of conquering by giving way, thus uniquely appropriate to Webb's style of masculinity; see Baron Evola's "The Serpentine Way" in his Introduction to *Magic: Rituals and Practical Techniques for the Magus* (Rochester, Vt.: Inner Traditions, 2001), where the Baron's disdain for "brute muscularity" may surprise his contemporary enthusiasts, as his ideal seems closer to Webb, or at least Bogart, than the likes of Mussolini or Ernst Rohm.

"The problem ... is [that] effective creation requires concentrated contemplation. ... Most of us, unfortunately, lack the willpower to focus so attentively on what we desire to achieve or create." [loc. 2135]

And as we shall see more in a moment, the main problem is that rather than contemplating, they are worried about results, and especially, making an impression on others, thus losing the single-pointed focus – Pater's "hard, gem-like flame" that is "success in life":

... when they propose to act ... it is because they want their act to be perceived by others [Plotinus, *Enneads* III-8-4; Hines, loc. 2217][30]

Belvedere introduces himself as a genius, but we see he is more than some theoretical nerd, like Sheldon Cooper of *The Big Bang Theory*.[31] Rather than being socially and physically inept, Belvedere is a master of many disciplines, a "jack of all trades." No wonder he thought himself qualified to answer an ad for a live-in babysitter. Pressed by Harry for a profession, he deigns to call himself a philosopher, which Harry glosses as someone who "just sits and thinks," but Belvedere immediately sets him straight: it is the key to restoring order to the world!

How does just sitting lead to such technical mastery? Of course, Belvedere does not literally just sit; he stands on his head in the mornings, and always takes a walk after dinner. And he insists that the only thing he hasn't been is an idler or slacker.

Let's get back to the movie, where we can see these themes play out.

The real charm, and advantage, of the path of *bhakti*, or devotion, is

---

[30] Brian Hines, *Return to the One: Plotinus' Guide to God-Realization* (Bloomington and Salem: Unlimited Publishing, 2004). For Pater, see the infamous "Conclusion" to his *Studies in the History of the Renaissance* (1873). In the same work, his equally infamous "Not the fruit of experience, but experience itself, is the end" is a kind of decadent, aestheticized version of Krishna's *karma-yoga*; the missing element of *dharma*, defining the correct action, is what makes Pater's version "quite poisonous" to George Eliot. The definitive work on Plotinus's doctrine of contemplation is also quite accessible to the layman: John N. Deck, *Nature, Contemplation, and the One: A Study in the Philosophy of Plotinus* (University of Toronto Press, 1969; Toronto Heritage series, 2017).

[31] Another TV hit from Hollywood Chuck Lorre, promoting messages that intelligence is socially isolating (so don't be smart) but if you are smart, then feel free to mock Christians and Middle Americans in general; the usual heads he wins, tails you lose strategy of the culture-distorter.

that it is also easier than the others, especially easier, because more natural (in the sense of "appropriate to their predominant qualities or gunas") for women and children. As we have seen, the children are easily converted to the cult of Belvedere, and by the time Harry gets home Tacey is smitten as well.

Of course, it is essential that she not like him "that way," which is where Belvedere's implied, and Webb's actual, sexual indifference become useful. "The fascination is not mutual" as Belvedere says on Day One. The scandals involving everyone from Oriental gurus to televangelists to Catholic priests are well-known. Within older Western traditions that had not been perverted by liberalism, we find strict rules and customs to limit this, from the systematic taboos of Hindu civilization — ignored by modern "gurus" East and West — to the monastic rules of mediaeval Catholicism. Perhaps most familiar to us are the rules of chivalry and courtly love; we recall how Bogart's treatment of women was called "courtly" while his "indifference" leant an authentic note of chivalry to his characters – Sam Spade sending Brigid to prison, Rick sending Ilsa on to Madrid with her husband (while striking up a beautiful friendship with Louis), etc. Belvedere is so strict he won't let the boys call him "Uncle," which is the traditional title for such a role, and one Darwinian explanation for the role of homosexuals in genetic success.[32]

Like countless men whose partners have acquired gay best friends, Harry nevertheless finds himself jealous, the very epitome of a useless and counter-productive emotion. Belvedere will, however, actually use this jealousy (remember, *yoga* is skill in action) just as Tantra uses the strategic breaking of taboos, to break down Harry and convert him. Harry is then subject to two trials.[33]

First, Harry is sent off on the usual "business trip." At first, he refuses, fearing to leave Tacey alone with Belvedere. Since he needs to

---

[32] The case of Franklin Jones of Long Island who became Da Free John of San Francisco and after many other whimsical name changes ultimately Adi Da of Fiji, is especially relevant and interesting; see most recently *Adi Da Samraj: Realized or/and Deluded?* by William Patrick Patterson (Arete Communications, 2012).

[33] Speaking of chivalry, we seem to be in a version of the tale of Gawain and the Green Knight in which the roles are reversed; in our version, it is the courteous knight who tests his host with his behavior toward his host's wife (in the winter scene — Gawain takes place at New Year's — Belvedere, like Gawain, receives a gift of clothing from his fair lady) which the host fails, but is ultimately forgiven and chastened by the lesson.

please his boss's "royal decree" Tacey agrees to stay with friends. In both his jealousy and obsequiousness toward his boss, we see Harry's other-directed nature.

One night, while he's gone, one of the children becomes ill, and Belvedere summons Tacey. Clarence, having seen the lights on, comes over to see (again, his obsession with spying) and finds them all in robes and pajamas. Rumor spreads, Harry's boss upbraids him for lowering the reputation of the firm, and Harry angrily confronts Tacey. Once it's all explained, he sheepishly backs down, but is still suspicious.

The second trial is set up when Tacey dances with Belvedere — like Krishna and the Gopis or milk maids[34] (remember, "You dance divinely." "Yes, I do") — at a hotel restaurant, and again Clarence is there to spy and gossip.[35]

This scene is really the pivot of the film. Once more, as in the shots of Belvedere and Clarence, we see them opposed, embodying opposite philosophies of life - Belvedere dancing with Tacey, oblivious to the crowd, Clarence on the other side of the room, wheeling his decrepit mother around, intently staring with hypocritical disgust.

Once more, Clarence spreads the rumor, Harry is upbraided by his boss, and this time his irrational response produces an ironic result - it's his wife who is driven out, leaving him at home with Belvedere!

But worse is yet to come; Belvedere has not been only meditating in his room; he's written an expose of the whole suburban community.

The resulting book is a bestselling scandal, of the Peyton Place type, and the entire community is outraged at its exposure - again, the motif of concern for others' opinion. That alone — apart from the revelation of his own philandering — makes Harry's boss feel justified in firing Harry for

[34] Although the Christian mystic tends to engage in rather masochistic forms of worship, and various Protestant sects have demonized dancing altogether, in the Gnostic Acts of John Jesus engages his disciples in the same kind of round-dancing as Krishna and the Gopis. In the Orthodox tradition, the Prayer of the Heart, aka the Jesus or 'Centering' Prayer, may correspond to Me-mindedness.

[35] One is perhaps reminded of Frank O'Hara's poem "A Mexican Guitar," which Camille Paglia reads as the gay poet's celebration of studio B-movies, like Webb's, in a later age of supposedly "realistic" method acting. As they dance the poet is impervious to the charms of his female friend, which are only displayed for onlookers — nuns, schoolboys, and Boston puritans — with "lavish envy." And say, isn't Tacey played by Maureen O'Hara? See her *Break Blow Burn* (Pantheon, 2005), pp177- 182.

31

harboring Belvedere, as well as firing Harry's best friend for standing up for him.

Harry has now hit rock bottom; wifeless, jobless, his reputation in the community in ruins, he returns home to find a film crew in his living room, interviewing Belvedere (who is also taking over the direction, having "done it many times before").[36]

Book published, bust sculpted by Tacey, newsreel interview shot, Belvedere has conquered all media and his image is available for the contemplation of his devotees everywhere.

Now, at the film's climax, Belvedere demonstrates his mastery of the situation, producing a better order out of the chaos he has created. Harry's boss and others, including Clarence, arrive to announce they plan to sue Belvedere for millions in damages. Belvedere announces he couldn't be happier, as the suit will only bring more publicity; and also provide a lucrative first case for the new law firm Harry and his friend will set up on their own.

At this point we note that Harry's boss, who issues "royal decrees" to Harry, is named Hammond – once more, Haman has been hoist by his own petard.[37]

And Belvedere also reveals that he's not the one they should sue anyway. He's gathered his information ... from Clarence! The others turn on Clarence and chase him out.[38]

The resolution of the Clarence subplot lets us revisit the use of Clarence as a foil for Belvedere.

When Belvedere reveals that his writing left no sound to give him away, due to his use of a quill pen — the Adept acts without leaving a trace — we recall that Clarence has throughout the film been using a feather to gather pollen throughout the neighborhood and thereby gather his gossip as well. The chiastic parallel is driven home when, in what Quinn Martin

---

[36] As someone who has published a book or two, book, I find the time compression here to be breathtaking; like the "Pilot" story arc on Seinfeld, we seem to go from publication to national bestseller to newsreel subject in about three days.

[37] On the "hang higher than Haman" trope, see my "Mad Men Jumps the Gefilte Fish: Part Three," loc. cit.

[38] There is also a secretary who provides information about Mr. Hammond's skirt chasing in the office, but Belvedere does not reveal her, no doubt from chivalry; we only see her in the set up to the dance scene, so she may as well treat her as a stand in for Clarence anyway.

would call the epilogue, we learn that Mr. Hammond has given Clarence a black eye; earlier, Harry had foolishly tried to strike Belvedere, who nimbly stepped aside to allow Harry's fist to hit the door frame. *Karma!*

Clarence lives in a Psycho-style house on top of a hill, where he dotes on his aged mother, who spies out the window and uses Clarence to gather more information on the neighbors, as he aggressively thrusts himself into people's lives through various pretexts, such as gathering pollen.

Belvedere lives in a room atop a normal suburban house, where others dote on him, and bring information to him, only approaching others when invited, as by Tacey's ad. As Plotinus has told us, Belvedere's contemplation is superior, since, though unmoving, it is creative: he sits, listens, and produces a book, a sociological study of the new suburban lifestyle.

This works both as a cinematic device — once more making Belvedere seem nicer than he otherwise would — as well as delivering a spiritual message. As we've seen before — in my essays on Brian DePalma's *The Untouchables*,[39] *Mad Men*, and Otto Preminger's *Advise and Consent*[40] — and will see again, in essays on *A Dandy in Aspic* and the apocalyptic cinema of Coleman Francis – one of the chief signs of the Enlightened One is the ability to "pass the buck": escaping *karma*, the consequences of action, by offloading it to another character. If Belvedere had been snooping around it would lower our opinion of him; instead, he has merely skillfully used Clarence's nosy nature for his own advantage, and in the process exposed and neutralized him (which, like Harry and the baby's cereal hurling, none of his victims has had the gumption to do).[41]

[39]   Reprinted in *The Homo & the Negro: Masculinist Meditations on Politics & Popular Culture*, Second, Embiggened Edition, edited by Greg Johnson (San Francisco: Counter-Currents, 2017).

[40]   For the last two, see the essays reprinted in my *End of an Era: Mad Men and the Ordeal of Civility* (San Francisco: Counter-Currents, 2016).

[41]   Belvedere will neither actively spy nor allow others to spy on him. Twice Tacey and Harry attempt to sneak into his room or peep through the window, and both times they are foiled by Belvedere. In the latter case, there may be some hint of the Garden of Eden or World Tree; Harry climbs up a tree but falls when Belvedere spots him from the ground. Spying on him is an unsanctioned use of Belvedere's providential incarnation, unlike the gazing upon his freely given form known in the Hindu tradition as *satsang*.

The King's snooping suggests a relation of some kind to a very different work. Two years before *Sitting Pretty*, Hermann Hesse received the Nobel Prize. In his 1927 novel *Steppenwolf*, another intellectual outsider with interests in *yoga* and Krishna takes rooms in an archetypally bourgeois house. However, in Hesse's book it's the outsider who is named

In the epilogue, Harry and Tacey, back together, announce that they will be adding another child to the mix. Apparently, although they have benefited from Belvedere's teaching, they have chosen to return to the householder's path. Though devoted to their children and each other, their love, and child raising abilities, can only have benefited from their brief stay among the devotees of Belvedere/Krishna. Belvedere may be disappointed but, as always, not nonplussed: he is also an obstetrician! A perfect metaphor for his Socratic, or midwife's, role. And no need to ever leave the gaze of Krishna again!

Writing on *How to Live 24 Hours a Day,* Arnold Bennett counsels that, when out for one of Belvedere's evening walks,

> Forget the goal; think only of the surrounding country; and after a period, perhaps when you least expect it, you will suddenly find yourself in a lovely town on a hill.

Perhaps the name of that town would be ... Hummingbird Hill?

If I seem to be overburdening this little screwball comedy, this *jeu d'esprit,* with too heavy a load of "significance," we would do well to recall that the motion picture, especially the popular movie, is the modern descendent or analogue of ancient public rituals and esoteric rites; thus, as Camille

---

Harry (Haller), and like our Harry, he's the one who needs an education in lifemanship. (Our Harry lives on Hummingbird Hill, H.H., which connects him to Harry Haller, just as Harry Haller suggests Hermann Hesse) The framing story includes the ingenuous account of what the landlady's nephew — one might compare them to the nosy Appleton and his dear Mother — discovers about Harry by surreptitiously entering his room, but when our Harry and Tacey try they find that Belvedere has anticipated them and changed the lock. There's also a book, or pamphlet, within the book, in which an abstract voice gives an objective, almost cosmic, perspective on Harry's angst-ridden life; in the movie, Belvedere writes a thinly veiled account of the goings-on at Hummingbird Hill. The main part of the novel, alliteratively titled Harry Haller's Records (Belvedere's bestseller, Hummingbird Hill?), involves Harry's attempt to come to terms with the vulgarity of modern life through a course in jazz dancing (Spengler's "death march of civilization") and opium under the guidance of a stern woman who reminds him of male friend of his childhood; in the movie, the stern and effeminate Belvedere undertakes the instruction of Harry by, among other things, dancing with his wife, and teaches the whole neighborhood a lesson about bourgeois vulgarity as well. In the end, Harry is still failing, he even tries to kill his girlfriend out of jealousy, but seems optimistic — Beckett's "fail again, fail better" — while in the movie Harry is successful in marriage and career and even expecting another child, though still under Belvedere's watchful eye.

34

Paglia says of poetry, "the sacred remains latent within."[42] This is precisely what makes it, along with the popular music concert, the dominant form of public art in our time. And we should also recall René Guénon's notion that Traditional wisdom has been encoded into folk art and traditions, safely, unknowingly, preserved and transmitted to later generations, who can recover it from the most unlikely sources, if they have eyes to see and ears to hear. We would do well to gratefully extract such lessons whenever we find them. Conversely, the decline of the Belvedere image, from "divine" to "jerkass," can serve as an index for the decline of modern culture in the Kali Yuga.

---

[42]   *Break, Burn, Blow* (Pantheon, 2005), p. xiv.

The Good Infinite and the Bad Infinite

"Game," Psychogeography, & Serial Killing in Groundhog Day ... & Others

> "Oh, good heavens!" Ignatius shouted, unable to contain himself any longer. Popcorn spilled down his shirt and gathered in the folds of his trousers. "What degenerate produced this abortion?"
>
> "Shut up," someone said behind him.
>
> "Just look at those smiling morons! If only all of those wires would snap!" Ignatius rattled the few kernels of popcorn in his last bag. "Thank God that scene is over." – John Kennedy Toole, *A Confederacy of Dunces*

IN RECENT MONTHS I've been finding more and more evidence in film and TV of an archetypal pattern in which our protagonist endures an indefinite repetition of events until he manages to escape by offloading his *karma* onto another and rising to a new, higher level; thus, the essays reprinted herein.

So it might seem natural to think I had seen, and possibly been inspired by, the Bill Murray/Harold Ramis comedy *Groundhog Day*. Truth be told, not really. I like a lot of Bill Murray's stuff, but in general I have a mulish resistance to seeing "what everybody is seeing," and especially if there's some kind of "uplifting life lesson" involved and/or "indie cred," as in too many of Murray's more recent, "Academy-worthy" works.[43]

However, since you Constant Readers have come to rely on this writer as an honest broker and committed profession — and it being the 20th

---

[43] Off the top of my head: such as *Lost in Translation* (saw first 10 minutes on cable), *The Life Aquatic* (bought the Criterion release, watched it, then sold it), *Rushmore* (watched it on cable 10 years later), etc. Conversely, the same quirk no doubt also accounts for my interest in films - lousy or just ignored — like the ones cited in the previous note.

anniversary, after all — I recently girded my loins to sit down and by God, watch this thing.[44] These thoughts are my results.

For the same reasons above, it's probably not necessary to give a detailed account of the plot (if necessary, you can find a synopsis all over the internet) but for convenience you can think of it as having a classic, Syd Field three act structure[45] with two plot points; it's even used in online courses:

Define the three acts according to the two main plot points.

At first his normal life where he is a weatherman, the second act would be once the days start repeating themselves and he feels like a lost soul and even killed himself a number of times, the third act would be once he starts doing something good with his gift when he tries to redeem himself and becomes basically a good citizen instead of the selfish and arrogant weathermen he was at first.[46]

And, of course, a character arc:

Describe the hero's transformation (called the character arc).

At the beginning he was a total jerk self-absorbed and arrogant weatherman, then with the day started repeating themselves and slowly he started to lose it, after a while he began to realize that maybe there was something positive he could do with all this time and started improving himself which at first was for personal gain (like when he used it to get with Nancy and the dozens of times he tried to get with Rita) but after a while he

---

[44] I felt rather like Walker Percy when forced to finally read *A Confederacy of Dunces*:

There was no getting out of it; only one hope remained – that I could read a few pages and that they would be bad enough for me, in good conscience, to read no farther. Usually I can do just that. Indeed the first paragraph often suffices. My only fear was that this one might not be bad enough, or might be just good enough, so that I would have to keep reading. In this case I read on. And on. First with the sinking feeling that it was not bad enough to quit, then with a prickle of interest, then a growing excitement, and finally an incredulity: surely it was not possible that it was so good. – Preface in Toole, John Kennedy: *A Confederacy of Dunces*, LSU Press, 1980.

[45] Although some guy named "Lon" argues for a 5-part model, based on Kubler-Ross's stages of dying, here: http://www.simplyscripts.net/cgi-bin/Blah/Blah.pl?b-screenwrite/m-1311035456/s-30/.

[46] Creative Writing 101 http://bbacreativewriting.wordpress.com/2012/01/18/groundhog-day/

realize that becoming a better person was the best way he could deal with what was happening to him, and so he did become a model citizen saved a number of lives. At the end of the movie Phil Connors was completely different to when he started being now kind, unselfish and generous ...

Or, for a more detailed analysis:

"Will Phil become a good person, get Rita, and get out of Groundhog Day?"

Answer: Yes.

Inciting incident: Phil and Rita go to Punxsutawney for Groundhog Day.

First beat: Phil wakes up stuck in Groundhog Day, is freaked out.

Second beat: (end of 1st act, point of no return) Phil wakes up in Groundhog Day again, realizes he is really stuck. He begins his journey by taking advantage of the situation.

Third beat: Phil, having grasped the ego-centric power of being stuck in the same day, begins to pursue Rita to no avail.

Fourth beat: (midpoint) Phil, stuck and miserable, tries to end his life and can't.

Fifth beat: (highpoint) Phil, humbled, finally becomes friends with Rita. She urges him to self improve.

Sixth beat: (end of 2nd act, emotional low point) In the process of self-improvement, Phil realizes that the old bum dies at the same time, no matter what Phil does to prevent it. As the bum dies in his arms yet again, Phil looks up to the heavens.

Seventh beat: (resolution beat) Phil has become great, and his greatness inspires Rita to bid on him at the Bachelor's auction.[47]

Obviously, the notion of indefinitely repeating the same day is the innovation here, and what fits it into my area of interest:

[F]ormer Monty Python member Terry Jones also included *Groundhog Day* in his top 10. "What's so remarkable about it," Jones observes over a pint in a north London pub, "is that normally when you're writing a

---

[47] The Hidden Structure of Movies, Rules #4 and #5, http://hiddenstructureofmovies.blogspot.com/2008/06/rules-of-screenwriting-4-5.html.

screenplay you try to avoid repetition. And that's the whole thing here, it's built on repetition."[48]

But Phil does not pass the buck; rather, he manages to overcome karma, or fate, by "changing himself."[49]

It's all expressed in the trajectory of his relationship with Rita. He wants her, he tries to seduce her – first with meanness, then by fraud, then with recitations of French poetry and engineered perfect moments. It is only when he gives up, when he accepts the blessing of her company, free from desire — at which point she, too, magically becomes a far more interesting character—that she is delivered into his arms.[50]

"Magically"? This is man-in-the-street magic, Disney magic. The 'magic' that Evola spoke of — and he was aware of the unfortunate connotations of the English word — was the serious, difficult, even dangerous science of the mages, or in other words, spiritual initiation.[51] And in line with the Disneyesque "boy gets girl" angle, our script analyst above adds this devastating sting to the end of the character arc:

... although you could argue that he became everything Rita said she wanted her ideal men to be, thus staying a selfish individual

---

[48] "Groundhog Day: the perfect comedy, forever" by Ryan Gilbey; *The Guardian*, Thursday 7 February 2013

[49] This is the reverse of what seems to happen online, where the equation is "Normal Person + Anonymity + Audience = Total Fuckwad ... normal people become more aggressive when they think their behavior carries no real-world social consequences." TVTropes.com, "Jerkass."

[50] "Reliving Groundhog Day" by James Parker; *The Atlantic*, February 20, 2013.

[51] See his *Introduction to Magic: Rituals and Practical Techniques for the Magus* (Rochester, Vt.: Inner Traditions, 2001). Reviewing it in *New Dawn*, Jay Kinney first notes that "Magic (or Magick, as it is sometimes spelled, in order to distinguish it from stage magic) is a word fraught with dubious connotations. It summons up images of robed figures, surrounded by clouds of incense, standing within magical circles, and conjuring demons to do their bidding" and then succinctly describes Evola's concept of Magic as "there is a capacity inherent in Man to raise consciousness above the call of the body and the distractions of the mind; a capacity that can lead to an immortal awareness. The means to this awareness is through a rigorous discipline wherein the transitory ego is shed, and the individual consciousness is wedded to the Eternal. In so doing, one passes beyond the conventional notions of Good and Evil, to a place where, in Gustav Meyrink's words, only "truth" and "falsehood" exist. To know this is not a matter of intellectual knowledge, but of spiritual experience, i.e. of gnosis." See "Magic and Awakening," http://www.newdawnmagazine.com.au/articles/Magic_and_Awakening.html.

only looking to please Rita and didn't do all those things out of pure kindness and generosity.

Is Phil's "transformation" anything other than what the manosphere would call "Game"? Act Two certainly looks like Phil is developing his game, and when that fails, does he "become unselfish" or merely develop a more subtle game?[52]

Perhaps that is, actually, a strength of the film; with all the talk about Game over the past few years, Phil's character is a bit more ambiguous than is realized by the hordes of "spiritual enthusiasts" who have claimed the movie for their own.

However, the simpler interpretation — Phil decides to be good — seems more in keeping with the simple gimmick of the repeating day. I confess that one of my qualms was that the movie would, in fact, repeat the same day, with Murray simply reacting differently, but the filmmakers have, admittedly, come up with many subtle and amusing ways to suggest the passage of time without hitting you over the head with it.

Still, how plausible is the whole idea? Anyone who takes seriously the ideas of the Right should find this more than a little dubious. After all, no less a pop culture authority than TV Tropes evinces it as an example of:

---

[52]   Phil first succeeds when gaming Nancy, then fails with Rita. The situation reminds me of *Overdrawn at the Memory Bank*, a wonderfully dreadful sci/fi tele-movie co-produced by US and Canadian public television. Imagine *Total Recall* crossed with Tron and done on a Wang computer. Anyway, Raul Julia (who must have thought he was signing on for some Masterpiece Theatre production) finds his mind sucked into a computer network, so, since he can now imagine his own reality, he decides to amuse himself by cyber-seducing one of his co-workers. His outside monitor, who rejoices in the name of Apollonia James and somewhat resembles Andie MacDowell, is disgusted by his "playing with himself" and inserts herself into the simulation, bearing stone tablets with rules of proper cyber-conduct, lest he be terminated; needless to say, they eventually hook up and escape from their dystopian world. Raul's control over the crap-cyberized world corresponds to Phil's predicament, frustrating them but also giving both godlike powers which they initially misuse, although in Phil's case it's the co-worker who lays down the law. Oddly, a reviewer at IMDB insists that "There was a time when I watched this film over and over because I was so addicted to it," while another insists that "*Red Zone Cuba* [wasn't] as hollow and boring as this."

On the other hand, TVTropes.com insists that Phil's transformation is, in fact, an example of the "Crowning Moment of Heartwarming" trope: "And the best part of this? He wasn't even really "arranging" it, and certainly not in any attempt to take advantage of Rita. The dance and all that follows is his "reward" for being able to earn genuine admiration and love from both Rita and the citizens of Punxsutawney under no selfish pretenses." We'll soon suggest reason to question how pure Phil's motives could be at that point.

41

Rousseau Was Right: The film's message: There is love, kindness and decency in everyone; you just need time to bring it out.

Just time? Isn't this just a variation the liberal shibboleth "we just need more education"? This all stems from the Socratic idea that people only hurt one another through ignorance; therefore if only everyone were educated and enlightened we could achieve a multiracial utopia where everyone is equal and peaceful because everyone understands one another. Of course, it's a childish idea of "good" as our default position that Nietzsche utterly destroyed in *Beyond Good and Evil*.

Is it really plausible that Phil would learn to be "good" at least as conventionally defined by the movie or by Rita? Let's look at some variations on *Groundhog Day's* three acts, based on some common film tropes, to see if they seem more likely.

*****

"California Doubling: The Movie was Shot in Woodstock, Illinois." - TVTropes.com

One immediately suggested itself when Ramis, on the commentary track, noted that the film was not shot in Punxsutawney, PA but in Woodstock, IL. The need to find a "more filmable" substitute for a run-down hick town, and the name "Woodstock" immediately called to mind *The Gilmore Girls* and my own meditations on what I've called "liberal psychogeography": despite their "big city," cosmopolitan airs, liberals, when they have the money and choice, prefer to live in small, even rural towns – once they've been cleansed of those actual unfortunate rural townsfolk (they don't have to worry about the darkies, since they're kept out by the same price of admission mechanism, which is "fair" because based on meritocracy; no need for embarrassing signs and bylaws, and the ones who do "make it" can be kept around to "show how diverse we are here").[53] Such towns,

---

[53] See Paul Kersey's "Because Life is So Brief and Time is a Thief When You're Undecided, here: https://www.unz.com/sbpdl/because-life-is-so-brief-and-time-is/. We can see the inverse process in the descent of Detroit from "The Paris of the Midwest" (*Wall St. Journal*)

ranging from Martha's Vineyard to The Hamptons to even small "college towns" like Ann Arbor or Madison, or remote outposts like Billings, MT, are the real life equivalents of movie stand-ins like Woodstock, IL.[54]

Thus did my mind turn to *The Gilmore Girls* as a more subtle version of Phil's Dilemma.[55]

The GG show pitch or set up[56] can be succinctly captured in the title of the first in a series of GG-inspired "TV novels": Like Mother, Like Daughter, which already hints at the repetition theme. Rather than one protagonist repeating, or trying not to repeat, the same day for an indeterminate lifetime while manipulating others, we see each generation of the Gilmores[57] seeking to manipulate the next into repeating their own life.[58]

The backstory is that at sixteen, the rebellious Lorelai Gilmore becomes pregnant with the boy next door.[59] Perversely, her parents are delighted,

---

to national punchline; see Kersey's Kindle book Escape from Detroit.

[54]   See "The Gilmore Girls Occupy Wall St.," reprinted in *The Homo & the Negro: Masculinist Meditations on Politics & Popular Culture*; Second, Embiggened Edition, edited by Greg Johnson (San Francisco: Counter-Currents, 2017).

[55]   Although, to be fair, it's easy to be 'subtle' when you're doing a TV show that could last, say, seven seasons rather than a 100-minute movie.

[56]   If you don't know the series, or haven't read my article previously referenced, you can get up to speed on Wikipedia or on any of dozens of websites. *Coffee at Luke's: An Unauthorized Gilmore Girls Gabfest* by Jennifer Crusie and Leah Wilson provides a mixed bag of essays in the "Philosophy and…" mode; for serious academic headaches, consider *Gilmore Girls and the Politics of Identity: Essays on Family and Feminism in the Television Series* by Ritch Calvin (2008); *Screwball Television: Critical Perspectives on Gilmore Girls* by David Scott Diffrient and David Lavery (2010); or most recently and most perhaps deadly, *Gilmore Girls Sieben Jahre in Stars Hollow: Der inoffizielle Guide zur Serie* by Peter Osterried (2013).

[57]   Lorelei named her daughter, known to most as Rory, after herself; an egotistical act that, typically, she cloaks as a half-assed "feminist" gesture. Later, we learn that she herself was named after her paternal grandmother, who also married her own cousin, which discovery is played as an "icky old rich people thing" while actually, of course, again demonstrating the deep strain of egotism in the family line as well as the almost Gothic repetition motif.

[58]   The mother/daughter of *Absolutely Fabulous*, despite occasional flashbacks to Edina's youth, are the opposite; daughter is completely different and openly hostile to mother's lifestyle. Watching "Modern Mother and Daughter," the French & Saunders skit that birthed Ab/FAB, it's easy to see now-a-comic-superstar Melissa McCarthy and whatever-happened-to Lauren Graham in the roles. Other than Ab/Fab once or twice appearing in the trademark pop cultural references on GG, I don't know of any influence.

[59]   Dr. Hannibal Lecter: "No. We begin by coveting what we see every day … You know how quickly the boys found you. All those tedious, sticky fumblings in the back seats of

since they view Christopher as an ideal match, but Lorelai ups the ante by running away to the impossibly quaint and conveniently nearby small town of Stars Hollow, raising the child herself in a potting shed out back of the bed and breakfast where she works first as a maid, then manager, and ultimately owns. As the series opens, Rory is now herself sixteen,[60] and to finance private school, Lorelai makes a deal with her estranged parents: in exchange for paying Rory's tuition, they will both appear each Friday night for dinner. The series follows Rory from entering Chilton Academy to graduating from Yale, as parents and grandparents attempt to help (or "control") both children.

We can begin to see the parallels here with *Groundhog Day,* especially when we realize that rather than playing out the same day over and over, it is Lorelai who, rather than changing over the last 16 years, has stayed the same, and is now trying to superimpose her life on the now 16-year-old Rory, under the guise of "don't listen to your controlling grandparents," while her own parents, especially the grandfather (the ur-WASP Edward Herrmann), see a chance to change Rory's life on their own terms and make her develop as Lorelai should have, into another WASP matron.[61]

Thus, we have a smug, egotistical, verbally quick and witty person[62] who is thrown out of their usual routine and lands in a bed and breakfast

---

cars, while you could only dream of getting out. Getting anywhere, getting all the way to ..." Stars Hollow, Conn.? The relevance of Lecter will become clearer as we move on.

[60]   The age difference of Lorelai and Rory is the same as Claggart and Billy Budd, another fun New England couple.

[61]   The superimposition of the two lives only becomes blatant in a late episode where Rory's father's new wife gives birth, and Lorelai – of course – spends the episode daydreaming about the events around Rory's birth.

[62]   Bill Murray of course is the master of this kind of pre-emptive verbal assault hiding as humor. According to Wikipedia, "The *New York Times* noted that the character talks fast and uses words to keep her "loneliness at bay" which, while opinion, seems to be a relatively insightful view of her ... On the characteristic of talking fast, Sherman-Palladino noted: "Just by listening to Lorelai's vocal patterns, it says volumes about this woman: First of all, that she's bright enough to put that many words together that quickly ... and it says a lot about her emotionally, that she's got a deflection shield that's sort of the way she gets through the world." Lorelai's ego-driven verbosity recalls James Joyce, at least as interpreted by Colin Wilson, who concludes that Ulysses "remains the kind of book that must be read while one is young and impressionable, and willing to take Stephen Joyce-Dedalus at his own valuation as a rebel who was determined to fly close to the sun. Once we begin to see him form the Wyndham Lewis point of view — as a rather tiresome young man clamoring for attention — it is difficult to read the book without impatience." *The Books in My Life,* Hampton Roads, 1998, p139.

in a charmingly eccentric small town, where they relive their life through another, while trying to "improve" not themselves but the other by more or less subtle manipulation. It's *Groundhog Day* without the redemptory third act.

Since Lorelai's smug hip leftist character is written from the perspective of smug, hip leftists, thus petted and pampered,[63] we have a chance to watch the second act of *Groundhog Day* from Phil's perspective: mocking the eccentric but dumb townspeople and doing everything to avoid making a commitment to others (except, Lorelai would point out in her pointing out way, her wonderful daughter, but of course she is her anyway). As Phil says, "They're hicks!"

The main character, Phil Connors, despises everyone around him. They are all his intellectual inferiors. So naturally, his version of Hell is to be stuck in a town with a bunch of dumb hicks. But Phil is not evil, so his Hell turns out to be a kind of Purgatory, from which he can only be released by shedding his selfishness and committing to acts of love.

> Phil … learns to appreciate the crowd, the community, the dumb hicks and their values. He decides to improve himself by reading poetry and by learning to ice-sculpt and make music. But most of all by shedding his ironic detachment from the world.[64]

This, of course, is what Lorelai — and Rory — never do shed their selfishness and ironic detachment, and certainly learn to appreciate the hicks and their values.[65] That, apparently, would be to give in to "the parents" — the elder Gilmores, or the Establishment in general — and join their world of coming out parties and D.A.R. teas; just as Phil has to become Rita's Mr. Right. By the series finale, Rory has dumped another guy after he, Good Phil-like, proposes, while Lorelai seems to be starting up, for the third time or so, with Luke, whom she left at the altar a few seasons back, to marry Rory's father 16 years too late, then dump him …

---

[63] We welcome Rory's ascerbic school rival, Paris Geller, who is acutely conscious that no matter how smart she is, everyone will always do whatever Rory wants, because "you look like birds dress you in the morning."

[64] http://www.guardian.co.uk/film/2013/feb/07/groundhog-day-perfect-comedy-for-ever.

[65] Again, there's a lot of Lecter (or in this movie, "Lecktor") in Lorelai: "I'm glad you came. My callers are mostly clinical psychologists from some cornfield university. Second-raters, the lot."

Speaking of Luke: if it seems odd to think of a female Phil, most of Phil's more masculine characteristics have been offloaded to Luke, who's sort of a ruggedly handsome Bill Murray; unshaven, sloppily dressed, misanthropic. His scraggly beard, backwards ball cap and open plaid shirt suggest nothing as fashionable as grunge but rather the classic Bill Murray dirtbags from earlier Murray/Ramis collaborations such as *Stripes*, *Meatballs*, and above all, Carl the Groundskeeper from *Caddyshack* (who fights his own repetitive war with a rodent).[66]

Lorelai, on the other hand, has Rita's list of Perfect Man requirements, at least implicitly, and presumably more PC, but not being, like Rita, "raised a Catholic" she never lets that stop her from bedding down with someone new.[67] Anyone hooking up with Lorelai would be well advised to follow Phil's advice and "rent first."[68]

Luke also facilitates one characteristic the Gilmore Girls share with Bad Phil: sitting around diners stuffing themselves with childish comfort food (smoking would be un-PC, though). Like Phil, neither one changes, so weight gain is not a problem. And speaking of diner owner Luke, director Ramis in the commentary track makes much of the diner waitress being played by one of his favorite comediennes, Robin Duke. Our Luke dispenses the junk food while ragging them for it, the odd combination — why is he serving it if he thinks it's bad for her? — bringing together Duke's waitress and Rita's censorial voice, underlining his oddly feminine role to Lorelai's Phil.[69]

As for the other locals, the Girls, like Phil, have acquired encyclopedic knowledge of the townspeople and their colorful foibles, but, as I pointed

---

[66] According to *The Onion's* AV Club, "Scott Patterson was just awful to deal with on-set, I've heard, much like Chevy Chase." http://www.avclub.com/articles/pilot,93236/.

[67] Lorelai even managed to dump the future Don Draper himself, Jon Hamm; he talked too much about his Porsche.

[68] There's almost a running gag of people buying or renovating a house for Lorelai, including Luke and her mother, only to get the shaft when Lorelai's adorable little mind changes. It's another manifestation of the "you look like birds dress you in the morning" syndrome.

[69] "For Luke Danes, food identifies the duality of his character. This is a man who runs a greasy diner… and yet is himself a health nut. … These contradictions symbolize the duality between what Luke projects on the outside — a gruff, belligerent, and uncharitable personality — and what he truly is on the inside — a sensitive softy who, despite his vocal protests, is always there when people need him." (*Coffee at Lukes* p123). Luke thus incarnates both Phils simultaneously, in keeping with the theme of superimposed rather than sequential time.

out my earlier essay, they exist entirely as figures of fun and mockery (in which Luke, though a townsman himself, joins in, thus underlining the doubling of Phil) for "brilliant" Lorelai and Rory, rather than, as with Phil, growing from "hicks" to "people to help." And since, as we said above, the show, unlike the movie, is conceived from her point of view, they are beloved by the naïve townsfolk, (well, maybe not Luke so much) and even subject to periodic festivals, just like Good Phil at the final dance.[70]

Rather than diss *Groundhog Day*, I should salute it for providing a contrast that opens up a new perspective on *Gilmore Girls*. Lorelai has stumbled into the same, or similar, time warp as Phil, but persists in her egotistic exploitation of others — just nicer than Phil does, since his misanthropy is offloaded onto Luke — passing the buck, I knew I'd find it somehow!

Real-Lorelai seems just as clueless about her role; in "the last Lorelai Gilmore interview," we are told:

I felt every year, even under Amy's leadership, that the show evolved. For the last episode, we tried to match the final shot with the first scene from the pilot, so we went back and watched the pilot – which I haven't seen for so long. And the show is really different from that pilot, which was more dramatic at the time than your typical WB show. And I think it evolved and got more comedic over the years; every year was an evolution.[71]

---

[70] Typically, despite thus adding to their number, the Gilmore Girls regularly mock the various local customs and traditions, just as Phil becomes more and more openly hostile to Groundhog Day. Either of these rants would easily be delivered by Lorelai or Luke:

Phil: "This is pitiful. A thousand people freezing their butts off waiting to worship a rat. (raising his voice) What a hype. Groundhog Day used to mean something in this town. They used to pull the hog out, and they used to eat it. (turns to the crowd) You're hypocrites, all of you!"

A few loops later ...

Phil: "Once again the eyes of the nation have turned here to this ... (silly voice) tiny village in Western Pennsylvania, blah, blah, blah, blah, blah ... (serious) There is no way ... that this winter ... is ever going to end, as long as this groundhog keeps seeing his shadow. I don't see any other way out. He's gotta be stopped. (beat) And I have to stop him."

[71] http://www.gilmoregirls.org/forum/index.php?topic=7340.

Really, evolved? They why on Earth try to match the last shot…

… with the final shot of the pilot episode; especially since no one knew the show was being cancelled yet?

In Stars Hollow, like Woodstock, it's always Groundhog Day.

Thanks for Watching

Awakening Through Repetition in Groundhog Day, Point of Terror, & Manhunter, Part I

I am awake only in what I love & desire to the point of terror – everything else is just shrouded furniture, quotidian anaesthesia, shit-for-brains, sub-reptilian ennui of totalitarian regimes, banal censorship & useless pain.

– *T. A. Z. The Temporary Autonomous Zone, Ontological Anarchy, Poetic Terrorism*, by Hakim Bey

IF GILMORE GIRLS 2.0 IS being rebooted as a "sleepy coastal town,"[72] then let's move on to a similar such town for our next movie.

We've been discussing *The Gilmore Girls* as an interesting example of putting a smug jerkass like Phil into a similarly timeless setting, but making him (or rather her, or even the two of them) the hero. Or heroine(s). But as we said, it achieves its advantage over *Groundhog Day* somewhat unfairly, as it luxuriates in an indeterminate, ultimately seven, year run rather than a tight 100 minutes. As Wagner proved, you can't write a five- hour comedy.

If you don't have the time[73] or interest to devote to the Girls (which until recently was running endlessly and sequentially on the Soap Channel) you can avail yourselves of a delightfully distasteful 88-minute piece of 70s sleaze called *Point of Terror*, which has just had a brand new DVD release, with enough re-mastering and interviews to make it look like as if it were a really worthy film.

---

[72]   A phrase mechanically repeated in everything dealing with Bunheads, from promo articles to Hulu streaming pages to Wikipedia.

[73]   "Time, get it?" – MST3K, Time Chasers.

49

It's not, of course. As one ironic fan noted, it feels like a 70s porn flick with all the sex cut out, and I can testify to it having just about that effect on me when I saw it on late night TV sometime in the mid-70s, in the days before cable porn when teenage boys would hunker down in the basement 'rec room' and channel surf all night for the obscure offerings of even more obscure local TV stations.[74]

Channel 62 in Detroit was one (weirdly, as the result of one of those TV for newspaper swaps, it's now become the local CBS outlet), which showed what one fan called "French symbolist cop dramas and Italian neo-realist sex farces."

Like the rest of films shown on Channel 62 and the like, the only reason to watch *Point of Terror* was the promise of numerous well-endowed women, among them Dyanne Thorne.

If *Gilmore Girls* gave us egotistical Phil as seen by a fellow egotist, thus cosseted and coddled rather than provoked to change, *Point of Terror* goes all the way: our protagonist is also the writer and producer himself, and quite possibly the director as well.[75] We thus have the chance to see Full Frontal Phil, and it's a greasy, unappetizing spectacle.[76]

As the "film" opens we get a heapin' helping of our auteur, doing a preview of his "act," resplendent in a red fringed suede jumpsuit that Elvis only dreamed of. Peter Carpenter, or at least his character here, has been rightly described as "Tom Jones without the looks or talent." I'll let the implications of that sink in.

Carpenter supposed worked in Vegas as a "jazz dancer" so I'll take his choreography as intentional. Inverting stereotypes, Pete can certainly swivel his hips with the best of them, but it's his arms that seem useless. He certainly makes the most of the famous "jazz hands" move, but the

---

[74] In the 80s, the USA cable channel created a 'legit' version called, of course, Up All Night; while the 90s brought us a show put together from the crap movies in a local TV station library: Mystery Science Theater 3000.

[75] The nominal director was Alex Nicol, the non-auteur of a handful of lousy films, most famously the MST'd *The Screaming Skull*; this, plus the title, trailer and poster, might have given credence to the idea that his is a horror or terror film, rather than just horrible and terrible.

[76] Although, unusually for a mainstream film, our auteur gives us almost as much of his own well-packed cut-offs, International Male swim wear, button-fly hip-huggers — I had those! — and even, in the uncut version, if you pardon the expression, several glimpses of his bare ass, as the three ladies involved. Truly a movie with something for everyone!

oddity is his stiff armed gestures — that's where the fringe comes in, in a big way — suggesting at times a crucifixion, at other times a puppet, perhaps, like Dante's Satan, upside down - the fringe again.[77] Both are recurrent — timeless— metaphors of the "block universe experience of total determinism and no free will" that Michael Hoffman has identified as the common central experience of mystery religions, entheogenic drug experience and psychedelic rock. Indeed, with its 70s vibe and garish red and green palate, perhaps PoT — get it? — is intended to be, or originated in, a classic "bad trip".

Despite internet legend, he does not repeat the same song over and over, although each is mind-numbingly repetitive in itself. The first one, now playing, is an up-tempo number, indeed, if the credits are to be believed, produced from the Motown stable. But when it came to the lyrics, it's like they took the pathos of "Across 110th Street" and re-wrote it for some smug slumlord. Pete, playing "Tony" has a 70s perm that recalls Tony Francioso's mobster in the original film, and Tony's frenetic flapping around suggests the inverse of Pam Grier's Stoic motionlessness — the metaphysical opposite of Pete's gyrations — as the song plays at the opening of Tarantino's *Jackie Brown*.

I lent a deafened ear to all the sounds of sadness
Watched with blinded eyes to all the looks of loneliness
Broke and heartless
Won't give a damn if you're down and dying, woah I'm
Broke and heartless
Running wild and running free
This is me, this is me
Born against the wall I had to learn the hard way
Armed with deafened mind [?] I had to stalk my prey
Broke etc.
And as proud as I can be
This is me, World, this is me
People say that love is stronger than fate [hate?]
But with my job [?] I guess that stuff will come too late
Born etc.
Broke etc.

---

[77] When his record company-owning sugar mama listens to the demo of the song, she'll mutter the suggestion "Maybe add strings."

Like a storm that drifts at sea
This is me
You can't change the way I am, this is me,
There's no one else I'd want to be, this is me,
Running wild and running free, this is me,
This is MEEEEEEEEE!

Etc. Just about at the point where the viewer is about to scream, we cut to Tony (as we'll soon be introduced to him) on the beach, screaming. So it was all a nightmare; indeed, that seems the best category for what we've just been though – eventually, we'll realize the red outfit and lighting are mean to suggest Hell.

Tony is soon appeased, however, by the approaching bosoms of bikini-clad future SS She-wolf Dyanne Thorne, who seems unaware or uninterested in Tony having been screaming his fool head off a few seconds ago. She quickly conveys that she is what today would be called a cougar, which is fine with Tony, since he's got a gig over at the local rich ladies hangout, The Lobster House [!] which does indeed resemble some decaying local fish shack cum nightclub of the sort one might find in a West Coast version of the Hamptons (more ersatz-rural psychogeography).

We briefly meet Tony's current regular Saturday night thing, and after apparently shagging her on the dressing room floor, our recharged Lothario enters stage right to begin his "act" proper.

Remember the odd "storm that drifts" where we would expect "ship"? The second song is a "slow dance" sort of thing that takes up the 'drift' metaphor. It would seem to be his public face, rather than the private one we just heard – indeed, this time there is indeed an audience. It's his "bad boy who needs love" game song.

This is what I am and what I'll always be
A drifter of the heart until love changes me
Take me for myself, let your mind run free
And find what lies ahead across the open sea

As you can imagine, the music at this point is eerily like the "*Love Boat*" theme. However, I can't help but point out that the lyrics are structured in the same inverted way as *Dancing Queen*: opening with what we will realize is the chorus. For the verse, the music moves into something like the bridge from Sly Stone's "Everyday People":

I've been right and I've been wrong and I've been in between
On the tip of my fingers I've balanced all my dreams
Love is something I can't keep I only seem to borrow
I play the game hard and fast like there's no tomorrow

Chorus:

If things go right and I'm on top love will be around
Like the wind they'll all be gone if ever I am down
My constant lonely searching life is the price I have to pay
To do the things I want to do and live this life my way

Chorus, repeated over and over until you just want to scream, again, but in Pete's movie it's a chick magnet, so good luck to him. Fortunately, his "act" seems to consist of just the one song, so it's good night and try the veal.

As Pete/Tony smarms his way through his "act" one can't help but recall that wonderful skewering of two-bit lounge acts on SNL, Nick the Lounge Singer; wait, that was Bill Murray! [78]

As Tony works his charms on the audience of lonely rich chicks (no disparagement intended, Dyanne's BFF calls her "Chickie") the camera circles around the stage from below, which I guess is supposed to be his hypnotic spell but it really suggests his career and life swirling around a drain. Metaphysically, these are the "Lower Waters" the Hero need to traverse, and the ever-spinning world of Samsara.

Anyhow, we now have had our two themes pile-driven into our skulls: this is who I am, and will be, until love changes me – a pretty fair approximation of *Groundhog Day*. Everyone all set with the premise?[79] Tony, like Phil, is a jerkass tool. [80]

Before getting back to the "plot" we might as well get the last song over with. We only get a fragmented listen to it, as it's the potential "big hit" that we watch Dyanne "producing" in the studio. Starting in mid-verse,

I've had dreams and desperation
Waiting for some world of time [?]

---

[78]   http://www.youtube.com/watch?v=dYl9R5wU980.

[79]   MST3K, *The Starfighters*.

[80]   The 'bots repeatedly add "I'm a jerk" to the game warden's explanations in the MST3k version of *Attack of the Giant Leeches*.

Now it's time for celebration
Lifebeats turning into lovebeats
Lovebeats turning into lifebeats
Lifebeats turning into lovebeats
Moving in and taking control of me

Verse:

Life's a drummer and my heart's a drum
Love the music gotta get me some.

The whole recording session looks like the Euro-crap song we see being recorded early in *Pod People*, and one wishes one of these actors would also give an ironic thumb-forefinger sign and add "It stinks." Incredibly, this Motown number was actually re-cycled a few years later for ... Diana Ross. Yet more incredibly, it was recycled again for ... Don Johnson in his early post-Miami Vice career. And in a final moment of awesome, it bears more than a little resemble to the end credit music for Michael Mann's pre-Miami Vice film *Manhunter,* which will take up our next section.[81]

The lyrics drive home the themes of dreams, desperation, helpless instrument of fate, etc., which the chorus evokes the endless repetition theme.

But we must tear ourselves away from these poetic heights and return to the mundane matters of the plot, which is a sort of smutty version of Double Indemnity[82] Tony takes Dyanne back to his swinging pad[83] where she reveals she is not merely rich but married to the head of "National Records," who, being wheelchair bound (thanks to Dyanne, as we will learn, along with the possibly useful fact that she — or they — murdered his first wife), has turned the day to day running of the business over to her.[84] Tony slaps on his ever-handy demo tape — that's where she tells him

---

[81]   At one point Pete sings 'heartbeat" not "lifebeat", either by mistake or as part of the rehearsal supposedly going on, which brings it even closer to the *Manhunter* song, "Heartbeat (It's a Lifebeat)".

[82]   Or, considering Dyanne Thorne's contribution, what Crow called "Double D Indemnity" in reference to a similar character in Coleman Francis' *The Skydivers*.

[83]   "Who's your decorator, Bela Lugosi?' she asks; which is a pretty odd line — it's beach bum bachelor pad, not a bit Transylvanian — until you realize later it sounds the note of vampire/zombie/living death.

[84]   He's portrayed as a virtual prisoner of their oceanfront mansion, despite a super-duper

he "needs more strings" — and before you can say "Wham bam, thank you ma'am"[85] Angie and Ziggy — I mean, Andrea and Tony — are in the studio recording his first big record! But first, after a midnight pool shag[86] Dyanne puts the finishing touches on her rather understandably jealous and bitter husband by pushing him into said pool.[87]

Although not part of Tony's plan, he figures he's got it made now, and proposes to Andrea, who turns him down with a laugh, pointing out that he's a boy toy, not husband material; she's now free, and doesn't need another ball and chain. Inexplicably, this obvious truth seems to surprise Tony, who pouts until Angela's step-daughter shows up for the funeral. When Andrea underlines her independence by a spur of the moment vacation, Tony turns on his irresistible charms, woos the daughter, and marries her in Tijuana.[88]

This doesn't sit well with the returning Andrea, and … well, I can't do better than Cinema de Merde's recap (although I will emphasize some symbolically important phrases):

[T]o say that Andrea throws a scene would be to say the very least. She clings to his leg as he drags her up the lawn. Oh by the way, in here is an obvious section where something was clearly edited out—using stone tools, by the looks of it—but one wonders what kinkiness was just too hot for us to hear. Anyway, through some bizarre, inexplicable edit, Andrea throws herself at Tony's FEET and somehow ends up hanging around his shoulders. At this point—listen here, this is amazing—he starts spinning around [as any one of us would do in such a situation] with such apparent speed that the centrifugal force is pulling Andrea's

---

motorized wheelchair so advanced it has its own line in the opening credits. "You know I can't come down to the office" he shouts into the phone at one point. Without getting into advocacy for the differently-abled, it's hard to see why, even for the 60s; it sure didn't stop Dr. Strangelove, now did it?

[85] "Suffragette City" was released as the B-side of the single "Starman" in April 1972.

[86] Impossible to watch now without thinking of the infamous pool scene in *Showgirls*. Kyle McLaughlin will of course become Mr. Mayor of *Portlandia*.

[87] Actually, in the film's most "psychotronic" moment, she goads him into chasing her around the pool, using a tablecloth like a matador until he falls in. This is all set to bullfight cheers and horns, I suspect this scene is Alex Nichol's contribution; since Pete's not in it, he likely had no interest in directing it. It's the sort of scene that Quentin Tarrantino would delight in, not that there's anything wrong with that.

[88] Where they get a better deal than in Vegas because the locals think he's Herb Alpert.

legs STRAIGHT out behind her. Now, Tony and Andrea WERE by the beach, but walked up the path to the house, which means that, when Andrea finally lets slip her grip, the force of Tony's spinning sends her body flying horizontally a MINIMUM of 95 feet, where she lands on the rocks of the beach, killing her instantly! Sadly, such accidents are ALL too common. And how many of us, when landscaping our homes, adequately guard against how surprisingly far our bodies might be horizontally flung in JUST such an everyday situation?[89]

Oh well, just another sunny day in California. Tony and sugar momma's step-daughter turned-wife prepare to move on, when Tony gets a call from his pregnant girlfriend. Wait, you forgot about the girlfriend back at the club? And that she was or got pregnant? So did everyone else. Tony rushes over, and she blows him away with a shotgun. Really, all this takes place in less time than it took me to type those sentences – again, were scenes cut, or a reel lost?

Before we have time to start asking questions Tony wakes up screaming. So, it was all dream! Thank goodness, we were really worried about what was happening to this wonderful guy we cared so much about. But wait, didn't he scream at the beginning? So it's starting all over again! And sure enough, here comes Andrea and her remarkable bikini. And Tony — and we — scream again.

And so ends our story. A cautionary tale, to be sure.[90]

Just as genre, and especially Grade Z flicks, can, thanks to their below the radar status, present us with more brutally realistic scenarios than standard "Hollywood" fare. In this small town, a heartless egotist repeats the last few weeks of his life endlessly, but without any change of character.

And why would he change? As Schopenhauer and Evola both assert, our character is fixed, indeed, given to us prenatally, and our lives are merely the unfolding of that eternal character in Time.[91] To break free of the Round of Existence requires spiritual initiation, which precisely grants a new character, a new being, to the initiate. But of course, it is also one's very character that grants one the indispensable qualifications for

---

[89] http://cinemademerde.com/Point_of_Terror.shtml.

[90] Delivered by Crow with a plummy English criminologist voice at the end of *Devil Doll* (Episode 818).

[91] See Julius Evola, *Ride the Tiger: A Survival Manual for the Aristocrats of the Soul*, trans. Joscelyn Godwin and Constance Fontana (Rochester, Vt.: Inner Traditions, 2003).

initiation – as well as providential birth in an area and time with access to a true spiritual current; only in the most exoteric, even sentimental sense, can it simply be distributed wholesale. As Evola says,

> What has to be negated most decisively is the transposition to this field of the individualistic, and democratic view of the "self-made man," that is, the idea that anyone who wants to can become an "initiate," and that he can also become one on his own, through his own strength alone, by resorting to various kinds of "exercises" and practices. This is an illusion, the truth being that through his own strength alone, the human individual cannot go beyond human individuality, and that any positive result in this field is conditioned by the presence and action of a genuine power of a different, nonindividual order. [92]

The appeal of *Groundhog Day*, both to the general public as well as the representatives of various spiritual paths of one or another level of legitimacy, perhaps lies in its presentation of profound spiritual truth – every day is *Groundhog Day* — with a comforting spiritual illusion — we can break free is only we try hard enough, or do just the right thing.[93]

Of course, it is true that the 'love of a woman' has frequently been used, either as a metaphor for initiation, and even sometimes as a means of initiation itself, in which case:

> the desire and rapture aroused by woman is not allowed to develop along material and profane lines, but is used as the means for a spiritual realization, which may even partake of the nature of an initiation. For such purposes a real woman is simply used as the starting point and as a support.[94]

---

[92] Op. cit, p. 214. See also *The Doctrine of Awakening: The Attainment of Self-Mastery According to the Earliest Buddhist Texts* (Rochester, Vt: Inner Traditions, 1995), Chapter 7, "Determination of the Vocations," p. 73f. Phil actually seems to cycle through the various spiritual (or rather, racial in Evola's sense) attitudes to *samsara*, from delight in transience to despair to a kind of "ascesis" in an attempt to transcend it.

[93] While Ramis has always disavowed any deep spiritual message, it's no surprise to learn he professes to be a secular Jew.

[94] See Evola's "The 'Mysteries of Woman' in East and West" in his *East and West: Comparative Studies in Pursuit of Tradition*, ed. Greg Johnson (San Francisco: Counter-Currents, 2018.

To read *Groundhog Day* along these lines, we would see Rita's (Rita = Rite?) list of the Ideal Man's qualities less as her equally selfish "counter-game" but as a real initiation.[95]

Women have learned well to be dubious of such male-derived cults of Woman; as Evola hints here:

> For such purposes a real woman is simply used as the starting point and as a support.

> The true object of the cult [of Chivalry] was indeed a woman possessed of autonomous reality, apart from the physical personality of the real woman, who could eventually serve as her support, and who could in a certain sense, incorporate and represent her.

and makes explicit elsewhere,[96] this is less about "worshipping the Goddess" or even taking out the garbage,[97] and more like ruthless exploitation. Indeed, Evola notes that some Taoist "texts give reason to suspect, that in some cases the purpose served is even a form of masculine vampirism.[98]

What can be said, is that both promiscuity, casual or frenetic, and marriage, seem to be either beside the point or positively harmful.[99] As the

---

[95]   In accord with our principle that Grade Z cinema is richer in more explicit themes of tradition, we recall from note 11 above that in *Overdrawn at the Memory Bank* Apollonia is portrayed more explicitly as a goddess delivering the Law. Phil is right to inquire "This is a man we're talking about, right?" less because of the list's Alan Alda, beta male features than because the Initiate, by transcending duality and achieving Wholeness, partakes of the Androgyne and even can be said to practice "Philosophical Incest," just as Tony marries his almost-step-daughter and displays his boy toy body throughout the film like a exploited female; or as the dominant, controlling Grandma Lorelai, who married her cousin and is nicknamed "Trixie". See Julius Evola, *The Hermetic Tradition* (Rochester, Vt.: Inner Traditions, 1995), passim.

[96]   See *Eros and the Mysteries of Love*, aka *The Metaphysics of Sex*, where flogging and deflowering are the recommended methods.

[97]   *Garbage and the Goddess* is the long since suppressed record of Bubba Free John's period of teaching through sex and drugs; see William Patterson, *Adi Da Samraj: Realized or/and Deluded?* (Arete, 2012).

[98]   Evola, in Part Two of "The 'Mysteries of Woman' in *East and West*," loc. cit. Another way to understand Andrea's weird line to Tony, "Who did your decorating, Bela Lugosi?"

[99]   As I have frequently pointed out, the traditional role of the homosexual or androgyne as a cultural and spiritual creator has been effectively co-opted by the culture-distortions of not only the Right-wing — punished as sin or crime — but more subtly, of the Left, in the form of post-Stonewall promiscuity and, post-AIDS, marriage and adoption. See the

path from duality to wholeness, initiation is inherently paradoxical.

This allows us to see the Tony/Andrea relationship in a surprising new light, particularly the odd scene where Tony proposes marriage. Tony has until now been portrayed as an aging rent boy or sexual predator, but now suddenly proposes marriage, which Andrea rejects with contemptuous laughter. As we have seen, both roles are alien to the process of initiation. Like Parsifal, Tony is a fool who has learned nothing from his encounter with Andrea.

If Tony is Parsifal, then Andrea's crippled husband, confined to his sterile 70s mansion, is the Fisher King. After Andrea "makes love" with Tony in the pool, he — the husband — is dumped in it and drowns. And now the bullfight noises make sense, referencing the lance that wounds Amfortas.[100]

His death summons the daughter from abroad, who we can think of as Andrea rejuvenated. Tony certainly thinks so, and proceeds exploit her naiveté by successfully renewing his pitch for matrimony.

If the initiation seems to be short circuited, we can find some clues by taking a close look — if you can stand it — at the curious sexual dynamics of Tony and Andrea.

Many later viewers and reviewers have noted, with either contempt or "campy" humor, that Andrea — and indeed, most of the older women among her rich set at the Lobster House — "looks like a drag queen." Whatever that expression may mean as an insult or endearment, it's true that with her big, bad blonde hair and rather hard features, the future SS Warden Ilsa does resemble a certain kind of big, often Southern, drag queen.

Meanwhile, her daughter has implausibly long hair — about waist length — that suggests a certain over-compensating, and first appears wearing a black leather overcoat that's sinisterly masculine and certainly

---

manifesto "The Homo and the Negro" in *The Homo & the Negro: Masculinist Meditations on Politics & Popular Culture*; Second, Embiggened Edition, edited by Greg Johnson (San Francisco: Counter-Currents, 2017).

[100] See Julius Evola, *The Mystery of the Grail: Initiation and Magic in the Quest for the Spirit* (Rochester, Vt.: Inner Traditions, 1996), especially Chapter 19, "The Dolorous Stroke." Is it cruel or trivializing to relate him to Baron Evola himself? We can note that while Andrea's husband dies under water, Evola, we are told, had himself wheeled over to a window so that he would die as a *kshatriya*, upright and in the rays of the rising sun.

recalls the future Ilsa.[101] And her aforementioned BFF is almost always falling down drunk and loudly wishing she "had tits like Andrea," while appearing in several scenes wearing an obvious and askew wig.

Above all, symbolically, their names; Andrea, with its masculine edge, is no doubt a favorite among a certain class of closeted cross dressers, as well as its suggestion of 'andro;' while the daughter seems to be named Helene, but according to the credits, it's "Helayne." And while I'm not going to suggest there's anything obviously "masculine" about Andie MacDowell, Andie is pretty close to Andrea, and her real name, Anderson, is even worse; to say nothing of her beginnings in the notoriously androgynous world of fashion mannequins.

As for Tony, there is a longstanding notion of the Don Juan or Lothario as, paradoxically, a feminine type, seeking affirmation from others. Tony's couch scene. Though a 'Z' movie, PoT is intended to be "mainstream" – i.e., not gay porn or a Kenneth Anger or Jack Smith style "avant-garde" piece. So the amount of 'beefcake' is extraordinary. His revulsion from Sally's pregnancy is perhaps mostly for its reminder that he is, after all, supposed to be the man here, while desperately seeking marriage to Andrea or Helayne like some spinster. "Tony" is as ambiguous as "Andrea".

What we see in this aspect of *Point of Terror* is well described by Camille Paglia in her musings on Coleridge's poem "Christabel":

An alchemical experiment whose main event is the crystallization of a *rebis* or hermaphroditic personality. The poem is an alembic of superheated psyche. Energy is released and rebounded. Vampires make vampires. ... Fascination, capture, possession, transfiguration.[102]

"Fascination, capture, possession, transfiguration" does seem to be the plot here, but Tony is unable to pull off the transfiguration part. Tony and Andrea are androgynous figures, but rather than vampirically making use of Andrea, he succumbs to the feminine role and seeks domesticity. As Evola explains:

---

[101]   The previous year, 1972, which I've speculated before as the highpoint of youth culture, brought us not only Ziggy Stardust but also the film *Cabaret*, which has some odd parallels to 1973's *Point of Terror*. Both movies open with a disembodied drum roll, the constant talk of money – "Money makes me class!" Andrea shouts at Tony — recall the "Money Song" ——"Money makes the world go around" — along with the club scenes, Andrea's BFF with her pixie hair, Tony's girlfriend is named Sally, and so on.

[102]   *Sexual Personae: Art and Decadence from Nefertiti to Emily Dickinson* (New Haven: Yale University Press, 1990), p. 341.

Since every symbolism is based on specific relationships of analogy,[103] it is necessary to begin with the possible relationships between man and woman. These relationships can be either normal or abnormal. They are abnormal when the woman dominates the man...

[I]t is necessary to refer to the normal relations between man and woman as the basis of the analogy and of the symbolism; hence the fundamental concept of a situation in which the virile principle retains its own nature. The spirit, *vis-à-vis* the masculine, is the "woman": the virile principle is active, the spirit passive. Even before the power that transfigures it and vivifies the hero, the virile principle retains the character that man has as the lord of his woman. In passing, we must note that this is exactly the opposite of the bridal symbolism prevalent in religious and especially in the Christian mysticism, in which the soul is attributed a feminine role, namely, that of the "bride."[104]

This is not to insist on any rigid kind of gender roles, only that each player needs to know where they stand. Tony turns out to be not man enough for Andrea. Tony fails to control and dominate the female.

All this is brought home in a remarkable scene I'll call the "Sofa Scene." It's the only thing I really remembered after all these years from seeing it once on late night TV, no doubt because of the enticing moment when Andrea lies back on a sofa and – well, it's not the sort of thing commonly seen on basic cable even today; but we'll get to that.

When Tony proposes to Andrea, she, as we noted above, laughs with contempt and points out that she plans to remain free, and that Tony is just a gigolo. Then, in a reversal of normal human, or even primate behavior — typical of what makes Grade-Z films so fascinating — she demonstrates her dominance by lying down on the sofa and spreading her legs. Tony, not to be outdone, reveals that he didn't go straight home and in fact witnessed Andrea's little bullfight scene. She gets up to protest his implicit blackmail threat — nice way to start a marriage, Tony; and say, didn't you see what

---

[103]   As Guénon points out, contrary to self-congratulatory secular mythologizing, symbolism is by no means an arbitrary assignment of this or that meaning to things, as occurs in mere allegory ("The Yellow Brick Road is the gold standard") but based on real, natural relations – if two things are called "flowers" they must also share "stems" and "seeds" as well; hence it can be understood by anyone, and passed on — *traditio* — without loss or alteration.

[104]   *Mystery of the Grail*, pp. 21-22.

happened to the last guy that knew too much about Andrea's homicidal tendencies? — and Tony then takes her place on the sofa, giving us an unwelcome shot of his own, um, area.[105]

Andrea then turns the, um, tables again threatening to reveal their relationship to Helayne. (What, she doesn't already know Tony is an unlikeable scumbag?), and it's back to the couch to wait for Tony to fail to call her bluff.[106]

This odd bit of stage business enacts the unnatural nature of Tony and Andrea's relationship. As Baron Evola quotes the hermeticist d'Espagnet:

> The Female at first is stronger than the Male and dominates him, in order to transmute him into her own nature. But then the Male recovers his vigor and in turn gains ascendancy, dominates the Female and makes her like himself. ... The Female must first be allowed to surmount the Male, and then the Male the Female.[107]

Andrea, in short, should seek to dominate Tony, using her masculine energies to attract this fundamentally feminine male; but having succeeded, she must be dominated in turn by the newly invigorated Tony. None of this, of course, can be accomplished with either a one-night stand or a happily married life in the suburbs.

The notorious whirling death scene also makes more sense. Tony is rejecting the path of Initiation with Andrea and choosing domesticity with Helayne. When Andrea returns to find that Tony, the invincible fool, has defied her and married Helayne, she attempts to drag him back, whereupon he flings her away into the sea – again, like the pool, and the swirling audience at the Lobster House, we have here the symbol of the Lower Waters.[108]

---

[105]   "Ahh! Mike, his batch! It's ... AH!" – MST3K, *The Legend of Boggy Creek*. If the characters weren't so vile, these would be examples of the trope known as "Fan Service."

[106]   Tony spends a lot of time supine. There's our first meeting with him on the beach; he's on the couch with Sandy; here, on the couch confronting Andrea; on the ground as Andrea attacks him at the climax; shot down by Sandy, then we cut to him back on the beach. Was he tired from all the singing and directing?

[107]   Julius Evola, *The Hermetic Tradition* (Rochester, Vt.: Inner Traditions, 1995), p. 72.

[108]   The odd geography and wild cuts also make sense in this Parsifal context; "Here time turns into space."

But this should be seen from the perspective of one of Hitchcock's reverse angle shots, as in Vertigo or especially the Statue of Liberty scene in *Saboteur*. It is Tony who is flung away and lost, not Andrea. As we will see in *Psychomania*, below, the withdrawal of the Realized Man — or in this case, the Shakti power — is perceived by the worldly as not just immobility but death.

This is confirmed in the immediately following scenes, where again jarring cuts and wonky geography indicate that time has changed into space, or at least is fragmented; Tony's girlfriend reappears, suddenly pregnant, as a sped-up version of his marriage, and puts an end to him – and the movie.

Speaking of Tony's long missing "girlfriend" Sandy, we recall that Tony — or rather, Peter Carpenter — gave himself a lost little boy scene with her soon after meeting Andrea — on the same couch! — complete with heart-tugging memories (his father shined shoes!), triumph over adversity ("When I sang, nobody laughed;" keep telling yourself that, Tony) and even tears. Hello, Oscar!

Anyway, Tony lets us know that

I want to be somebody. Not much time left for me, that's what I want to be – somebody. That's all I've ever wanted, to be – somebody. I'd do anything.

Now, as Andrea taunts Tony from the sofa, she warns him:

You'll have nothing. Nothing but self.[109]

Tony has confused the personality and the Self, rejected transcendence of the ego for the more familiar personal triumph – singing career, marriage. Like the Modern Woman, he wants it all!

No matter how many times he repeats the cycle, "A drifter of the heart, that's what I'll always be."[110]

---

[109] Unless, of course, she just blew the line "but yourself" and no one noticed or cared.

[110] There's also this exchange, driving home the 'puppet' motif:

Sandy: I'm gonna buy you a kite.
Tony: With my luck, the string would break.

Tony fails because he insists on marrying Andrea, then moves on to her daughter.[111] Weirdly his mundane swinger lifestyle encompasses both promiscuity AND settling down, both inappropriate here choices for the initiate.[112]

Groundhog Phil is wiser; although he seems all to ready to settle down with Rita, he immediately starts to hedge:

"Let's rent first."

Unless he's just crazy to begin with, we can assume that Tony screams at the beginning for the same reason he screams at the end: waking up to the realization that it's the same day again; only now we're in on it too, having — unfortunately for us — seen the preceding film. So far, pretty much like *Groundhog Day*, only with a longer cycle of several weeks or months. In fact, *Groundhog Day* was going to open the same way, already in *Groundhog Day* mode but not telling us, letting us wonder why Phil always already knows what's going to happen next.

Except – since Tony, the first time we see him, doesn't continue screaming, or trying to get out of the loop like Phil does, we can assume further that he immediately forgets what happened, and then relives essentially the same events. In fact, since Tony himself, unlike Phil, is denied any knowledge of what is happening to him, he has no motive to even try to "reform" himself, especially since everything seems to be going his way, chick and career wise. Until it doesn't, and rapidly spins down the drain, only to start up again.[113]

---

[111]   Given its "mother like daughter" premise, and its view of men as disposable, easily manipulated tools — in several senses — its odd that *The Gilmore Girls* never took up this theme explicitly, if only from its post-feminist Girl Power viewpoint, not *Point of Terror's* Penthouse Forum sleaze. There were hints, though; the very first scene of the pilot introduced us to the Girls and the theme by having a passing hitchhiker first try to pick up Lorelei, then unknowingly move on to Rory. And the second episode, entitled "The Lorelei's First Day of School" is widely hated by fans for her bizarre decision to dress like Daisy Duke for Rory's first day at private school, and for immediately flirting with all the fathers among the parents; in fact, she soon begins a romance with one of Rory's teachers. And we recall that Lorelei's grandmother not only shared her name but married her (second) cousin.

[112]   We might see a parallel here to the modern Left's neutering of the traditional cultural role of the homosexual by promoting the only apparently different "lifestyles" of bathhouse promiscuity and gay marriage.

[113]   It's rather like the scene in *Hitchhikers Guide to the Galaxy*, where there's a crashed spaceship whose suspended animated passengers are re-awakened every couple hundred

There's no telling how long this has been going on, but considering the very time-specific hair, clothes, music, technology, etc., and assuming each reiteration is, like the one we've just seen, the same, it must be fairly recently. Still, like any dream, the actual time passing could be minute, so this could be the 10,000th cycle.

If Phil is in Purgatory, Tony is in Hell.

If he's lucky, perhaps it's a Buddhist hell.

> Thirst is, if only strong enough, almighty. At the moment of my death it will make me find out in the infinite universe the beloved being which had died before me; moreover, my thirst will infallibly bring about my attachment within the beloved being's range. Thus we shall meet again, though both in a new shape; although we shall not recognize one another, this reunion will deeply move both of us, calling forth a "love at first sight." All this may repeat several successive existences.[114]

Our Buddhist author, however, also provides us a ray of hope

> Naturally, in the course of time, even in such a case estrangement shall gradually set in, wherewith even this love transcending death shall prove to be impermanent.

Contrary to the childish nightmares promoted by Christianity, all is impermanent, even Hell. We can imagine that Tony's obsession will gradually decay, until — again, should his essential character, created by past karma — some insight into his condition arises; perhaps then he will perceive suffering, the cause of suffering, and the path leading to the cessation of suffering.[115]

If Tony is in Hell, it's a kinder, gentler version, since he seems only aware of his situation at the moment of awakening. With all due suspending of disbelief, I find it hard to believe that Phil, or anyone, could literally live the same day over and over again without going mad long before they had the

---

years, thrash about screaming and trying to get out, then re-suspended, and so on.

[114] *Buddhist Wisdom: The Mystery of the Self* by George Grimm; translated by Carroll Aikins; edited by M. Keller-Grimm (Delhi: Motilal Banarsidass, 1978), p. 35.

[115] There is perhaps a hint of this in *Gilmore Girls*, in a curiously self-aware opening bit where Lore and Rory are watching *Grey Gardens*, and suddenly realize that they are Big Edie and Little Edie, but of course nothing comes of it and after the comedic blackout things go on.

chance to make any improvements in themselves and thus, inadvertently, end the cycle. We'll look at that idea — Mad Phil — in Part Two.

From Punxawaney PA to Woodstock IL to Stars Hollow, CT to a sleepy Coastal California town; in Part Two let's complete our geographical circle to the Deep New South, whose Gothic/Futurist horror has been well mined by Michael Mann, first as Miami Vice, then in the Georgia, Kansas City and Alabama locales of *Manhunter*.

Phil & Will

Awakening Through Repetition in Groundhog Day, Point of Terror, & Manhunter, Part II

W E'VE BEEN USING a variation on what Baron Evola called The Traditional Method, in which various historical traditions, each more or less incomplete, are held up against each other to provide a mutual critique of each one's imperfections, and suggest the presence of the higher truth each imperfectly embodies.[116]

Point of Terror, despite its somewhat endearing sleaziness, critiques *Groundhog Day*'s premise, and suggests the more Traditional notion that one's character is a given, perhaps selected pre-natally but subject to very little variation in life, no matter how many repetitions one is given; in fact, the more likely result of endlessly repeating one's life would be a kind of living Hell rather than resolution, reform, and living happily ever after.[117]

Or perhaps, madness. The film *Manhunter* suggests that an unlikable jerk-ass in Phil's situation is far more likely to develop into a serial killer than a saint, secular or otherwise.

Constant Readers will not be surprised when I disclose that I am a Big Fan of *Manhunter*, Michael Mann's post-Miami Vice pastel-and-neon take on Thomas Harris's *Red Dragon*.[118] Yes, we have here another Neglected

---

[116] See *Mystery of the Grail*, pp. 9-10.

[117] See "Thanks for Watching: Awakening Through Repetition in *Groundhog Day, Point of Terror, & Manhunter*, Part I."

[118] Hollywood legend has it that producer Dino De Laurentis demanded the name change since he was superstitious about 'dragons' after the failure of Michael Cimino's *Year of the Dragon*. The failure of the latter was due less to its title than to the critical backlash against Cimino for his studio-killing mega-bomb *Heaven's Gate*, an absurd fantasy of noble Slavic

Masterpiece; perhaps one may suggest, neglected precisely because it's a American Masterpiece? Despite all the "controversy" over the casting, the photography, and the music, if you listen closely, you can tell it's hated because it's so American.

It is indeed a very American film, meaning that, like America of old, it is an unself-consciously, taken for granted Caucasian world. Will Graham, the retired FBI profiler (or "manhunter" as the tabloids dub him) is called back — having retired after first entering the mind of, and then being gutted with a linoleum knife by Hannibal Lecktor — to find the killer of two large, well-off families in the New South (Birmingham and Atlanta, no less). His task is to save the next family – as so often in fiction, the psycho has provided a handy timetable for the authorities.[119]

Graham's mission is to save American families; he's well-suited for the role, since he has one of his own – his very '80s rail-thin and frizzy-haired wife (Kim Greist) and his very blond son.

Jack Crawford: Oh, for Christ's sake, it's a foregone conclusion! It's 11:30 P.M., the full moon is happening tonight. Give it up. Forget this month. It's too damn late.

Will Graham: I gave it up! Till you showed up with pictures of two dead families, knowing God damn well that I'd imagine families three, four, five and six. Right?

Jack Crawford: You're fucking right I did! And I'd do it again!

Will Graham: Great! But don't talk to me about late, pal! I'll tell you when it's too fucking late! Until then, we go as late as I wanna take it!

It's such an American film that even the bad guys are Caucasian: Hannibal Lecktor and Francis Dollarhyde.[120] Lecktor, whom Brian Cox plays very

---

immigrants to Wyoming (?) being mass-murdered by evil cattle barons that bears no resemble to any part of Earth's known history; see Steve Sailer's discussion: https://isteve. blogspot.com/2013/08/heavens-gate.html

[119] Thus, an instance of the trope known as "You Have 48 Hours": "Since the Tooth Fairy "operates on a lunar cycle," the FBI has until the next full moon to catch him before he kills again. They start out with two weeks, but end up taking it right down to the last minute before the killer claims another victim." Of course, this parallels Phil's repetition day.

[120] It is speculated online that Mann changed the spelling of "Lechter" and "Dolarhyde"

differently than Anthony Hopkins did, still seems to be vaguely British, and obviously likes to read; two very suspicious traits.[121]

Doctor Hannibal Lecktor: But you haven't threatened to take away my books yet!

Dollarhyde's Otherness is more intriguing. Played by Tom Noonan, he's very pale, nearly an albino, identified by a blond hair on his note to Lecktor and as a Caucasian on van permit at work. Yet his more striking characteristics seem to suggest a villain. When we first meet him, he jumps up and towers over a female co-worker; his absurd height, chrome dome, gangly limbs and powerful build suggest an NBA thug.[122] His obsession

---

because they were "too Jewish"; if so, that would make the Red Dragon re-make, by restoring both, more "ethnically insensitive."

121   The online controversy over *Manhunter* vs. *Silence of the Lambs*, or more recently the *Red Dragon* re-make, has two particularly stupid aspects. First, Cox vs. Hopkins. I'll discuss Cox in a bit, but comparing the two is pointless because each takes place in very different films, and are played accordingly; you couldn't switch them out without producing a jarring discontinuity. *Manhunter* is essentially a police procedural, a film noir version of *Miami Vice*. (In the same year, Mann, who was still executive producer of MV, produced an episode, "Shadow in the Dark," that actually seems like a dry run for the film, with Don Johnson replacing William Peterson as Will Graham and Edward James Olmos replacing Dennis Farina as Crawford. So if *Manhunter* is *Silence* as a *Miami Vice* episode, "Shadow" is that *Miami Vice* episode squared; I haven't tried a detailed comparison for fear of falling into a black hole.) The Hopkins films are grand opera or grand guignol, harkening back to *Phantom of the Opera* or *Dracula*. Thus, in reference to our discussion just now, Cox is in white prison uniform, in a white cell in a white prison/hospital (presumably Baltimore, but, in keeping with the New South theme actually filmed in some soulless postmodern art museum in Atlanta); Hopkins, by contrast, sits in a dank, subterranean cell, wearing grey against a palette of black and blood red.

The second stupid controversy is the music; "It's so outdated; it's so '80s!" Even Brian Cox can't resist putting the boot in: "The only thing I'm not mad about, when I look at it — though I saw it recently and I was a little bit more forgiving — but I was never a fan of '80s music. So that always dates the film, for me, the score. Visually, I think the film's a hundred per cent. Musically I think it's 50 per cent." (http://www.denofgeek.com/movies/18119/brian-cox-interview-manhunter-hannibal-the-cannibal-adaptation-michael-mann-and-brett-ratner).

We'll look at the music in a bit, but really, since the film takes place in the '80s, what music should it have – Grunge? Electo-pop? Tin Pan Alley? By contrast, *Scarface's* disco soundtrack is arguably anachronistic, and the idea of replacing it with the kind of rap inspired by the film itself would be clever, if the actual "music" wasn't so vile.

122   According to the book, he would also have an NBA-worthy full body tattoo, the

with sight, his outsized vampire dentures, and his disfigured lip all suggest stereotypical villainous features that set him apart from others – eyes, teeth, lips. Even the blind Reba knows there's something different about him, and when she tries to compliment him on it, she sounds like Joe Biden complimenting Barack Obama:

> Reba: You know, you speak very well, although you avoid fricatives and sibilants.[123]

However, Dollarhyde's preferred method is nothing other than the suburbanite's great fear: home invasion. But then, it's all the same in the dark:

> Doctor Hannibal Lecktor: Have you ever seen blood in the moonlight, Will? It appears quite black.

It's always great to find a film that, even in the '80s, takes place in an implicit suburban utopia. Things will be perfect again as soon as that pesky Tooth Fairy is taken out. As far as I can tell, there are only two African characters. One, who appears so briefly that I only noticed him on my most recent re-viewing, is a jogger that is mistaken for Dollarhyde when he runs into the trap Graham set for the Tooth Fairy.

> The Runner: [to the cops] What you movin' in slow motion for, man? I'm being mugged.

The other is some kind of police officer near the end, essentially a servant, whose job is just to relay information to the men in the plane overhead; significantly, neither he nor any other cop plays a role in capturing Dollarhyde, only Graham himself.[124]

Anyway, I'm suggesting that our two bad guys, Lecktor and Dollarhyde, are examples of what Phil would likely become if someone like him were to find themselves in an endless loop.

---

eponymous *Red Dragon*, but Mann wisely decided it "cheapened" his menacing look; the remake brings it back, with comical effect on the scrawny Brit Ralph Fiennes.

[123] A great example of Hollywood screenwriter bullshit: fricatives are sibilants, and Dollarhyde just delivered a line full of them.

[124] On the other hand, the actor will reappear as "Willie the Orderly" in the next three films, thus becoming the only actor to appear in all four Lecktor/Lechter films, although in two different roles.

According to TV Tropes,

No Endor Holocaust: The movie glosses over two things. ... 2: Given the suggested timespan there must have been days when he did incredibly cruel things to relieve his frustration, but those days aren't shown. ... Ramis and his co-writer Danny Rubin have said they deliberately avoided one of the logical extremes that Phil could have done: create despair and kill people with no consequence. They decided to avoid the sadistic possibilities of the time loop. Presumably, the fact that even at his worst Phil has enough of a moral compass to avoid murder and overt sadism is one of the things that helps him on the road to redemption.

If it sounds strange to think of Phil as Lecktor, that's because you're thinking of Hopkins' Count Dracula. As someone once said online, Cox's Lecktor is the sort of ordinary guy who might sit down next to you on the bus, or the DMV, and engage you in a casual conversation that suddenly finds you in his basement, hogtied.

Cox's most Murray-moment comes at the end of the scene where he makes a late night call to convince a temp to give him Graham's home address – today's hackers would call this "social engineering." The look on his face, literally tongue in cheek, as he chews the gum whose foil wrapper enabled him to re-direct the call supposedly to his attorney, is pure Bill Murray, and miles away from Hopkins feasting on rare lamb chops.

And I'm glad to see that image has been chosen for the recent "Brian Coxfest."

Both Phil and Lecktor are smug jackasses, who seem to have some kind of unearned omniscience. Lecktor, like Sherlock Holmes — or Dr. House — is supposedly so damn intelligent they can "deduce" just what you're thinking or about to do. Although Phil was already a condescending jerk, we know that his thousands of repetitions of the same day have given him omniscience the easy — or perhaps the hard — way. In fact, if Groundhog Day had been filmed as originally planned, Phil would have appeared at first without back-story, leaving us to wonder how he was able to know everything that was going to happen.

It's Lecktor who will, unwillingly, provide Will — get it? — with the essential clue he'll need to find Dollarhyde. Will, as a profiler, is able to enter the mind of the likes of Lecktor or Dollarhyde, making him another

Double of both. As such, we can see him as a Good Phil, while Lektor wants him to become a Bad Phil like Dollarhyde. To do so, he gives him the same counsel about the exchangeability of character we've already emphasized – as usual in movies, it's the psychopaths who speak for Tradition:

> Will Graham: I'm sick of you, Lecktor. If you've got something to say, say it!
>
> Doctor Hannibal Lecktor: 1 want to help you, Will. You'd be more comfortable if you relaxed with yourself! We don't invent our natures, they're issued to us with our lungs and pancreas and everything else. Why fight it?
>
> Will Graham: Fight what?
>
> Doctor Hannibal Lecktor: Did you really feel depressed after you shot Mr. Garrett Jacob Hobbes to death? I think you probably did. But it wasn't the act that got to you. Didn't you feel so bad, because killing him felt so good? And why shouldn't it feel good? It must feel good to God. He does it all the time. God's terrific! He dropped a church roof on 34 of his worshippers in Texas last Wednesday night, just as they were groveling through a hymn to his majesty. Don't you think that felt good?
>
> Will Graham: Why does it feel good, Dr. Lecktor?
>
> Doctor Hannibal Lecktor: It feels good because God has power. If one does what God does enough times, one will become as God is. God's a champ. He always stays ahead. He got 140 Filipinos in one plane crash last year. Remember that earthquake in Italy last spring?

Groundhog Day presents us with Good Phil, who after some initial shenanigans gets with the program as outlined by Rita (as we noted in Part One, the Sanskrit notion of rule or order) and worked to become a better person. Being a comedy, the screenwriters know they can only go so far; Phil can attempt to harm himself, but not others.

Tasked with producing a "thriller," Harris and Mann have a freer hand, and we can see the whole dialectic played out. Lektor is a Satanic figure who tempts Will into accepting his murderous impulses (which enable him to "profile" actual serial killers) and become as God is; Dollarhyde has already accepted this Faustian bargain.[125]

Lecktor's coded message, "inherit my mantle and surpass my achievements" is directed at Will as much as Dollarhyde. But Lecktor is a false Guru, who would trap Graham in the endless repetition of Samsara; the climax shows us Graham somehow summoning up the Will to resist, disrupting rather than joining the Tooth Fairy's fantasy world.[126]

Will Graham: I'm sick of you crazy sons of bitches, Lecktor

While Phil/Murray looks even less like Dollarhyde than Lecktor, we'll see that he has even more in common. Graham has previously imagined his way into Dollarhyde's mind and intuited the reason for his crimes –

Will Graham: You ... rearrange the dead families into an audience. You think what you do makes you into something different. You're becoming ... What is it you're becoming? The answer is in the way you use the mirrors. What do the mirrors make you dream?

The parallel with TV weatherman Phil, whose automatic, couldn't care less greeting is "Thanks for watching" should be clear.

Graham is then able to "put it together" (using a clue his "sick of you" outburst goaded Lecktor into giving him):

Will Graham: He dreams about being wanted and desired. So he changes people into beings who want and desire him.

Jack Crawford: Changes?

Will Graham: It's a word. Killing and arranging the people to imitate it. And Lecktor told me something: "If one does what God does enough

---

[125] As with the music, we'll see that Mann's much abused "Miami Vice" color scheme is rigidly appropriate, with splashes of acid green in Lektor's cell and Dollarhyde's home to connect them with Lucifer's emerald; see Evola, op. cit.

[126] Thus Lecktor resembles such false Männerbünde leaders as Melville's Gnostic Ahab, as well as De Palma's Al Capone, as we've seen in my review of *The Untouchables*. Capone, played there by Robert De Niro, was known as "Scarface" which links him to Dolarhyde; *Scarface* was in turn another gangster film directed by De Palma, starring Al Pacino, who would later make Mann's *Heat* with De Niro.

times, one will become as God is." You put it together, you get: If our boy imitates being wanted and desired enough times, he believes he will become one who is wanted and desired and accepted. It'll all come true.

I think this is clearly what Bad Phil would be doing, especially after a couple hundred or so repetitions; not change himself, but change other people. And if that seems too dark, remember, no one "really" dies, since the day repeats; Phil can't even kill himself.

> Phil: I have been stabbed, shot, poisoned, frozen, hung, electrocuted, and burned.
>
> Rita: Oh, really?
>
> Phil: .... and every morning I wake up without a scratch on me, not a dent in the fender ... I am an immortal.

Indeed, Phil has become as God is.

> Jack Crawford: But finally, how does he select his victims?
>
> Will Graham: Jack, all the women have a bloom on them. He didn't win them in a lottery – he picked these women! There's selection and design in his choices.

As Graham obsessively replays the tapes made of families' home movies[127] he suddenly intuits that the killer has already done the same thing:

> Will Graham: But he doesn't take anything. He needs souvenirs from the houses, so he can relive the event. So he can see himself accepted over and over and over again.
>
> Crawford: Maybe he records it somehow. VTR's, Polaroids, stills, what? – How do I know?
>
> Graham: And you know you need a bolt-cutter and every other Goddamn thing. Because everything with you is seeing, isn't it?

---

[127] The pride with which the cop offers to transfer the home movies to "three quarter inch video tape" is almost as charmingly nostalgic as Graham's gigantic "mobile phone."

Your primary sensory intake that makes your dream live is seeing. Reflections. Mirrors. Images. ... You've seen these films! Haven't you, my man?

Both families' films were developed at the same lab, leading the FBI to Dollarhyde.[128]

In effect, Phil is in the same situation. Just as the repetitions allow him to develop Lecktor's level of omniscience, so they serve the same function as Dollarhyde's viewing the films and planning his invasions. The parallel, as Holmes would say, is exact.[129]

The Phil/Rita and Dollarhyde/Reba doppling is most apparent in two scenes, or rather, two particular shots.

In *Manhunter*, Dollarhyde, who works in a photo processing plant and has just killed two entire families so as to get them to look at him, meets Reba, a blind woman who, unrepulsed by his unseen harelip, not only finds him "a sweet, thoughtful man" but initiates a night of lovemaking. In the morning, we have a shot from the ceiling, showing the two in bed, Reba asleep. As the camera glides lower, Dollarhyde places her hand over his mouth (hiding the harelip) and, in a remarkable bit of acting by Tom Noonan, we seem to see his entire face collapse into a kind of corpse or skull, as the realization sinks in that he has found redemption, but it is too late, his stupid "posing the victims" idea has doomed him already.[130]

Will Graham: This started from an abused kid, a battered infant ... My heart bleeds for him, as a child. ... At the same time, as an adult, he's irredeemable. He butchers whole families to pursue trivial fantasies. As an adult, someone should blow the sick fuck out of his socks.

---

[128] If it's still hard to see "funny" Murray as Dollarhyde, consider "funny" Robin Williams in *One Hour Photo*, where he is a lonely photo shop technician (again, technological nostalgia!) who develops (!) an unhealthy and ultimately violent obsession with a suburban family.

[129] "The Empty Room"

[130] As Gob and others would say on *Arrested Development*, "I've made a huge mistake." Noonan's performance seems as if it were a homage to the sometimes suppressed final shot of *Psycho*, where a skull seems to be superimposed on Anthony Perkins' face; Norman of course has his own problems with spying on people and making things — birds, mothers — stay put.

There's a remarkably similar shot in *Groundhog Day*, looking down on Phil as he wakes up yet again on February 2nd, and apparently hit's the rock bottom of his despair:

But Phil, as we know, hasn't murdered anyone, and Rita is still available. Phil breaks the cycle by changing himself – he stops obsessing with being seen ("Thanks for watching!") and instead listens to Rita.[131] In the end, the Dollaryhyde/Reba shot is repeated, but as a happy ending.

Will, like Good Phil, resists Lecktor's fatalism and chooses — wills — to save the families, not kill them – or at least not let them be killed.[132] He makes that decision in a very blunt way, at the very climax of the film, when, having reached Dollarhyde's house, he sees him about to kill Reba. Here's Mann's original script:

GRAHAM (whispers in radio) It's happening again, Jack ...

CUT TO:

INT. DOLLARHYDE'S KITCHEN - DOLLARHYDE + REBA - NIGHT

On the right we see Dollarhyde's right arm with the aluminum shafts ... Beyond them, THROUGH THE WINDOW we see Graham has stepped out from the tree line. He stands on the grass. He looks helpless. His gun hangs idly at his side.

CLOSE: GRAHAM

It's his worst nightmare. About what he's seeing:

GRAHAM(low) ... stop it.

INT. DOLLARHYDE'S KITCHEN - DOLLARHYDE + BEYOND HIM THE WINDOW: GRAHAM

---

[131] One odd bit that the existence of Serial Killer Phil would explain is Phil winning an ice sculpture contest by executing a bust of Rita - with a chainsaw. "I know your face so well, I could have done it with my eyes closed."

[132] Those who have felt that this, or my previous, film work have been a tad too obsessive are welcome to go to the "Can Analyze" blog and feast on his 99-part analysis of the "hidden plot" of Manhunter: http://cananalyze.blogspot.com/2009/11/running-table-of-contents-to-manhunter.html. Hint: Lechtor is Hermes Trismegistus, and he is ultimately trying to get Will to murder his own family! Actually, it is rather odd that Will falls asleep on the plane while looking at photos of the slaughtered families - and dreams of his own.

We and Graham see Dollarhyde's arm arc back for an uppercutting thrust into Reba. Dollarhyde's left hand clutching her dress, raises her two feet up the wall. And now Graham starts running forward. And his face is distorted and he's shouting:

GRAHAM (roars) STOP IT!!!

Dollarhyde turns to the window in time to see:

128.

WINDOW + GRAHAM

— his arms across his face and his body angled sideways
— CRASHES through the glass.[133]

We see Graham with his arms hanging, helpless, in the open countryside, watching it "happen again" through the window of a rather Modernist house. Somehow, he musters the will to shout "Stop it," run forward, and then crash through the window that separates him from Dollarhyde and Reba.

At this point, I have to stop and go back to what I mentioned in a note earlier about the "controversy" over the music in the film. As Constant Readers will intuit, I just love the music, which is implicitly American, and those who profess to hate it are, to the extent that they have real opinions and are not just mouthing received wisdom, objectively vulgar.

Anyway, a few minutes ago in the film, as Dollarhyde begins to stalk the blind Reba in his house, the music changed abruptly; like Mia in *Pulp Fiction*, Dollarhyde has punched a button on his ultra-modern sound system and cued up a golden oldie: Iron Butterfly's "In-na-gadda-da-Vida." Even most critics of the soundtrack will admit that choreographing the final showdown to that song is a crowning moment of awesome.

Now, several subtle things are going on here. Up till now, the music has been "diagetic" as the professors say; it relates not to the world on screen but to the character's inner worlds, and suggests to the viewers the feelings they themselves should have.[134] (In the same way, the much

---

[133]   http://www.imsdb.com/scripts/Manhunter.html.

[134]   Wikipedia: "*Manhunter's* soundtrack 'dominates the film,' with music that is 'explicitly diegetic the entire way.' Steve Rybin has commented that the music is not intended to correlate with the intensity of the action portrayed alongside it, but rather to signify when

maligned "unnatural" Miami Vice palette throughout gives subtle cues to the viewer.[135]) And that music is American '80s music.

Thus, the music is telling us that we are not just in Dollarhyde's house, which exists in our world, but in his head, as it were. Just as Dollarhyde is a creature of the past, what "They" have made of him, constantly reliving the past, so his mental space is revealed to us by the way he, like some demonic Boomer, is still listening to the music of the past.[136]

Jack Crawford: You feel sorry for him.

Will Graham: This started from an abused kid, a battered infant ... My heart bleeds for him, as a child. Someone took a kid and manufactured a monster. At the same time, as an adult, he's irredeemable. He butchers whole families to pursue trivial fantasies. As an adult, someone should blow the sick fuck out of his socks. Does that sound like a contradiction to you, Jack? Does this kind of thinking make you uncomfortable?

Of course, the music is shortened a bit, but more than that, it's been extensively "remixed" as the kids say. Even at full length, it makes no sense in narrative time – Graham couldn't possibly have flown from Atlanta to St. Louis, and driven out to Dollarhyde's house, within one LP side, unless Dollarhyde had it on a loop, and just chased Reba around for the sadistic fun of it.

---

the viewer should react with a 'degree of aesthetic distance' from the film, or be 'suture[d] into the diegetic world' more closely." John Muir (!) suggests that this helps identify the character of Graham with the 'goodness' of the natural world, and Dollarhyde with the city, 'where sickness thrives.' This strongly stylized approach drew criticism from reviewers at first, but has since been seen as a hallmark of the film and viewed more positively."

[135] Wikipedia: Cinematographer Dante Spinotti made strong use of colour tints in the film, using a cool 'romantic blue' tone to denote the scenes featuring Will Graham and his wife, and a more subversive green hue, with elements of purple or magenta, as a cue for the unsettling scenes in the film, mostly involving Dollarhyde. Petersen has stated that Mann wanted to create a visual aura to bring the audience into the film, so that the story would work on an interior and emotional level ... 'There is nothing in *Manhunter* ... which is just a nice shot,' says Spinotti. '[It] is all focused into conveying that particular atmosphere; whether it's happiness, or delusion, or disillusion.' This 'manipulation of focus and editing' has become a visual hallmark of the film.

[136] We saw this with the Boomers of *The Big Chill*: "Don't you have any music from this century?" "There is no other music, not in this house."

In addition to the time-distortions in the music, Mann filmed the climax with several cameras running at various speeds, "giving the final scene ... an "off tempo," "staccato" feel."[137] Not only are Dollarhyde's motions choreographed to the music,[138] but the herky-jerky motions, particularly at his death scene, suggest exactly the totally-determined, puppet on a string; a theme we will return to elsewhere.

The roles are reversed; now it is Dollarhyde whose weapon hangs from his limp arm.[139]

Just as post-Traditional Western music has depended almost entirely on the simple use of modulation to build tension and then release it with the return to the home key, so George A. Martin (not, presumably, the Beatles producer) created a version of the Iron Butterfly jam which "build[s] tension towards the long-delayed return of the tonic bass riff, the exact moment when Graham literally bursts through the glass wall ... into the red dragon's metadiegetic realm."[140]

Graham, in other words, is outside Dollarhyde's world of repetition; he can crash through the glass wall, like the Gnostic's Alien God, and stop it. Dollarhyde, however, has become hopelessly entrapped in it; even Reba can't help.

Presumably, Graham's agonizing glimpses into Lecktor's mind, coupled with Lecktor's knife attack, has acted as a kind of initiation, which, as in the Traditional doctrine, is the only real way to "change" oneself — precisely by transcending this world and obtaining a new character, a new will — a new Will, a New Man.[141]

---

[137]   Wikipedia, "*Manhunter*," quoting cinematographer Dante Spinotti.

[138]   "'The music belongs only to the killer's space, and its representation of his subjectivity is increased by the gradually ever more dance like quality of his actions, responding to the rhythm and line of the music." Daniel Goldmark, *Beyond the Soundtrack: Representing Music in Cinema* (University of California, 2007), p. 199.

[139]   "Can Analyze" seems to have been reading my previous discussion of the puppet meme: "UPDATE 4/21/13: Since the time of the last update to this post, various discoveries have been made while analyzing some of the other Lecter movies, as well as while analyzing A Space Odyssey, which suggest an alternate interpretation of Dollarhyde's jerking motions to that given above [i.e., magic]: Dollarhyde's motions are like those of a marionette, i.e., of a puppet operated from above by strings."

[140]   Loc. cit.

[141]   This ties in with Graham's flight from Atlanta, which much have been a shamanic act, explaining the collapse of time that allows him to reach St. Louis within the time of an LP side; he arrives a Superior Man, able to shift time and crash through the glass wall – an

Manhunter uses a somewhat clunky metaphor for Will's supervening instinct to protect rather than destroy – before leaving his family, he builds a wire enclosure to protect newborn turtles; when he re-unites with them, he checks on the turtles, finds them doing fine, and mutters "most of them made it." When Thomas Harris came to write the sequel, of course, he seems to have decided that lambs would make for a more snuggly symbol. But *Groundhog Day* finds a more amusing way to subvert the image. Phil seems to conflate the eponymous groundhog with both the Tooth Fairy and the cycle of repetition he, and Phil, are trapped in, and as he becomes "better" he tries to save the town — and himself — from the demonic groundhog:

> Phil: This is pitiful. A thousand people freezing their butts off waiting to worship a rat. (raising his voice) What a hype. Groundhog Day used to mean something in this town. They used to pull the hog out, and they used to eat it. (turns to the crowd) You're hypocrites, all of you!

A few cycles later, using Will's exact words ...

> Phil: Once again the eyes of the nation have turned here to this ... (silly voice) tiny village in Western Pennsylvania, blah, blah, blah, blah, blah ... (serious) There is no way ... that this winter ... is ever going to end, as long as this groundhog keeps seeing his shadow. I don't see any other way out. He's gotta be stopped. (beat) And I have to stop him.

Will kills Dollarhyde to stop him, and save the families/turtles/lambs; Phil tries to kill the symbolic animal itself to end the cycle.

Lecktor has been thwarted, his gospel of defeatism defeated[142] by a man of True Will, like the Green Lantern.[143] Or has he? The Gods of Repetition have a little surprise for us at the very end of *Groundhog Day*. TV's Phil would be nothing without his ... cameraman.

---

inverted "glass ceiling" actually between the Upper and Lower Realms?

[142] Unfortunately, in true Hollywood style, he'll be back, three more times, each one less necessary than the previous, even remaking this very film. Repetition seems to be the very essence of the Lecter saga.

[143] See the title essay in my *Green Nazis in Space! New Essays on Literature, Art, & Culture*; ed. by Greg Johnson (San Francisco: Counter-Currents, 2015). In this film, however, green is associated with Dollarhyde's scenes.

Larry the Cameraman: People just don't understand what is involved in this. This is an art form. You know, I think most people just think that I hold the camera and point it at stuff. There is a lot more to it than just that. Would you be at all interested in seeing the inside of the van?

He seems familiar. Where have we heard that unctuous tone?

Lecktor: Would you like to leave me your home phone number?

Wait a second – that's Chris Elliot. Say, wasn't he in... *Manhunter?*

There's no real reason for me to be in that movie other than the fact that it was, like, the height of my appearances on Letterman. ... I was cast through a casting agent who'd seen some article on me, and had told Michael Mann, "Oh yeah, it would be cool to have him in this movie," I guess. So I knew right from the start, "Oh, I really shouldn't be in this." In *Manhunter,* I was supposed to be an FBI forensic investigator. And I don't know, I was 23 or 24 at the time, with a giant beard and long, stringy blonde hair – I just didn't look the part. I remember when the movie premièred, I appear in the scene where everybody's putting together the final information that leads to this killer, and the camera panned the table and cut to me, and there was this big blast of laughter from the audience that broke the whole tension of that scene. I can only imagine that Michael Mann was not happy about that.[144]

Forensic investigator, giant beard, long stringy blonde hair, camera man, van ... Perhaps he was the one who wrote the FBI's phony personal ad from Lecktor to the Tooth Fairy: "Inherit my mantle and surpass my achievements."

[144] "Random Roles" by Tasha Robinson at *The Onion AV Club*, December 5, 2007, http://www.avclub.com/articles/chris-elliott,2097/.

Evola on Wheels

Psychomania as Hermetic Initiation

HERE'S ANOTHER FLICK I fondly recall from some late night broadcast in my teens or so, which has been made accessible again through the miracle of DVD.[145] Needless to say, it has its 'net fans as well, one of which give this summary:

> If you haven't ever seen *Psychomania* it's a unique British horror and is quite hilarious in terms of language and actual horror, but remains a classic all the same. The opening title with these Bikers from hell weaving in and out of a large stone circle has to be the most memorable you will see. Briefly it's the story of a gang of Bikers called the Living Dead. The gang leader (Henson) has a weird mother (our Beryl) who is immortal, as is her sinister butler (Sanders). Henson finds the secret of his mother immortality (this involves a frog), then tells his gang members how they can comeback alive and wreak havoc. They then all commit suicide. It really is funny. They all get turned into stone at the end. There are some great scenes and some superb furniture along the way. Only the British could make such a daft movie.[146]

---

[145] Actually, there's a Blu-ray that just came out, "packed" with special features, which I can't afford at the moment, but dig it if you can. Like similar low-budget Brit horror films of the time — such as *The Wicker Man* — it seems to exist in various different versions with various cuts and runtimes. Oddly enough a version close to the Blu-ray can be had on an otherwise disgusting "Laugh Track" DVD – a "white rapper" version of MST3K that, mercifully, can be run without said rapping, and for only a couple of bucks on Amazon.

[146] http://www.trunkrecords.com/turntable/psychomania.shtml

OK, everyone set with the premise?[147] That opening scene was really the only part I recalled, due to either falling asleep or being sent to bed, so I can attest to it really being memorable.

A group of motorcyclists — The Living Dead, we'll soon learn — perform various maneuvers in and around a sort of mini-Stonehenge – as we'll also soon learn, a local monument, the "Stone Witches," a coven supposedly turned to stone for some devilish misdemeanor — all shrouded in fog, filmed in slo-mo, and above all, accompanied by some amazing creepy prog-music — not unlike to music being created at the same time in Germany that we now know as Krautrock – that instantly catapults this film into *Suspiria* (Goblin) or even *Manhunter* (Shriekback) territory.[148] Or maybe not.

It would be hard for any movie to keep up with that opening, and this one sure doesn't. But there are some rewards here for the metaphysically inclined and politically incorrect.

First, this is not just a British film, but a very British film. That means, apart from a subdued, vaguely melancholy color palette of foggy grays and damp greens and blues – the whole film looks like it was filmed at the bottom of an aquarium, which is appropriate, given the unusually large role frogs play. It's quite a relief, in today's culture and environment, to sink into this cooling British aquarium of a film, like a soothing ice mask after a hot day.[149]

"British" also means we can expect the subtle pleasures consequent on a low-budget and a strangely reticent, almost downright shy approach to film making.

Take, for instance, a very early scene that presents us with one of the gang's "outrages." Now I for one will admit that having a motorcycle, to say

---

[147]   MST3k 612, *The Starfighters*.

[148]   It turns out to be the veddy British John Cameron who recently reminisced for the release of the soundtrack: "Jazz and session musicians playing pre-punk 'trash-rock' for a tale of supernatural gore and mayhem, on a Shepperton recording stage more suited to the LSO than a rock line-up, complete with 'suit-and-tie' recording engineer is one of my more unexpected memories. In a pre-synthesizer age every trick was used: Musser vibes through phase and wah-wah pedals, phased bowed bass, drumsticks inside a grand piano, electric harpsichord through a compressor, Hammond organ fed through a phase unit and Leslie speakers, and wordless solo voice ... Sorry my recollection is a little blurred, hell, it was the 1970s!"

[149]   "In the morning if my face is a little puffy I'll put on an ice pack while doing stomach crunches. I can do 1000 now." – Patrick Bateman, *American Psycho*.

nothing of half a dozen or so, zip right by you while out walking around the town shopping center would be a rather unpleasant, perhaps even scary, experience. But really, this is supposed to be a horror film, and the sight of the Living Dead, even with their home-made skull visors, zooming alongside shoppers at quite reasonable speeds, knocking over a few prop fruit stands and what not, doesn't even bring to mind the rather sedate The Wild One but rather the *Monty Python* sketch, "Hell's Grannies"; even a Benny Hill skit would have speeded things up. In fact, the gang's suicides, as they follow Tom's lead, are rendered in a quick sequence all played for laughs.

On the other hand, cheapness and restraint can produce remarkable effects themselves, as any connoisseur of B-films can attest. In a later scene, when — not give too much away — our now back from the dead gang dispatches two constables and an inspector who are waiting unsuspecting in the morgue, the camera simply shifts away from the three, slowly revolves full circle to reveal — hey presto! — our three new corpses laid out in their conveniently see-through drawers, with nary a sound, mark or drop of blood, leaving Martin Scorsese to ask, "how'd they do that?"

But the film's greatest and most famous sequence occurs when Tom, having driven himself off a bridge and then buried by the gang — on his motorcycle — revs up from underground and explodes up and out of the burial mound, good as new and ready for some more of the old ultra-violence.

I defy anyone to watch this amazing sequence without screaming out: "Like a bat out of Hellllllllllllllllllllllllll!"[150]

It's when Tom learns the secret of immortality — or whatever it is; as we'll see, it's a little hard to pinpoint just what kind of state he achieves — that my Traditionalist spidey-sense started to tingle.

---

[150] One can only imagine there must have been some influence here on the cover of Mr. Loaf's 1977 opus; I don't know of any other previous use of this trope. One might also compare Mr. Loaf's character, Eddie, in another Brit-horror film, 1975's *Rocky Horror Picture Show*, who rides a motorcycle out when he escapes from the freezer prison-grave [?], only to also wind up dead again. There is also a terribly similar looking character (though still, as noted, very neat and clean) in the Living Dead named – Chopped Meat. Both Tom and Dr. Frankenfurter live in very British gothic mansions with all the latest mod cons, though Riff Raff is a sadly decayed Shadwell. The swaggering, always in leather Tom is sort of a combination of Eddie and Rocky, and thus would have made a more suitable companion for the Dr. than either.

The secret turns out to be: kill yourself, but only if you can maintain constant, unwavering concentration on the belief that you will live again.

The secret, in fact, turns out to be a kinda suicidal version of Oprah's beloved Secret, the dumbed down residuum of America's 19th-century "New Thought" movement.[151]

But where had I heard this before? Of course – Baron Evola!

As is well known, Evola was quite pessimistic about the possibilities of finding a true source of initiation in today's world; ultimately passing from pessimism to nihilism. Unlike Guénon, who held out slender hopes, Evola simply denied the existence of a valid and effective initiatory stream, without contact with which no chance of enlightenment, or immortality, is possible.

What to do? Evola counseled the "differentiated man," the man aware of some element of the transcendent within himself — which would be the requisite material to be acted on by initiation — to:

> Give ever more emphasis to the dimension of transcendence in oneself, more or less concealed as it may be. Study of traditional wisdom and knowledge of its doctrines may assist, but they will not be effective without a progressive change affecting the existential plane, and more particularly, the basic life force of oneself ... that for most people is bound to the world and is simply the will to live.

One can, then, with some effort and luck, and of course a predisposition, effect a change of polarity, like "the induction of magnetism in a piece of iron" and thereby reverse the direction of one's life force: from willing to live ordinary life to the urge to attain "the life which is more than life."

> When the orientation toward the transcendent no longer has a merely mental or emotional character, but has come to penetrate a person's being, the most essential work is done, the seen has penetrated the earth, and the rest is in a way, secondary and consequential.[152]

---

[151] Derived from colonial readings of Hegel and Emerson, and serious enough to warrant William James devoting a chapter — "The Religion of Healthy-Mindedness" — in his lectures on the Varieties of Religious Experience. For an alt-historical account, see *The Secret Source* (Feral House) that traces it back to the Egyptian Hermetics – rightly so, as we shall soon see. For more on New Thought, see my *Mysticism After Modernism: Crowley, Evola, Neville, Watts, Colin Wilson & Other Populist Gurus* (Melbourne, Australia: Manticore Press, 2020).

[152] Julius Evola, *Ride the Tiger: A Survival Manual for the Aristocrats of the Soul*, trans.

As I read this, the idea seems to be that one should concentrate as much of one's consciousness as one can on the Transcendent, within oneself, so that a certain direction, and even force or momentum, is built up, allowing one to spring forward at death, into the Beyond, rather than passively submitting to the dispersal of the elements and return to the racial root that is the fate of the un-initiated. [153]

Although Evola counsels against suicide in the same book, as an all-too-human failure of will — except for those who are already enlightened, who may well choose to take themselves off the scene — we might draw a parallel to Evola's own ill-advised "testing of my fate" by walking about Vienna during Allied bombing runs, which ultimately resulted in the injuries that left him unable to walk.[154]

And now the occult synchronicity of Tom's burial becomes clear; buried upright, astride his motorcycle, no doubt facing East (the movie gives no clue), just as Evola, by his request, was wheeled over to a window so that he would die as his *kshatriya* ancestors would wish, upright and facing the rising sun.

The Evola connection also solves the major puzzle critics have with the movie. The re-born cyclists are usually called "zombies" by critics but they bear no resemblance to the now canonical rotting, brain-eating ones. TVTropes has cited the film under the trope "Our Zombies are Different" but observed:

Psychomania has gained some notoriety as "zombies on motorcycles," but are really zombies only in retrospect. More accurately, they're willing participants in a ritual that grants eternal life. The ritual

---

Joscelyn Godwin and Constance Fontana (Rochester, Vt.: Inner Traditions, 2003), pp. 216–17. See also the remarks on the very last page, p. 227.

[153] Evola discusses these contrasting fates in many places, for example, Chapter 8 of his *Revolt Against the Modern World*, trans. Guido Stucco (Rochester, Vt.: Inner Traditions International, 1995), "The Two Paths of the Afterlife."

[154] Evola himself discusses the incident in *The Path of Cinnabar; An Intellectual Autobiography*, trans. Sergio Knipe (London: Arktos, 2009), pp. 183–4, where he disavows any "occult attack" interpretations. If it seems rude to speculate thus around Evola's personal situation, there are distinguished precedents; no less than Eliade speculated in a letter that Evola had been wounded in the *chakra* that governed pride and arrogance — "and what do you think about that?" I discuss Evola, occult attacks and New Thought in "Immobile Warriors: Evola's Post-War Career from the Perspective of Neville's New Thought," Counter-Currents, Sept. 16, 2020 (https://counter-currents.com/2020/09/immobile-warriors/).

requires that they first die. On revival, they carry on as before; they are essentially their own creator.[155]

"Their own creator." This is a tremendously important point, which links the film's formula of immortality with Evola's discussion of the "magical heroes" who are a "kingless race" of "self-rulers" after having, unlike the contrary archetype of the "religious saint," taken control of their own destiny and fate.[156]

Here we also find the significance of the "turn to stone" motif, in which Tom and the gang are "punished" at the end of the film by being transformed into megaliths, presumably just as the Seven Witches were years before the film began.[157]

The Stone, briefly, symbolizes The Center, the *Axis Mundi* along which transformation is accomplished (rising to a higher level); thus the stones are fittingly located on the lush green heath, which alludes to the equally central symbol of the Garden of Eden. The Stone also signifies the Transformed Man himself, solid, unmoved, upright; as well as the instrument of transformation, the alchemical Philosopher's Stone or even perhaps The Grail (which Evola suggests was fashioned from the green gem — or stone — that fell from Lucifer's crown. The color green ties in with the green frogs and the green frog medallion — the frog is the snake in the Garden which is also Satan — that are involved in the rituals conducted by Shadwell and Tom's mom. [158]

We're already starting to find here elements of both repetition and the phenomenon I've called "passing the buck" – the Superior Man does not "work off" his own karma, as in so many crypto-protestant interpretations,

---

[155]   http://tvtropes.org/pmwiki/pmwiki.php/Main/VoodooZombie.

[156]   See Evola, *The Hermetic Tradition* (Rochester, Vt.: Inner Traditions, 1995), especially the "Introduction to Part One: The Tree, the Serpent and the Titans."

[157]   It's a not too impressive time-lapse effect. Brit John Boorman, in 1974's *Zardoz*, will subvert this trope, ending with a time-lapse disintegration of Sean Connery and Charlotte Rampling, who have accepted mortality. This "self-creation" seems to correspond to the process Evola describes as the sage re-creating his body cell by cell, producing an immortal, indestructible "body of light" or, in Pauline terms, a "resurrection body." See *The Hermetic Tradition*, op. cit., but especially his *The Yoga of Power*, trans. Guido Stucco (Rochester, Vt.: Inner Traditions, 1992), Chapter 15, "The Diamond Thunderbolt Body."

[158]   See Evola, op. cit., and also his *The Mystery of the Grail: Initiation and Magic in the Quest for the Spirit* (Rochester, Vt.: Inner Traditions, 1996), especially Chapter 15, "The Luciferian Stone."

but instead demonstrates his superiority precisely by offloading it onto some sucker or mark.

To explore the Stone some more, we need to look at some of these repetitions. The basic repetition occurs in the First Act, when Tom demands to be allowed into The Locked Room in order to learn The Secret, an ordeal that his father failed, fatally. As Evola explains, in the traditions of the "religious saint," the quest for immorality or enlightenment or perfection is presented as a danger; as a result of our ancestor's catastrophic failure — Adam and Eve, of course — the pursuit is not only forbidden, but we are subject to a sinful debt that will result in our own damnation unless we can obtain Jehovah's forgiveness.[159]

Tom, however, presents us with the Hero of the alchemical traditions, who dares – and succeeds.

Of course, we've seen that in the film, Tom and the gang are "punished," but that's just the exoteric cover story; "turning to stone" is the esoteric goal, or the reward, of their efforts. (We can assume that the Witches succeeded as well). This is also presented as a punishment because to the naïve, worldly man, the Enlightened Man seems more dead than alive; impassive as a stone, unmoved, not subject to the worldly man's endless, unsatisfied desires that "make life worth living."[160]

It's the usual "he tampered in God's domain"[161] cautionary tale, dating back from Frankenstein through Faust through Don Juan through Dante all the way back to the Eden myth – but we don't care about that, nor whether the producers had any of this in mind. It may be the case, as Trevor Lynch suggests, that under contemporary conditions — and really, that would be the whole post-Constantine period — Traditional ideas can only appear in the mouths of villains and madmen. But even beyond this,

---

[159]   In fact, Christianity recognizes that the debt is so great as to require Jehovah to kill his own Son; a titanic example of "passing the buck."

[160]   Towards the end of *The Hermetic Tradition* Evola devotes some pages to considering how the Realized Man may well appear as a broken down failure beset with worries, due to his desire not to stand out, as well as the results of "karmic repercussions" from his activities in the higher dimensions – hence our idea of the need to "pass the buck" to someone else. Guénon, at the end of his book *Man and His Becoming According to the Vedanta*, has an interesting discussion of how the Realized Man, having climbed the World Axis, would literally pop out of view, like a three-dimensional being in Flatland.

[161]   The verdict delivered in Ed Wood's *Bride of the Monster*; see the collection of these tropes at http://tvtropes.org/pmwiki/pmwiki.php/Main/TheseAreThingsManWasNotMeantToKnow.

this is how Traditional ideas have always been transmitted – embedded in "folk" tales that the folk grooved on but never really understood, hidden safely in plain sight until someone like Guénon or Evola could decode them for us once again.

On the purely cinematic level, Tom is channeling Alex from 1971's *A Clockwork Orange*. Of course, Kubrick was an American and had a big budget, so although made and set in England, the film seemed startlingly brightly lit, violent and explicit at the time.

And yet, Tom, though admittedly a nice lad who lives with Mum — in a very groovy, all too British manor house with just the right swinging '60s touches, unlike Alex's futurist hellhole — is far more violent than Alex; just more reticent about it. No sooner do we meet him than he's forced a car off the road and sent some British git through the windshield – I mean, windscreen. Of course, being British, we don't see any exploding heads or even a slight cut, so it's hard to tell if he's unconscious or dead. No one in authority, at least, seems too concerned; whereas Alex's one murder results in a very British "now you've done it lad" and straight to the Ludovico room.

On revival, though, all bets are off. Tom kills a couple of blokes just on general principle, then heads for a pub to chats up a couple birds. The scene looks like it will play out like Alex's teenage girl *ménage a trois*, but instead he winds up killing everyone else in the place – off camera of course.[162]

We've already commented on the Pythonesque qualities of the shopping center attack. And of course, as we now expect, they return. But TVTropes is wrong to say they "carry on as before." No, this time they do it right, mate. Dozens of people are injured or worse as the gang invades a Sainsbury — Sainsbury's! — on wheels; red leather girl even runs over a baby carriage, child inside - now when did you ever see that, outside of an Andy Warhol film? But again, no blood, no flying limbs; no need to blow the special effects budget this late in the film.

And speaking of Kubrick and repetition, doesn't this village morgue look a lot like the cryogenic tubes in 2001? And hey, isn't that *Star Trek's* Scotty?

---

[162] In fact, the most British thing about Tom, as opposed to Alex, is that he's more interested in the ultra-violence than the old in-out. He seems only to be interested in the red-leathered bad girl in the group as a partner in crime, while constantly hectoring his still-living goody-goody girlfriend to just off herself already, though what he intends to do with here is unclear. No sex please, we're British!

Given the andro-centric nature of the *Hermetic Tradition*, we can anticipate that the sucker will be a woman. There's Tom's goody-goody girlfriend – unlike the rest of the gang, she wears a denim jacket, with her name cutely appliquéd to the front, not the back, in Holly Hobby font — who refuses to join him in the — overlife? — and will no doubt be psychologically scarred for life.

But mostly, it's Tom's mom, who resolves to stop his reign of genteel terror by reneging on her "oath" (of what? Who knows?) and, rather than petrifying, turns into a frog. Finally, the frog motif resolved, Chekhov-style![163]

The circular, literally "hermetic" structure of the film — like the Locked Room itself — is now clear. We begin with the Living Dead – ordinary men and women, but with some spark of the transcendent that renders them unable to tolerate the banality of "the whole Establishment" (as Tom describes the targets of his undead mischief). Dying to this world, they are reborn as Immortals subject to no authority but themselves; but ultimately, having thrown off karmic ties, they are fully transformed into Men — and the red leather chick — of Stone, no longer weaving among the stones but upright and unmoving; truly Men Among the Ruins.

Finally, as usual with horror flicks, the creepiest story is backstage. George Sanders is the star name here, but unlike later work by Christopher Lee or Peter Cushing, he doesn't look like he's having any late career fun in this two-bit Brit flick.[164] He mumbles his lines throughout — unless that's an artifact of the poor production or the DVD transfer — and looks bored – terminally so. As it happens, as soon as the picture wrapped, Sanders killed himself. Perhaps he was more inspired by the script in real life than he seems on film? Whether he came back is unknown.

---

[163] The producers of the German version seem to have thrown up their hands and titled it "Der Frosh."

[164] Either by design or incompetence, it's not clear until the very end that Tom's mom is a mortal who's made a deal with some occult power, perhaps an occultist in over her head, rather than being a witch or demon herself. Sanders' character is never clear, right to the very last shot, when he drives up at the stone circle ... what? Is he just a butler, a fellow initiate, perhaps of a higher level, like Crowley — whom Sanders seems to be channeling — a minion of Satan, or Satan himself? As the 'bots say, perhaps I should just relax.

Breaking Badge

Touch of Evil *Through the Lens of* Breaking Bad

"'Bad' to the Bone; *'Breaking Bad'* Creator Vince Gilligan Brings More Than a *Touch of Evil* to a New Season."[165]

L EAD ACTOR BRYAN CRANSTON stated in an interview that: "The term 'breaking bad' is a southern colloquialism and it means when someone who has taken a turn off the path of the straight and narrow, when they've gone wrong. And that could be for that day or for a lifetime."[166]

Mad Men and *Breaking Bad* are sort of the Beatles vs. Stones of the AMC network universe.[167] Constant Readers will recall that I've described Detroit culture in the '60s as involving such things a sovereign independence from coastal media driven trends such as Beatlemania and a preference for such working class acts as the Stones or the Who.[168]

Now you might think that this would incline me to *Breaking Bad*, but you'd be wrong. First, *Mad Men's* story arc lead up into and through that

---

[165] Article by Neal Justin, *Minneapolis Star Tribune*, July 14, 2012, here: http://www.startribune.com/entertainment/tv/162294376.html.

[166] http://breakingbad.wikia.com/wiki/Breaking_Bad.

[167] Of course, Don Draper doesn't "dig" the psychedelic Beatles, unlike his younger second wife. She leaves a copy of *Revolver* around and suggest Don listen to "side one, last track" — i.e., "Tomorrow Never Knows" — but Don turns it off after a few measures. (Season 5, Episode 8) Like James Bond, he thinks that "some things just aren't done ... like listening to the Beatles without earmuffs"(*Goldfinger*); Don returns to compliment by listening to "You Only Live Twice" on a bar-room jukebox (Season 5, Episode 13).

[168] See, of course, the title essay of *The Homo & the Negro: Masculinist Meditations on Politics & Popular Culture*; Second, Embiggened Edition, edited by Greg Johnson (San Francisco: Counter-Currents, 2017).

very period (making Don's oldest son my Doppelgänger), while *Breaking Bad* is all too contemporary. Moreover, I found the whole "guy recovers his manhood by shaving his head and becoming murderous drug dealer" motif to be to be far too dull to be of any positive interest.[169]

Recently, however, I obtained the 50th Anniversary release of *Touch of Evil*[170] around the time of AMC broadcasting a multi-week marathon of *Breaking Bad*, and once I finally sat down to watch the latter with the former still in mind, I experienced a sense of imaginal déjà vu.

Having previously suggested that *The Gilmore Girls* is a seven-season long TV version of Orson Welles' *The Magnificent Ambersons*,[171] I may be forgiven for imagining that Breaking Bad is a 5 season long TV version of Welles' *Touch of Evil*.

Walter White is a loser of a high school chemistry teacher who is diagnosed with inoperable lung cancer. Not only is the treatment unaffordable, but his inevitable death will also leave his family destitute. Walt decides to make lots of money, fast, by turning his skills to the manufacture of meth, and it turns out he's pretty good at it — both the manufacture itself as well as the related distribution and, inevitably, enforcement. He revels in being good at something,[172] but periodically expresses some concern about his transformation into the criminal genius known only as "Heisenberg."

I suspect this is what interests viewers; as Jack Donovan would say, Walt was a good man who was bad at being a man, while "Heisenberg" is a bad man, who is good at being a man.

This is a love-affair story of Walt and his love of science, and ["Blue Sky" meth] was his greatest product – his greatest triumph as a chemist. It wasn't about Walter White as a criminal or a murderer or an awful person. It was him ending on his own terms. It felt creatively right.[173]

---

[169] Ibid.

[170] An "outrageously good re-release: Two discs, all three versions of the film, four commentaries, two featurettes – and a print version of the infamous memo, so you don't have to squint at your screen to read it." – DVD Verdict, http://www.dvdverdict.com/reviews/touchofevil50th.php.

[171] See "The Gilmore Girls Occupy Wall St.," reprinted in ibid.

[172] "He develops a skill set." – Bryan Cranston on his character, "Walter White," interviewed during AMC's 2014 "Breaking Bad Binge."

[173] "Why '*Breaking Bad*' Chose Badfinger's 'Baby Blue' – Music supervisor Thomas Golubić explains Walt's send-off song" by Steve Knopper; *Rolling Stone*, October 1, 2013.

Walt may love science, but it hasn't loved him, and that's why he has no money, and his family will be left destitute:

Once a promising chemist who greatly contributed to the breakthrough of a multi-billion-dollar company Gray Matter Technologies, Walt abruptly left the company and sold his financial interest for $5,000. The founders of the company Elliott Schwartz and Gretchen Schwartz later married and made a fortune. Walt harbors animosity and blames Elliot and Gretchen for stealing his hard labor and contributions to become a highly successful foundation, without giving Walt any credit. Walt then bitterly blames Gretchen for his financial problems and his lot in life.[174]

Watching and listening to Walt repeatedly returning to this aspect of his situation, I began to hear another voice: Orson Welles' Hank Quinlan, justifying himself as, unknown to him, the end is near:

Quinlan: "Don't you think I could have been rich? A cop in my position. What do I have ... after thirty years, a little turkey ranch – that's all I got. A couple of acres."[175]

One difference, since this, as I said, is a movie, not a series, is that *Breaking Bad*, luxuriating in the kind of time and budget and studio regard Welles could only dream of, presents us with the full transformation of Walter White,[176] while Hank Quinlan, when we meet him, has already become the local Heisenberg:

Adair: "Vargas, you've heard of Hank Quinlan, our local police celebrity."

Vargas: "I'd like to meet him."

Coroner: "That's what you think."[177]

---

[174] http://breakingbad.wikia.com/wiki/Walter_White.

[175] The turkey ranch, we later realize, is the first thing we hear about Quinlan, right at the start — "Where's Captain Quinlan? Got him out of bed at his ranch. He's on his way," providing a neat cyclicality.

[176] "Vince Gilligan, who had spent years writing the series *The X-Files*, expressed interest in creating a series in which the protagonist of the story became the antagonist. Gilligan has stated numerous times that his goal was to turn the protagonist, Walter White from Mr. Chips into Scarface." – https://breakingbad.fandom.com/wiki/Breaking_Bad.

[177] "You clearly don't know who you're talking to, so let me clue you in: I am not in danger,

But I see I've started talking about *Touch of Evil* without cluing some of you in. Here's a neat summary from DVD Verdict:

A car crossing the border from Mexico into the U.S. blows up, killing the driver, a wealthy older man, and his passenger, a blonde stripper. Witnessing this are Mexican narcotics investigator Mike Vargas (Charlton Heston) and his American wife, Susie (Janet Leigh). Soon, the "legendary" local police captain, Hank Quinlan (Orson Welles), arrives on the scene and commences the investigation.

Vargas has been running an investigation of his own, bringing down the Grandi family, drug-dealing gangsters headed up by Uncle Joe Grandi (Akim Tamiroff). The trial of Joe's brother is about to start, and the Grandis want Vargas to call it off. ... Uncle Joe has [an] idea of how to persuade Vargas, and it involves terrorizing Susie. When she goes to an out-of-the-way motel to wait for her husband, the Grandis get their chance.

Meanwhile, Vargas is tagging along on the murder investigation. Quinlan's fabled instincts tell him that the killer is the Mexican boyfriend of the dead man's daughter. During an interrogation at the man's home, some incriminating evidence turns up in a shoebox – but Vargas had seen the shoebox before, and it was empty.

Now, Vargas realizes that Quinlan is corrupt and that his "legend" has been built from planting evidence and framing possibly innocent suspects. But Vargas has bigger problems: the police found his wife passed out and reeking of drugs in a strange hotel room – with a dead [Joe Grandi].[178]

Already we see a metamorphosis: "local police celebrity." Walt becomes Heisenberg, but Hank is already the Bad Captain.

Pete Menzies: You're a killer.

Hank Quinlan: Partly. I'm a cop.

Skyler. I am the danger. A guy opens his door and gets shot, and you think that of me? No! I am the one who knocks!" – Walter White.

[178]   http://www.dvdverdict.com/reviews/touchofevil50th.php.

Now, talking about "bad," what I want to be suggesting here is that in both works we find an idea that I've called *Passing the Buck*. It's the notion, disconcerting to many, that the Enlightened or Realized Man is not necessarily — or perhaps necessarily not — the Good Man. Since the goal of enlightenment is usually thought of as being "beyond the contraries," including those of good and bad, why should we imagine that the path involves conventional "goodness"?[179] More particularly, perhaps the way to reach the state of freedom from karma is to dump it on some poor sucker and just keep moving.

You could say that this is a metaphysical version of Jack Donovan's thesis: the (conventional-morally) good man versus the man good at being (the Realized or Universal) Man. Thus, any really compelling dramatic work — as opposed to some "morality tale" — will involve men who are mad, bad, and dangerous to know.

The men of Walt's world are killers and kingpins and assassins – but at least they are men. One of the larger philosophical issues raised by this series — too large for me to explore here — is the tension that sometimes exists between masculinity and law and order; or: between primal masculine virtue and the virtues necessary to sustain civilization.[180]

Hence, the curious ambivalence audiences — and creators — feel towards characters like Walter White and Hank Quinlan.

---

[179] The Christian might object here, and this indeed divides Christianity, in its original or "purest" form, from the other (or the real) Wisdom traditions. This is why the "good Christian" presents such a sorry spectacle: a goody-goody like Ned Flanders; Hell seems so much more interesting than Heaven, and the Devil has all the good tunes. The pagan notion survives or intrudes into Mediaeval Europe in the form of chivalry and knighthood; the hermit wonders at Parsifal: "Never has the Grail been won by violence [until now]." Even Protestantism, rejecting "good works" as a path to salvation, still finds itself obsessed with worldly morality. ("The Church has become a moral regulation society" — Alan Watts). We see the same notion in the Greek mysteries, where the philosophical conundrum arose at why a great criminal, if initiated, could merit a better posthumous fate than a "good man," and of course in Tantrism. See *Introduction to Magic: Rituals and Practical Techniques for the Magus* (Rochester, Vt.: Inner Traditions, 2001), p. 182, for the former; his *The Yoga of Power: Tantra, Shakti and the Secret Way* (translated by Guido Stucco; Rochester, Vt.: Inner Traditions, 1992) for the latter. "Rascal gurus" (As Alan Watts calls them) like Gurdjieff follow the "Way of the Clever Man" and regard their disciples as "Idiots." Uncle Joe: "Why should I be tailing him [Menzies], he's an idiot."

[180] See Jef Costello, *"Breaking Bad*: A Celebration," Counter-Currents, April 2, 2012; https://counter-currents.com/2012/04/breaking-bad-a-celebration/.

Walt ends up saving the day by beating the big bad neo-Nazis with ingenuity. He goes on to avenge his brother-in-law's death, releases "old yeller" from captivity so he can personally kill that "Opie dead-eyed piece of shit," poisons the (other) crazy "bitch" that dared to challenged his potency, gives the original emasculating bitch a get out of jail free card and gets all that money to his estranged son via payback to the couple that wronged him in the first place. Instead of emerging as a defeated anti-hero, Walter White's evil alter ego somehow rises from the ashes like a superhero. [181]

Again, as music supervisor Thomas Golubić said about the finale:

> It wasn't about Walter White as a criminal or a murderer or an awful person. It was him ending on his own terms. It felt creatively right [182]

But let's get back to how this all plays out in the film and TV series under review. Since Sr. Vargas, the "Good Cop," has implicitly pushed his way into our reflections, just as he pushes his way into Quinlan's sweet little setup, let's look him over. Vargas is our nominal hero, not only a gang-busting cop (he's just put the head of the Grandi gang in jail, a kind of south of the border Tom Dewey) but a romantic leading man, escorting his new, American wife over the border for an ice-cream soda. Everything about him exudes smug rectitude (his "I'm a Latin Lover" moustache actually recalls Tom Dewey), but the first problem is that he's played by Charlton Heston.

Now, this is a faux pas so legendary that it's become a pop culture reference point:

> Ed Wood, Jr.: Do you know that I've even had producers re-cut my movies?

> Orson Welles: I hate when that happens.

> Ed Wood, Jr.: And they always want to cast their buddies. It doesn't even matter if they're right for the part.

---

[181] "Why Do We Feel So Good About Walter White's Bad Behavior?" by Steven Aoun at PopMatters, 7 October 2013; http://www.popmatters.com/feature/175686-cop-out/.

[182] Knopper, op. cit.

Orson Welles: Tell me about it. I'm supposed to do a thriller for Universal. They want Charlton Heston as a Mexican.[183]

Like many such pop cultural memes, it's more about what pleases current dogmas than historical truth.[184] We "know" that studios are philistines; we "know" that Caucasians should never play non-white roles (though the opposite is just fine). But in reality, Heston was already cast, and it was Heston who used his star power to force Welles on Universal as director instead of just actor. And that star power is important to the film as well, since, as we'll see, our nominal hero proves to be so lame, so paper-thin, as written, that only an actor with the screen presence of a Heston could prevent him from fading away entirely, lost in the malignant shadow of Welles' monstrous Hank Quinlan.[185] And there simply weren't any Hispanic actors in Hollywood who could act alongside Orson Welles – Caesar Romero, you think? [186]

As for his Spanish, it sounds pretty good to me, although I don't, like Quinlan, "speak Mexican." I'm not an expert, just an ordinary movie-goer, and isn't it all about creating an illusion? [187]

Quinlan: I don't speak Mexican. Let's keep it in English, Vargas.

Vargas: That's all right with me. I'm sure he's just as unpleasant in any language.

[183] *Ed Wood* (Tim Burton, 1994).

[184] These are the people who sneer that "wrestling is fake, man"; sure, and I bet Spielberg didn't "really" kill anyone on Schindler's List either.

[185] After filming wrapped, Heston told Welles he had only made one mistake: there were several scenes that were only there to show Vargas was the hero, but really, "The film is about the fall of Hank Quinlan." Welles said "I know. So we won't have any problem with the cutting, will we?" – DVD commentary.

[186] The liberal elite "knows" Heston must be a bad actor, since like Reagan, he's a "conservative"; asked about his politics, people will say "gun nut" rather than, say, "marched in Washington arm in arm with Martin Luther King" or "gave jobs to blacklisted actors."

[187] Welles crafted a whole backstory about Vargas coming from a wealthy family, attending Stanford, etc., making him more Anglo than your standard illegal. Mexico, like most Third World countries, is ruled by a caste of light-skinned, European natives, as a look at the last few Mexican presidents would confirm. Speaking of Universal, I understand that when Edgar Bronfman, the Seagram's heir who "always wanted to own a movie studio," if I may paraphrase Kane, put together the Seagram's/Universal/Vivendi deal, he was easily outsmarted by his French counterparts since, though a native of Quebec, he understood French not at all, having, like the rest of the Jewish elite, spent his life entirely among the anglophonic; French was for the peasants.

Sanchez: Unpleasant? Strange. I've been told I have a very winning personality. The very best shoe clerk the store ever had.

Oddly enough, Heston's supposedly fractured Spanglish provides yet another link to *Breaking Bad*, in the person of Gus Fring. For some reason Fring seemed to get most of the supposedly Spanish lines, and I remember trying to follow along, as I usually do, especially with the Spanish cable channels, to try and pick up some of the lingo and test my knowledge thereof. Apparently, Gus was doing the same, earning the show an entry at TVTropes, right alongside *Touch of Evil*, for

> Not Even Bothering with the Accent: Many people singled out the show *Breaking Bad*, and the character Gustavo "Gus" Fring, for falling flat on language. Tamara Vallejos writes, "Gus' Spanish and accent were so painful to listen to, and it made me super angry that such a pivotal and fantastic character would have such a giant, noticeable, nails-on-a-chalkboard flaw."[188]

Well, I would think that such a delicate flower shouldn't be watching such a violent show in the first place. And here too Gus provides a link to the film. Another way *Touch of Evil* reminds one of *Breaking Bad* is that both, for their own time, are remarkably violent; in fact, even the movie, from 1958, has moments that can match anything in the cable show.

Adair: An hour ago, Rudi Linnekar had this town in his pocket.

Coroner: Now you can strain him through a sieve.

Quinlan: An old lady on Main Street last night picked up a shoe. The shoe had a foot in it. We're gonna make you pay for that mess.

There's even that B-movie staple,[189] "acid to the face":

> In an alley outside the club, Vargas is attacked by one of the Grandi gang members who throws acid at Vargas's face. In Welles' original script, the acid misses Vargas and hits a cat asleep in the trash. This

---

[188] http://www.npr.org/blogs/codeswitch/2014/10/04/353516402/does-television-spanglish-need-a-rewrite.

[189] Joe Bob Briggs, intro to the Guilty Pleasures DVD release of *The Incredibly Strange Creatures Who Stopped Living and Become Mixed-Up Zombies* (Ray Dennis Steckler, 1963; 2004).

was changed in the film and the acid instead explodes in a smoky hiss against the poster of the dead stripper.[190]

Speaking of faces, even the TV show's most infamous scene, where Walt kills Gus Fring with a bomb that leaves him staggering out of Uncle Tio's room with half his face gone — the episode is cutely titled "Face Off" — is matched by the equally infamous quick shot of another dead uncle, Uncle Joe Grandi; lending perhaps a new significance to Uncle Joe's earlier speech, leading Quinlan into the scheme that will, unknown to Uncle Joe, lead to his own death:

> Uncle Joe Grandi: "We are both after the same exact thing, Captain. If Vargas goes on like this, shooting his face off ... Somebody's reputation has got to be ruined. Why shouldn't it be Vargas's?"

Welles was quite aware of how much he was pushing the envelope:

> As Welles said in conversations with Peter Bogdanovich (This Is Orson Welles by Orson Welles and Peter Bogdanovich) "It was perverse and morbid ... one of those go-as-far-as-you-can-go–in that kind of dirty department ... when [Tamiroff] looked at the gun, it was every cock in the world. It was awful, the way he looked at it–made the whole scene possible." Make no mistake about it, this is an ugly scene. Tamiroff is a much smaller man than Welles, and is just about consumed by Welles. Tamiroff's character is dragged around the room, his shirt torn at the chest, his toupee knocked off. Eventually Quinlan strangles him with one of Susan's stockings, leaving Uncle Joe's face hanging over the bed, eyes bulging out by a nice effect of using painted contact lenses. [191] Welles wanted the shot of the bulging eyes short enough so it would be almost subliminal — something people wouldn't be quite sure they saw — but the studio added extra frames to that shot.[192]

While we're on the face, let's talk about hair. Walt sports the aforementioned iconic chrome dome, first due to chemo, then presumably to cement his

---

[190] http://newimprovedgorman.blogspot.com/2012/05/really-extraordinary-piece-by-dave.html.

[191] And a cow tongue.

[192] http://newimprovedgorman.blogspot.com/2012/05/really-extraordinary-piece-by-dave.html.

"gangsta" image. Is Quinlan bald? Like most men of his era, he wears a hat. But if you stop and think about it, he always wears a hat – that is, we literally never see him without it, from the first time we see him, getting out of his car, to the last, as he floats dead in the river.

We do on one occasion see the hat without him – we see it at Tanya's whorehouse, where Quinlan is presumably off-screen, passed out from his drinking binge; even here, it's that hat that tells us he's there somewhere. Thus the hat is effectively the same icon, depriving or at least hiding his hair, a symbolic castration.

Uncle Joe is an inept stand-in for the real Grandi boss, whom Vargas has on trial in Mexico, as shown by his constantly lost or misplaced toupee.

The same with his candy bars, which he supposedly gnaws on to avoid drinking, as some people do for smoking. The whole scene is chock-full of sexual defeat:

Quinlan: Have you forgotten your old friend, hmm?

Tanya: I told you we were closed.

Quinlan: I'm Hank Quinlan.

Tanya: I didn't recognize you. You should lay off those candy bars.

Quinlan: It's either the candy or the hooch. I must say, I wish it was your chili I was gettin' fat on. Anyway, you're sure lookin' good.

Tanya: You're a mess, honey. [193]

Quinlan might also seem symbolically un-manned by his cane, but Quinlan, like Ahab, has turned it into a source of strength. He needs it not due to old age but from a heroic act, stopping a bullet aimed for his partner/stooge, Menzies.[194]

---

[193]   Audiences today need to remind themselves that Welles, though no longer exactly boyish, was still a handsome enough Hollywood leading man, not the bloated, shambling talk-show clown he later became. The fat-suit and fake nose are far more convincing than the "old Kane" makeup (although at times, like while thrashing Grandi around in the tiny hotel room, his he recalls middle-aged Kane smashing up Susan's room – here, it's Vargas' wife, Susie), and audiences in 1958 would have been genuinely shocked by his appearance. In a classic Hollywood story, Welles attended a party right after a day of filming, without time to clean himself up. He hadn't been in Hollywood for a few years, and was created with cries of "Orson, you haven't changed a bit! What's your secret, you old dog?" and the like.

[194]   Menzies, as befits his stooge role, is truly unmanned when Quinlan finally shoots him

Most importantly, the cane/wound gives Hank his power, his "famous intuition," a twinge that supposedly tells him who's guilty, which he then "proves" by planting evidence. And when Vargas first suggests that Quinlan planted the dynamite in the shoe clerk's apartment, Quinlan raises his cane between them as if to strike him dead.[195] One might indeed compare it to Wotan's spear, and Quinlan's one mistake is to leave it behind, symbolic of a temporary loss of wits, thus implicating himself as Uncle Joe's murderer.

So, back to Vargas. As Heston and Welles agreed, Vargas is only the Hero by genre conventions. He's actually quite inept: no competent cop, certainly not one of Vargas' supposed importance, would poke his nose into some hick town murder, on the other side of the border, even, and certainly would not have done so with his new bride by his side. When Susie is kidnapped, his only tactic is to go around the bars beating up random people, and when he speeds out to confront Quinlan he roars right past the hotel where his wife is hanging out the window, screaming for help.

In fact, so inept is Vargas that I was reminded of the disgusted crew of the Satellite of Love, faced with the continuing, irritating ineptness of the protagonist of *Manos: The Hands of Fate*, generally agreed to be one of the Top Five candidates for the worst movie ever made: "When is this guy going to demonstrate some simple competence!?"[196]

The resemblances start with the fractured Spanish title (*manos* means, as even I know, "hands," so the title amounts to *Hands: The Hands of Fate*. Wow, how long did they take to dream that up?) and the Southwest background (the director was a fertilizer salesman in El Paso and shot it on weekends in nearby locales, as Welles did in Venice, California; the main action was filmed at a judge's decrepit ranch, not unlike Quinlan's I suppose). In both movies, the supposed "hero" (here played by the director, again like Welles), also named "Mike," (Heston plays Ramon Miguel 'Mike' Vargas) takes his wife (and child, here) on a pleasure trip that turns into a nightmare. Along the way she's groped in a motel-like room, like Susie, there's a creepy, oddly gaited "night manager" (here, the immortal Torgo), gunplay at the end, etc.

---

at the end: unlike Quinlan, he loses his hat, and even after shooting Quinlan he drops his gun as well, as Quinlan sneers "That's the second bullet I've stopped for you, partner."

195   Is "raising Cain" related to "breaking bad"?

196   For more on *Manos,* see the essay to come.

The two most important similarities, however, are that along the way, our "hero" proves to be immensely incompetent, and, at the "twist" ending, he is apparently (the film is too badly made to make any sense) reincarnated as ... the new keeper. Both these themes can be found in *Touch of Evil*, and may help us better understand the *Breaking Bad* finale.

Vargas, then, is our "good man" who is far from "good at being a man." Even if we grant that he's a good cop (he does, at least, have the head of the Grandi gang locked up) he's a pretty piss-poor husband, either romantically or as a protector. If Menzies hadn't killed him, Quinlan likely would have succeeded in framing Vargas, and he seems genuinely surprised that Quinlan doesn't care when he points out that he can't arrest him in Mexico (if only Vargas had been so wise in the first place!), since he plans to shoot him anyway.

Vargas doesn't prove himself when he decides Quinlan is corrupt and goes after him (that's more Ned Flanders bein' a busy-body and all) but precisely when he realizes Susie has been kidnapped.

> Vargas: Listen, I'm no cop now. I'm a husband! What did you do with her? Where's my wife? My wife! (Grabbing and slapping people around left and right)

But what's interesting here is that Vargas doesn't, say, figure out how to use his cop skills to rescue his wife; instead, the only way he knows how to go about rescuing her is to stop being a cop. What he really means, is, stop being a Good Cop and become a Bad Cop. To be good at being a man, and save his wife, he must become Quinlan.

> Schwartz: Intuition?

> Vargas: Why not? Quinlan doesn't have a monopoly on hunches.

What's happened is that our two themes have coalesced: Vargas, a (morally) good cop, to become good as a man (find the killer, stop Quinlan's reign, save his wife), must become a bad cop, like Quinlan himself.

> Schwartz: Well, Hank was a great detective all right.

> Tanya: And a lousy cop.

And thereby Quinlan is able to escape his karma, passing it off to the perfect sucker: Sr. Vargas.[197]

Like all genre films that last and become objects of fascination ("cult" films) there's more going on here than meets the eye, or even than the "auteurs" know. We have at least three levels here:

> There's the superficial plot, which satisfies the studios and the audience, seeking either pastime or reassurance in a cruel world: the Good Guy (Vargas) wins, the Bad Guy (Quinlan) vanquished.

> At a more profound level, the audience must get the masculinist message that to be good at being a man may require becoming, however briefly, a Bad Man.[198]

> Menzies: You didn't have to make it dirty.

> Quinlan: I don't call it dirty. Look at the record ... All those convictions.

> Menzies: Convictions, sure. How many did you frame?

> Quinlan: Nobody.

> Menzies: Come on, Hank. How many did you frame?

> Quinlan: "No one — nobody that wasn't guilty, guilty, guilty. Every last one of them — guilty." (And indeed, "the last one," Sanchez the shoe clerk, does confess, off screen).

---

[197] Menizies had been, as he himself says, Quinlan's "sucker" all along, unknowingly helping to plant evidence and build Quinlan's reputation, but, as Uncle Joe says, he's too much of an "idiot" to replace him. Instead, like Judas, his role is to betray Quinlan. He switches sides, and when he shows up at the whorehouse, after Vargas wires him up, the drunken Quinlan says "I thought you were Vargas." After discovering the bug, he shouts "I'm talking to you, now, Vargas, through this walking microphone [Mike-rophone] that used to be my partner." Menzies is, at best, what Jack Donovan would call a "runt"; see my use of this concept in my review of De Palma's *The Untouchables*, reprinted in *The Homo & the Negro: Masculinist Meditations on Politics & Popular Culture*; Second, Embiggened Edition, edited by Greg Johnson (San Francisco: Counter-Currents, 2017).

[198] As we quoted Cranston at the start, to "break bad" means to "turn off the path of the straight and narrow, when they've gone wrong. And that could be for that day or for a lifetime."

Vargas and Quinlan are more alike (one anti-Mexican, the other anti-corruption) than either would like to admit. Vargas is famous enough to be recognized by the border guards, and almost immediately he meets "our local police celebrity."

More particularly, both men's metamorphoses are tied to their wives (as Walt's, at least officially, is to his family). At the start of his police career, Quinlan's wife was murdered – supposedly strangled by a Mexican whom he was never able to bring to justice.

In fact, although I can't find many critics explicitly making this inference, it seems clear to me that Quinlan was the murderer, and the Mexican, who conveniently died in WWI, is simply a racially-charged alibi. He has dealt with his guilt by a life-long, obsessive pursuit of "justice," finding and punishing the guilty by whatever means necessary.[199]

As Lawrence Russell says, "All his murder cases have become a replay of his own psychodrama, wherein he plays judge and executioner in the unproven affair of his dead wife and her lover. He strangled his wife ... and now he hunts the shadows of the border town Los Robles for the surrogates who must pay the price for his ancient trauma."[200]

Menzies: Yeah, yeah, yeah. Drunk and crazy as you must have been when you strangled him. I guess you were somehow thinking of your wife, the way she was strangled.

Quinlan: Always thinking of her, drunk or sober. What else is there to think about? Except for my job, my dirty job.

Menzies: You didn't have to make it dirty.

Quinlan: I don't call it dirty. Look at the record ... All those convictions.

Menzies: Convictions, sure. How many did you frame?

Quinlan: Nobody.

Menzies: Come on, Hank. How many did you frame?

---

[199] "He mother never really love him / He crimefighting covers up a basic insecurity" is one of the lines in MST3k's English "translation" of the Jet Jaguar theme song's Japanese lyrics in "Episode 212: *Godzilla versus Megalon.*"

[200] http://www.culturecourt.com/F/Noir/TEvil.htm.

Welles' genius was such as to allow him to view his characters objectively. Though Welles was a hard-line com-symp, Quinlan gets more than enough sympathy as portrayed by Welles himself. The eye-rolling he gives Vargas's little speech about a police state —

Quinlan: Our job is tough enough.

Vargas: It's supposed to be. It has to be tough. A policeman's job is only easy in a police state. That's the whole point, Captain – who's the boss, the cop or the law?

— is intensely funny (Welles the ham is in his element) but it also meets the audience's eyes, thus implicating them as well — "Can you believe this guy?"[201]

And finally, at the most profound level, it is insinuated that to reach Realization, one must find a way to offload one's karmic attachments and given a demonstration of just how to do it.

Now, I mentioned just now how Vargas uses a wire to entrap Quinlan, and that reminds me that I should give some attention to the Other Hank, TV's Hank,[202] Walt's brother-in-law, and half-witted Holmes to Walt's Prof. Heisenberg.

Is it Walt White who is Hank Quinlan? The most natural doubling is Hank Quinlan/Hank Schrader. Both are Southwestern border-town lawmen, named Hank – duh! Hank matches Welles's bulk, and like Quinlan speaks no Spanish (or as he says, "I don't speak Mexican"). Unlike

---

[201] On the other hand: "Amusingly, Bazin is indeed forced to admit that 'in the interviews which he gave me ... Welles challenged this interpretation. He maintains that his moral position is unequivocal, and he condemns [Quinlan] absolutely.' 'The personal element in the film is the hatred I feel for the way the police abuse their power ... The things said by Vargas are what I would say myself ... that's the angle the film should be seen from; everything Vargas says, I say.' You can get pretentious about it all you want, and bring to bear political views that the film doesn't support (after all, within the film Quinlan is punished for his crimes and the 'mediocre' [Truffaut's word] moral hero triumphs), but sometimes a spade is a spade; sometimes a villain is a villain; sometimes your disgusting moral perspective isn't being covertly supported by a film that seems to condemn it." (http://100filmsinayear.wordpress.com/2014/09/24/touch-of-evil-1958/). Of course, I will argue that Quinlan isn't "punished" at all (death being a successful release from a realm of material futility), Vargas hardly "triumphs," and Welles' second-hand ACLU platitudes are irrelevant to what the film actually presents. Pretentious, moi?

[202] Not to be confused with TV's Frank of the MST3k cast.

Quinlan, he's a basically honest cop, but not above roughing up a suspect — his beating of Jesse matches up with Quinlan's "third degree" of the shoe store clerk (but smarter — Quinlan knows how to not leave a mark, while Hank's beating of Jessie gets him in some hot water).

> Quinlan (off camera): What're you scared of? I'd only slap you again if you got hysterical. Wouldn't be brutal. Even in the old days, we never hurt people in the face. It marks 'em up. We gave it to 'em like this. [Sound of blow landing, Sanchez grunting]

Movie Hank walks with a cane, the result of a bullet intended for Menzies:

> Quinlan: That's the second bullet I stopped for you, Pete.

TV Hank is also crippled, temporarily, by a bullet. Movie Hank's cane will betray his presence at Grandi's murder. TV Hank's medical bills are secretly paid by Walt, which enables Walt to stymie Hank's subsequent investigation.

Most interestingly, Hank delivers the line that most directly links the two works:

> While wiring Jesse for audio surveillance in the scene at the plaza, Hank instructs him, "Don't cross your arms, if you can help it." In Touch of Evil (1958), Charlton Heston as Vargas delivers a similar line, "Now remember, don't cross your arms," while wiring Sgt. Menzies to record Orson Welles' character Hank Quinlan.[203]

The line is Vargas', though; this emphasizes that TV Hank stands for a generalized notion of the Good Cop, what Movie Hank was but now can only perceive as a threat. Movie Hank is both TV Hank and Walt; by making Movie Hank himself a cop the film helps fit Walt's story arc into 100 minutes, and intensify the story, by absorbing TV Hank's story as well. Movie Hank shows the corruption of TV's Hank/Walt combo.

It's at the end, appropriately enough, that we witness the transfer of karma, and find the clearest similarities between the two works.

Touch of Evil, of course, opens with a legendary three-minute uninterrupted crane tracking shot, that covers four blocks from start to finish. But it is implicitly connected to the end, where Vargas crossing the

---

203   IMDB on *Breaking Bad* episode "Rabid Dog" (2013).

Mexican border on foot with his wife is echoed by Vargas running over the bridge from Mexico[204] and jumping into Susie's car and then roaring off, forgotten by the action and ignored by the camera.[205]

Breaking Bad ends with a crane shot, frequently discussed not so much for its technique, which is run of the mill today, as its emotional implications.

> "But in came the dailies, with that wonderful crane shot moving over Walter White, and once we played the song, [we thought], 'Oh, I get it now,'" Golubić continues. "This is a love-affair story of Walt and his love of science, and this was his greatest product – his greatest triumph as a chemist. It wasn't about Walter White as a criminal or a murderer or an awful person. It was him ending on his own terms. It felt creatively right."[206]

I'm not sure if a crane was used at the end of *Touch of Evil*, but Welles is now being shot from above, rather than the previous shots from below that emphasized Quinlan's menacing bulk. These shots show the similarity of their ends:

Conventional movie grammar has these kinds of shots symbolizing the defeat of the Bad Guy, his "fall" if you will. As I've suggested many times, this can also be given a positive meaning, at least esoterically. The body falls horizontally, resolved into the elements, (with Quinlan, water) while the spirit is released, upwards, freed from the burden of karma.[207]

---

[204]   Border and bridge are archetypal liminal locations, appropriate to such alchemical procedures; see my De Palma review referenced above.

[205]   As the car chase starts up at the beginning of Coleman Francis' *The Beast of Yucca Flats* (another Southwest epic) the camera "incompetently" lingers on the second car while the first roars off-screen. "Off-camera excitement, the Coleman Francis way." – MST3k, Episode 721.

[206]   Knopper, op. cit.

[207]   The finest example of this I know of is the last scene of the last movie of supposedly "bad" director Coleman Francis. Here, in *Red Zone Cuba*, Francis, like Welles, stars as the, literal, heavy. He runs across a field (the warp and woof of the material universe) and is shot down from a helicopter (a Francis trademark, replacing the crane shot and allied to shamanistic themes of flight); as he falls, he spins around (the whirl of manifestation, symbolized by the polar symbol of the swastika). Is this "the end of Rico" (as in the iconic end of *Little Caesar*)? No! A narrator suddenly appears for the first time, and it Coleman Francis himself, his character obviously delivering the epitaph — "Griffin. He ran all the way to Hell" — from a higher realm. I explore the entire Shamanistic oeuvre of Coleman

Tanya: Isn't anybody going to come and take him [the corpse] away?

Quinlan, thanks to Menzies' betrayal, can now find rest; his karmic burden has been passed on to the naïve, inane Vargas, who happily speeds away:

Vargas: It's all over, Susie; I'm taking you home.

Of course it isn't; Vargas has changed, and will likely spend the rest of his career enjoying the application of the third degree in Mexico's notorious jails.

But who, then, is Walt's sucker? His partner, Jesse.

Like Menzies, Hank Quinlan's apprentice sucker, Walt takes a bullet for him and, like the second bullet Hank Schrader takes, it kills him. Like Vargas, the ultimate sucker, he jumps in his car and roars away, laughing with glee.

At least one fan has put his finger on exactly why this denouement fails to satisfy:

I thought the ending sucked. What the fuck was Jesse so happy about? He was still destined to be a miserable (and now broke) fuck having to live with his shitty life choices.[208]

Both endings also have music which is "non-diagetic," as the critics say, meaning it is not natural but presumably conveys a character's POV. Quinlan's corpse is eulogized by the gypsy/madam Tanya (Marlene Dietrich!) as the sentimental pianola music from his brothel is, through the magic of the movies, somehow audible way out by the bridge. Tanya had already clued us in on its archeofuturistic significance: "The customers go for it – it's so old, it's new."

And indeed, Hank — or his karma — is now Vargas.

Also "so old it's new" is the music of *Breaking Bad*'s finale, "Baby Blue" by Badfinger. The first line, "Guess I got what I deserved," is clearly ironic in this context; in terms of the threefold analysis I proposed earlier,

---

Francis in a later essay below.

[208] http://www.theburningplatform.com/2014/10/16/either-youre-the-butcher-or-youre-the-cattle/. This fan also "was never sold on Walt being a badass tough guy so that never worked for me. He was more of an extremely lucky, bumbling idiot!"

Walt has I suppose received his conventional comeuppance, but we know that on the levels of manhood and metaphysics, he has found both true manhood and transcendence.

To those of us of Walt's generation (I admit to being somewhat creeped out by the realization that I've outlived him), Badfinger's song irresistibly recalls an even older tune, Bob Dylan's "It's All Over Now, Baby Blue," which not only seems appropriate enough for a finale, but also literally recalls Vargas' valediction: "It's all over now, Susie."

As we've said, nothing could be more false than Vargas' naïve happy ending. But if we're looking for the proper epitaph for both Quinlan and Hank, nothing can beat Tanya's famous line:

Schwartz: Is that all you have to say for him?

Tanya: He was some kind of man ...

St. Steven of Le Mans

The Man Who Just Didn't Care

"Though they may not always be handsome, men doomed to evil possess the manly virtues."
– Jean Genet, *The Thief's Journal*

L E MANS IS A "RACING MOVIE," and if that makes you want to run the other way – don't. If this essay can't convince you, then at least catch the documentary, *Steve McQueen: The Man & Le Mans*, on Showtime or Amazon Video. If that still doesn't convince you, you may be dead, or at least, have no soul.

Le Mans is a "racing movie" but this is no Tom Cruise "vehicle" with a pretty-boy romance to bring in the ladies like *Days of Thunder*. Nor is it a "people are so stupid" "comedy" like *Talladega Nights: The Ballad of Ricky Bobby*. And, as we'll see, it certainly isn't some thunderingly loud and visually disorienting CGI'd fantasy for nerds without driver's licenses.

There's been a lot of talk on websites about various writers' personal history with various icons of masculinity, especially (given our times) the cinematic sort, especially in the realm of espionage. In the latter context, names from the '60s like Sean Connery or James Coburn seem to predominate.[209]

Now, I don't want to get into any pissing contests here, but perhaps McQueen's taciturn model of the quietly efficient doing of one's job[210] with only the private satisfaction of some inner amusement could serve

---

[209]   See especially Jef Costello's *The Importance of James Bond & Other Essays*; ed. by Greg Johnson (San Francisco: Counter-Currents, 2017).

210   In the words of the Buddha, *Katam karaniyam,* "that which has to be done has been done," a phrase that will acquire pertinacity here soon.

as a more relevant, or accessible, role model than the wise-cracking, showboating Connery/Coburn?[211] You'll see what I mean in a moment.

Frist, let's get some perspective from, of course, Wikipedia:

Terence Steven "Steve" McQueen (March 24, 1930 - November 7, 1980) was an American actor. Called "The King of Cool," his "anti-hero" persona, developed at the height of the counterculture of the 1960s, made him a top box-office draw of the 1960s and 1970s. McQueen received an Academy Award nomination for his role in The Sand Pebbles. His other popular films include *The Cincinnati Kid, The Thomas Crown Affair, Bullitt, The Getaway,* and *Papillon,* as well as the all-star ensemble films *The Magnificent Seven, The Great Escape,* and *The Towering Inferno.* In 1974, he became the highest-paid movie star in the world, although he did not act in films again for four years. McQueen was combative with directors and producers, but his popularity placed him in high demand and enabled him to command large salaries.

After an archetypically bad childhood,[212] McQueen left reform school to take up a rather archetypally masculinist life:

At 16 McQueen left Chino and returned to his mother, now living in Greenwich Village, New York. He then met two sailors from the Merchant Marine and volunteered to serve on a ship bound for the Dominican Republic. Once there he abandoned his new post, eventually being employed as a "towel boy" in a brothel. Afterwards

---

[211] Steve McQueen, it's been said, is the only man who could make wearing a turtleneck look cool; Coburn barely succeeds at that. As for Bond, am I the only one who thinks Daniel Craig, as he emerges from the end of the *Casino Royale* titles, is channeling McQueen? In fact, according to Wikipedia, "Spy novelist Jeremy Duns revealed that Steve McQueen was considered for the lead role in a film adaptation of *The Diamond Smugglers,* written by James Bond creator Ian Fleming; McQueen would play John Blaize, a secret agent gone undercover to infiltrate a diamond-smuggling ring in South Africa. There were complications with the project which was eventually shelved, although a 1964 screenplay does exist."

[212] McQueen was dyslexic and partially deaf; he alternated between street crime and parental beatings. "McQueen was caught stealing hubcaps by police, who handed him over to his stepfather, who beat him severely, ending the fight by throwing McQueen down a flight of stairs. McQueen looked up at his stepfather and said, 'You lay your stinkin' hands on me again and I swear, I'll kill ya.'" (Wikipedia)

McQueen made his way to Texas and drifted from job to job. He worked as an oil rigger, a trinket salesman in a carnival, and a lumberjack.

Ultimately — and again archetypally — the Marines seemed to straighten him out:

> Initially he reverted to his prior rebelliousness and was demoted to private seven times. He took an unauthorized absence by failing to return after a weekend pass expired, staying with a girlfriend for two weeks until the shore patrol caught him. He resisted arrest and spent 41 days in the brig.

> After this he resolved to focus his energies on self-improvement and embraced the Marines' discipline.[213] He saved the lives of five other Marines during an Arctic exercise, pulling them from a tank before it broke through ice into the sea. He was assigned to the honor guard, responsible for guarding then US President Harry Truman's yacht. McQueen served until 1950 when he was honorably discharged. He later said he had enjoyed his time in the Marines.

By the late '60s he had managed to become "the King of Cool" and arguably the biggest male star in the world. Now there's self-improvement!

There were two additional elements to McQueen's success: his frequent director, John Sturges, and the interestingly named Alan Trustman, a successful lawyer who retired at 37 and decided to become a screenwriter. His first two were the iconic McQueen vehicles, *The Thomas Crown Affair* (written for Sean Connery but rewritten for McQueen; the 1989 remake would go to Bondian Pierce Brosnan) and *Bullitt* (written in 20 hours and grossing 68 million). With the first, Trustman felt the script had to be rewritten for McQueen and spent a week of 16-hour days at United Artists in New York screening film on McQueen and making lists of what McQueen liked, didn't like, did well, and could not do.[214] McQueen loved

---

[213]   McQueen seems to have discovered for himself the value of practicing visualization during the hypnagogic states that precede and follow sleep:

"I like daydreaming. You know that state before you get to sleep? Except in my life my daydreams came true." – from the end of *Steve McQueen: The Man & Le Mans*, an interview given while he was dying from lung cancer in 1980. For more on this, see my *Mysticism After Modernism: Crowley, Evola, Neville, Watts, Colin Wilson & Other Populist Gurus* (Melbourne, Australia: Manticore Press, 2020).

[214]   "Director Steven Spielberg said McQueen was his first choice for the character of Roy

the rewrite, and told everyone "I don't know how but the son of a bitch knows me."

"Knows" or "created"? Let's say Tribesman Trustman, a clever middleman,[215] was able to perceive the essence of McQueen's persona and then distill it into a handy formula; a mantra for McQueen to recite before each scene, "no matter what the director says":

I decide what is right and what is wrong, and I don't have to explain it to anybody. I like women, but I'm a little afraid of them. If you make a commitment to a woman they can hurt you. I won't pick a fight with you, but if you pick a fight with me or back me into a corner I will fucking kill you.[216]

There, see? Now there's a mantra for the modern man. Worth a whole gigabyte of game blogs.[217]

They let me meet with him a few times so I could explain [compare?] the character to Humphrey Bogart, hard-bitten, not loquacious.[218] All

Neary in *Close Encounters of the Third Kind.* According to Spielberg, in a documentary on the *Close Encounters* DVD, Spielberg met him at a bar, where McQueen drank beer after beer. Before leaving, McQueen told Spielberg that he could not accept the role because he was unable to cry on cue. Spielberg offered to take the crying scene out of the story, but McQueen demurred, saying that it was the best scene in the script. The role eventually went to Richard Dreyfuss. (Wikipedia)." One wonders if Ben Stiller was riffing on this in his *Tropic Thunder.*

[215] "I'm a nice Jewish boy from Boston." "'Thomas Crown Affair' screenwriter Alan Trustman talks films, working with Steve McQueen" by Mike Jaccarino; *NY Daily News,* August 28, 2011, http://www.nydailynews.com/entertainment/tv-movies/thomas-crown-affair-screenwriter-alan-trustman-talks-films-working-steve-mcqueen-article-1.950830.

[216] As his son, Chad, says later in the documentary, regarding his suborn insistence on making Le Mans his way: "He didn't give a shit, you know? If there was a fight he wouldn't turn away."

[217] So much for "method" acting nonsense. Not that he was "ignorant" of the Method. According to Wikipedia, "In 1952, with financial assistance provided by the G.I. Bill, McQueen began studying acting in New York at Sanford Meisner's Neighborhood Playhouse. Purportedly, the future "King of Cool" delivered his first dialogue on a theatre stage in a 1952 play produced by Yiddish theatre star Molly Picon. McQueen's character spoke one brief line: "Alts iz farloyrn." ("All is lost."). During this time, he also studied acting with Stella Adler."

[218] See my review, "Humphrey Bogart: Man Among the Cockroaches," reprinted in *The Homo & the Negro: Masculinist Meditations on Politics & Popular Culture;* Second, Embiggened Edition, edited by Greg Johnson (San Francisco: Counter-Currents, 2017).

116

the sentences had to be short, a character of internal integrity who's not afraid of a fight ...

McQueen understood the camera and understood that the camera loved him, and that's an exceptional ability for an actor to have. Yes, he was consistent, but people loved that character. And it was very much like the real Steve McQueen.[219]

TCM recently had a double feature of *Bullitt* (1968) and *Le Mans* (1971). Although I'm a big fan of *Bullitt*,[220] I've seen it many times and did not mind not noticing it was on until it was almost over. *Le Mans* was the movie I wanted to catch for the first time, having seen the documentary *Steve McQueen: The Man & Le Mans* a few days before. However, for our purposes, if not those of Turner Classic Movies, it would be good to start with *Bullitt*.

The novel *Mute Witness* has an elaborate plot which, whatever its merits,[221] the film, (retitled for its McQueen character), like most successful films — much to the annoyance of Tolkien and comic book fan-boys — puts on the back burner or largely ignores, in favor of sound and vision.

Much of the joy of watching *Bullitt* comes from what it captures: San Francisco in the 1960s, Steve McQueen when he was young, action sequences which are believable, and a sense of space and stillness. The dialogue is kept to a minimum, the acting is understated, we observe the characters from a distance. This contrasts with the films they make today which are too busy, with too much going on, too many special effects, unreal action sequences, and with characters who display too much

---

[219]   *Joccarino*, op. cit.

[220]   "BULLITT" is a trademark of Warner Bros./Chad & T. McQueen Testament Trust, used here for review purposes only. In other words, "Don't fuck with Steve McQueen."

[221]   "[At some point in the '60s] Penguin began to publish anything, and an orange spine ceased to be an indicator of quality. I've yet to establish exactly when the change occurred, but this book provides an upper bound. Simply put, this book has no merit whatsoever. It is just a story; pulp fiction. The characters are not believable, their conversations are inane, it tells us nothing new about the world it describes, and the author has no observations to make on life. There are no lessons here. This book gives the reader nothing but a way to pass some time. It is what Graham Greene would have described as 'an entertainment', but even that description would be generous. The book has a single saving grace in that it was the source of the film *Bullitt*, which is an amazing film, but one in which the plot is very difficult to follow." A Penguin a Week blog, "Penguin no. 2999: Bullitt (Mute Witness) by Robert L. Pike," http://apenguinaweek.blogspot.com/2010/12/book-2999-bullitt-mute-witness.html.

attitude and sarcasm. You can watch *Bullitt* 10 times and still find elements of the story you hadn't noticed before, which usually provide some crucial insight into understanding the plot. Important aspects of the story are revealed in places you don't expect, such as behind the opening credits and before the main characters are introduced. Understanding this film is an iterative process, a better detective story than the one embedded within the plot. It never gets boring.[222]

"An iterative process" – in short, exactly the kind of movie ripe for our paranoiac-criticial method. But that will have to wait for another time. All the elements this blogger singles out for praise will be found in the much less appreciated *Le Mans* and (perhaps because) at an even higher level of intensity.[223]

And a trip to San Francisco in the late '60s as well.[224] Like Clint Eastwood's Carmel and Monterey, this is still a world where "hip" means smooth West Coast jazz.

One audio-visual element left out in that appreciation — perhaps it goes without saying — is the famous, indeed iconic "car chase" through what a later TV show would call "the streets of San Francisco."[225] At the time, for a long time after, and largely still today, it's considered the Gold Standard for such sequences; especially since, of course, there's no CGI.

---

[222] Pike, loc. cit.

[223] Although I have to admit that I can't claim you can watch it "10 times and still find elements of the story you hadn't noticed before, which usually provide some crucial insight into understanding the plot," as I haven't had the chance to do that.

[224] Check out the somewhat frighteningly detailed assembly of "*Bullitt* Locations" http://www.rjsmith.com/bullitt-locations.html.

[225] "The famous car chase features a wild drive through several picturesque parts of San Francisco. The chase was filmed in a variety of disparate locations and there is little continuity. It took two weeks to film the chase, not surprising since the locations are spread out over a considerable part of the city. The lack of continuity is due to the logistics of filming in a working city. There are several basic locations from which the film crew operated and many shots were filmed at locations close to these areas. For example, San Francisco General Hospital is close to the chase scenes filmed around 20th Street, Kansas Street, and Rhode Island Street, while Russian Hill served as the base for many of the chase scenes, with the Marina District only a short distance away. The chase continues west toward the Golden Gate Bridge on Marina Boulevard. According to several printed sources, the chase was supposed to continue across the Golden Gate Bridge but the Golden Gate Bridge and Highway District refused permission since even in 1968 it would have created a traffic nightmare, so the chase picks up again on University Street, which is all the way across the city to the south." "*Bullitt* Locations," ibid.

And *Le Mans* does the same for the "racing film" – upping the ante with 50 cars, twenty-four hours, and the greatest track in the world. And just as *Bullitt* pitted the two greatest street-legal cars — the Ford Mustang and Dodge Charger — against each other,[226] so the latter film uses the greatest racing cars of all time, the Porsche 917 and the Ferrari 512S; and again, no CGI.[227]

All these elements would be carried forward into *Le Mans*, which is pretty interesting, since the only common elements are the time period and McQueen; and fast cars, of course. Otherwise, *Le Mans* jettisons plot altogether, other than the ready-made narrative provided by the 24 hours of the race.

First, back to McQueen. Inspired by the character he played in *Thomas Crown Affair*, he had decided to parlay his acting cred into becoming something that really mattered: a filmmaker. He would no longer be "some candy-ass actor" but a mover and shaker. Filmmaking meant something, both as a massive industry and as a total art form: "Film is a very important medium."

Here, McQueen is on the same page as film reviewer Trevor Lynch:

By integrating so many art forms, film can communicate more, and more deeply, to more people, than any single art form. ... Second .... movies are a force. They are the greatest tool ever invented for shaping people's ideas and imaginations. In the right hands, they can be a force for good. In the wrong hands, they are a force for evil.[228]

---

[226]   "The production company used two Mustangs and two Dodge Chargers to film the chase scenes. The Highland Green Mustangs had 390 cubic inch engines, while the Chargers had 440 cubic inch engines. The Chargers were 4-speeds, as were the Mustangs. The Dodge Charger was driven by Bill Hickman, who also played one of the hitmen in the film. The Winchester shotgun-toting hitman was played by Paul Genge. The Mustangs were driven by Bud Ekins, Carey Loftin, and McQueen. The camera car, built upon a Corvette chassis, was driven by Pat Houstis." "*Bullitt* Locations," ibid. Note that McQueen did (some) of his own driving; he'd do the same in Le Mans.

[227]   A reviewer of *Le Mans* at IMDB laments: "Sadly, this is probably the last of the true racing movies. The world today is impossible to make a movie out of real racing car (every single race car in *Le Mans* is real: the Porsche 917, the Ferrari 512S, the Lola T70. Driven uses mock CART car based on Indy Light, plus a whole lot of crappy CGI car, Grand Prix uses the F2 car that looks like the F1 at the time. A movie like *Le Mans* probably will never be made again."

[228]   "Why I Write," here: https://counter-currents.com/2011/08/why-i-write-11/

As Lynch goes on to point out, films today are mostly a force for evil, since the views and values they embody and promote are those of the elite. McQueen's production company would promote — if only implicitly — the "cool" masculinity of the Western Man.

The name of his company would be, of course: Solar Productions.

There was another element — also implicitly Western — to be added as well: auto racing.

Maybe it's being from Detroit, but I've never understood the loathing of NASCAR. Well, except I understand it as a status marker posing as cultural sophistication. This is Euro-style Grand Prix racing, not NASCAR, which really did have some cachet domestically at the time, but now I suppose unless it's bike (or "cycle") racing, it's all the same.

As usual, you can tell it's a status thing from the banality of the reasons offered. "They just drive in circles!" Sure, no talent required, like horse racing — the sport of kings! — Roman chariot races, and all those track athletes. It's like "Wrestling is fake!" Sure, unlike, say, a Hollywood movie.

Speaking of fake, McQueen's racing was, like his acting, not an act. According to Wikipedia,

> He began to earn money [in 1952] by competing in weekend motorcycle races at Long Island City Raceway and purchased the first of many motorcycles, a Harley-Davidson. He soon became an excellent racer, and went home each weekend with about $100 in winnings (equivalent to $900 in 2015).

> When he had the opportunity to drive in a movie, he performed many of his own stunts, including some of the car chase in *Bullitt* and the motorcycle chase in *The Great Escape*. Although the jump over the fence in *The Great Escape* was done by Bud Ekins for insurance purposes, McQueen did have considerable screen time riding his 650cc Triumph TR6 Trophy motorcycle. It was difficult to find riders as skilled as McQueen. At one point, using editing, McQueen is seen in a German uniform chasing himself on another bike.

By 1970, McQueen would drive the 12-hour Sebring race, actually finishing second, despite driving with a broken foot. As an interviewee puts it, "it took Mario Andretti and two Ferraris to beat him."

"I am a driver, an actor, and a filmmaker."

McQueen was now perfectly positioned to draw on all three talents to produce a "racing film" that would be the greatest racing film, the greatest documentary, possibly the greatest film, ever made. *Le Mans* would combine the tycoon of *Thomas Crown Affair* with the barely scripted hard driving of *Bullitt.*

The Guardian, of course, provides a perfect example of how a modern cultural cockroach would view this film and this documentary thereon, as well as McQueen himself:

> A weird mood of solemnity settles like rain on this interesting, odd documentary about the petrol-head Hollywood star Steve McQueen and the film he took on in 1970 at the height of his celebrity prestige. It was to be a big budget movie about the *Le Mans* 24-hour auto race in which he would be producer-star: he wanted all the real thrills of the sport he loved.
>
> It was soon horribly clear that this film was something between a vanity project and a midlife crisis. McQueen could never decide on a script or story, and the movie went wildly over budget as McQueen's team of professional drivers risked their necks shooting hours and hours of ambient race footage.
>
> Another type of documentary, with a little more ironic detachment, would have played up the hilarious tinseltown nightmare of McQueen's Le Mans, and been much more candid about him being an egomaniacal pain. But not this film, which has the cooperation of McQueen's family and so respectfully insists on how poignant and sad it all was. It could be that this documentary defeats your hopes for fun and interest in exactly the same way as the original film – which is, however, still admired in certain quarters for its almost wordless documentary realism. But it's still an interesting study in how even the biggest movie stars can bump their heads on a career ceiling. Like Brando, McQueen was discontented with pretty-boy fame. He yearned for producer-power and producer-control, but finally had to settle for being the world's biggest acting star instead.[229]

[229]   Peter Bradshaw, *The Guardian*, Thursday 19 November 2015, http://www.theguardian.com/film/2015/nov/19/steve-mcqueen-the-man-le-mans-review.

I honestly had to take a shower after reading that. My God, it's all there, isn't it? Racing fans are morons ("petrol head"). "Another type of documentary" — you know, a clever, postmodern one — might salvage some "fun" by revealing the naked Emperor for laughs, but this benighted one takes it all seriously. Oh, my goodness, can you believe it? Of course, I suppose it has its crude fans in "certain quarters,"— inhabited by fans like this one at IMBD: "Steve McQueen, & *Le Mans* — SCREAMS Alcohol, Tobacco, Drugs, Women, Violence, Man Cave ... !" – but you couldn't pay me to visit those inbred, Bible-thumping shitholes ...

Anyway, back to 1970.

Le Mans was supposed to be an unprecedented production, both a racing film — no one, all agreed, had really captured the sport on film — and at the same time a storyline of some sort. McQueen would tie the two together, starring in the story and driving in the race.

Things began to go to Hell almost immediately.

They began without a screenplay. Not, without a completed screenplay — a not at all uncommon occurrence — but no screenplay at all. *Le Mans* would be a kind of cinematic "nonfiction novel," with the filmmakers as participants in the events, and the storyline emerging along with the race.[230]

The first blow was that the insurance chappies refused to let McQueen actually drive.

Director Sturges continued as he had started, filming everything in sight, using both the race itself and staged sequences with stunt drivers. But he continued to press McQueen on coming up with a screenplay with a suitably "romantic" storyline, which McQueen refused to countenance.

Eventually Sturges quit the film — after most his footage proved unusable — with the classic parting remark, "I'm too old and too rich to put up with this shit."

---

[230] Somewhat in the manner of the French New Wave, or the way Hunter S. Thompson's failed coverage of the Mint 400 motorcycle race the next year eventually produced *Fear and Loathing in Las Vegas*. MarkM comments: "I've always seen this movie as a sort of fictional documentary, as though the scripted scenes are of course staged & filmed, the feel of it is akin to watching a documentary on the race itself, albeit with fictional protagonists & something resembling a plot." https://wondersinthedark.wordpress.com/2013/05/15/when-people-risk-their-lives-shouldnt-it-be-for-something-important-steve-mcqueen-and-lee-katzins-le-mans/.

Next to go was Trustman. Despite "knowing" McQueen, the trusty screenwriter could not go along with McQueen's idea of abandoning his macho image and playing a loser. In the doco, Trustman asks plaintively:

"He wanted to lose, and I don't know why."

We'll get back to that. McQueen decided to jettison the story altogether, but eventually, the financiers (of course) moved in:

Cinema Centre considered shutting down the film completely, but eventually struck a deal with Steve in which he gave up his salary, his percentage of profits, and his control of the film, in order to "get it finished."

The same old story: the Western Man creates, begins to succeed, and the financiers bring him down and take it over.[231]

The film got finished 2 months later than planned and 1.5 million over budget. One driver lost a leg during production, and Steve was nearly killed twice.

After *Le Mans* was released in the US, Steve went bankrupt, his main Solar partners left the company, and Solar as a 'real' production company had folded. Also, his marriage to Neile was collapsing.

Le Mans did make money ($19 million at the box office), but in typical Hollywood fashion Steve never saw a cent of it.[232]

Le Mans is surprisingly not a disaster itself, although it proved to be a disaster for all involved. McQueen's career never really recovered, and he died of lung cancer in 1980. Trustman, for example, says he went from the biggest writer in Hollywood to a complete unknown — "the phone stopped ringing" — after quitting the film. We'll look at the significance of winning by not winning in a bit.

---

[231] See, for instance, my "This Ain't Funny – This is Genocide! The Rise & Fall of the National Lampoon," Counter-Currents, January 28, 2016, https://counter-currents.com/2016/01/this-aint-funny-this-is-genocide-the-rise-fall-of-the-national-lampoon/, and "From Ultrasuede to Limelight: Aryan Entrepreneurs in the Dark Age," reprinted my *Green Nazis in Space! New Essays on Literature, Art, & Culture;* edited by Greg Johnson (San Francisco: Counter-Currents, 2015).

[232] The doco reveals that McQueen asked Cinema Centre to earmark a share of the profits for the injured driver, Dave Piper, but he never got anything and in fact never knew, until now, of McQueen's gesture.

I've frequently suggested that with Grade Z filmmakers like Edward D. Wood, Jr., Coleman Francis, and Merle Gould, the utter lack of conventional "talent" results in a kind of negative capability that allows, in Zen fashion, interesting things to "just happen." Freed from Hollywood expectations (Sturges: there must be a romance; Trustman: he must be a hero), the films not only evade liberal agendas (Ed Wood, for example, was a pro-family, anti-smut Republican under his angora sweater) but are free to become remarkably accurate time capsules of the period (true *cinéma vérité*)[233] as well as be open to the arising of archetypal and Traditionalist motifs.

The lack of a script isn't B-movie incompetence, blockbuster no-brainer, or art house superciliousness. It allows *Le Mans* to be a hypnotic meditation on racing and is appropriate to McQueen's no-talk character. The ending avoids both contrived Hollywood schmaltz (Even Rocky had to come back and win in *Rocky II*) and hip nihilistic romanticism (unlike *Easy Rider*, say).

Some other online comments from the review at *Wonders in the Dark* are perceptive:

> This film has fascinated me for years – not just its checkered production history, but its refusal to play it conventional in terms of narrative storytelling. The filmmakers understand that for this kind of film, visual storytelling is of paramount of performance –hence the surprisingly lack of dialogue and, at times, *cinéma vérité* approach. (JD)

> [*Le Mans* only has] something resembling a plot. What plot there is is driven, (no pun intended), by the race, & the sketchily drawn characters are in turn driven entirely by the plot, & are never driving it, which is a microcosm of racing & real lit itself. The characters are sketchily drawn on purpose, as they are as incidental to the movie as the plot is, both being the framework to hang the images on that actually drive the movie. (Mark M)

---

[233] As the three homicidal hoboes of *Red Zone Cuba* struggle to raise the top of their stolen convertible, Crow T. Robot exclaims, "Your everyday annoyances should not be filmed!" (MST3k, Episode 619).

The time capsule element is built right into the race documentary angle. The saturated color easily evokes the '70s. The most notable element is the silence – except for the cars, of course. No ever-present Muzak as in today's public spaces. No iPhones, iPods, etc. Drivers and crews talk directly to each other, over the car noise, no headphones or mikes.

As for narrative, *Le Mans* has the thinnest plot thread of any big-budget, supposedly "Hollywood" film I've ever encountered. It's not intended to be an "experimental" or even "art" film, but as I'm insisting, it subtly winds up as wildly innovative and unique. I suppose we should be glad that McQueen was restrained enough not to go full Andy Warhol and offer us a 24-hour film.

It's called *Le Mans* because the race is the major component, one that simply goes on its own for 24 hours. Inserted into this is a woman (whose name I can't be bothered to recall, so little does it or her matter) whose husband died at *Le Mans* the year before. McQueen is a driver who cracked up elsewhere, to avoid a hitchhiker in the road. Their eyes meet; they know each other's backstory.

He says, "It must have been hard for you."

She replies, "At first. But now I'm alright … Was it difficult to return to racing?"

If this was a "Hollywood" film this encounter would lead to a "romantic encounter" as per Sturges's idea; I've seen online reviews that actual say there is one, so great is the Hollywood preconditioning. But McQueen is in charge now, and so it doesn't. Eventually, near the end, they meet in a trailer, and a typically awkward male/female conversation occurs.[234]

"When people risk their lives, shouldn't it be for something important? What's so important about driving faster than anyone else?"

"A lot of people go through life doing things badly. Racing is important to men who do something well … When you're racing, it's life … Anything that happens before and after, it's just waiting …"

---

[234] "This checkmate has forced him to devise a better response, a response his face and body reveal to be peculiarly agonizing, his being a pronouncedly (and necessarily) laconic take upon dynamics. Barely audible, he takes a stab at conveying the nub of his involvement with fast cars." *Wonders in the Dark,* op. cit.

Then McQueen goes out and finishes the race. The end.[235]

Here's what I think is happening: the race, of course, is a Circle. The widow is returning to the scene of her husband's death, McQueen, who unlike her husband crashed without dying, is returning to racing. By connecting with him, if he can finish the race without dying she will have broken the broken the chain of karma that would keep her returning again and again to the race (the circle of *samsara*). The vicious circle will become a virtuous spiral.[236]

Meanwhile, McQueen has concocted a brilliant subversion of the Hollywood Hero ending. McQueen's character, Mike Delaney (oh, yeah, that's the name, it hardly matters, it's Steve McQueen!) also evades *karma*. He has crashed again, become *hors de combat* before talking to the widow. But the team manager does not trust his teammate to maintain the lead; he sends McQueen back in solely to stymie the Ferrari driven by his longtime rival and enable the other Porsche driver to win;[237] thus he acts without concern for the fruits of action, he "wins" without "winning."[238]

Remember when Trustman (what a name!) asked plaintively: "He wanted to lose, and I don't know why."

Well, I'll suggest that answer to that, or at least, call on Baron Evola to explain. The "differentiated man" (the man who stands out from the mass) that *Ride the Tiger* is a study of, and a manual for, faces the lack of initiatory tradition in the modern world by structuring his life as a series of tests or challenges, by which he confronts death, symbolic or otherwise, in order to discover and reaffirm (contra Heidegger) his connection to something Transcendent within.

---

[235] There also an even slimmer subplot of the second driver who's thinking of retiring, but no one, including McQueen, cares about this plot.

[236] Needless to say, all this recalls the theme song from *The Thomas Crown Affair*, "The Windmills of your Mind," a classic bit of '60s Euro-Pop with lyrics that at first may sound like typically meaningless Euro-Pop babble: "Like a circle in a spiral, a wheel within a wheel. Never ending or beginning, on an ever-spinning reel." The song is by Michel Legrande, who would also score *Le Mans*, although, like all the others his contributions — merely some atmospheric "cool jazz" that prefigures ambient music — are muted almost to nothing in McQueen's single-minded pursuit of The Race Itself.

[237] An interesting combination of such macho clichés as "taking one for the team" and "cock-blocking."

[238] "So, you lost. But by admitting you lost, you won. That's some Zen shit, there." *World's Dumbest Brawlers 12* (TruTV, 2012).

The valid attitude toward the beyond is the same attitude that I proposed for life in general: that of a transcendental confidence, joined on one side by the "heroic" and "sacrificial" disposition (readiness to actively take oneself beyond oneself), or the other by one's capacity to dominate his soul, impulses, and imagination: just as one who, in a difficult and risky situation does not lose control of himself, doing lucidly and without hesitation all that can be done ... the disposition of being ready "to bear lethal blows on ones won being without being destroyed."[239]

"The 'heroic' and 'sacrificial' disposition" would suggest McQueen's subversion of the "winner" cliché in the climax of Le Mans. "One who, in a difficult and risky situation does not lose control of himself, doing lucidly and without hesitation all that can be done" – would be an excellent description of race driving, filmmaking along the lines of Le Mans, and life itself, lived along the lines of the King of Cool.

Le Mans manages to be a bravura celebration of technical mastery — of race driving and filmmaking — along the lines suggested by Ernst Jünger; combined with a proud non-mastery, a sovereign contempt, for the niceties of screenwriting and audience-catering to. As commenter "JD" says,

> Y'know, one could argue that in some respects, McQueen is the auteur of this film. It was obviously a passion project for him, one that almost bankrupted him and that refused to compromise on, which resulted in an uncommercial film, but one that his vision represented his vision. He saw a beauty and sense of purity in racing – the whole man and machine thing where you're not only racing against an opponent(s), but yourself in terms of mental and physical endurance, which I think LE MANS explores in fascinating ways.[240]

Indeed, McQueen's whole persona, the "man who didn't give a shit," suggests Baron Evola's description of the true Western "race of spirit":

[239] Ride the Tiger: A Survival Manual for the Aristocrats of the Soul, trans. Jocelyn Godwin and Constance Fontana (Rochester, Vt.: Inner Traditions, 2003), p. 221. It's interesting to imagine Evola as a Gran Prix driver; Ferrari or Porsche, do you think? In his own case, it was "mountain climbing at high altitudes" that allowed him to "seek dangers as a tacit way to put fate to the test." See his Meditations on the Peaks (Rochester, Vt.: Inner Traditions, 1998) and also his autobiography, The Path of Cinnabar (London: Arktos, 2009), pp. 183–84, where he also discusses the "rumor" that his crippling injury in wartime Vienna was a result of a similar "testing" of fate.

[240] Wonders in the Dark, loc. cit.

It is not said that the realization that something is impermanent is *eo ipso* a motive for detachment from and renunciation of it. This depends on what we have elsewhere called the "race of the spirit." ... Only in those in whom this race [the 'heroic"] survives ... can it arouse the reaction that follows from "No, I want no more of it," from "This does not belong to me, I am not this, this is not my self." The work, then, has one single justification, it must be done, that is to say, for the noble and heroic spirit, there is no alternative. *Katam karaniyam*, "that which has to be done has been done," this is the universally recurring formula that refers to Ariya that have destroyed the *asava* and achieved awakening.[241]

Speaking of circles and repetitions, blogger Sam Juliano at Wonders in the Dark, though writing in somewhat impenetrable Euro-cinema lingo, has uncovered several fascinating parallels between *Le Mans* and our old favorite, *Kiss Me Deadly*![242]

Beginning with the beginning: both movies commence with our protagonist, named Michael (Delaney/Hammer), driving his expensive sports car (Porsche/Jag) at night on a country road, and swerving to avoid a female hitchhiker.

He even makes this remarkable claim:

It is, though, the other side of the camera we have to pay some attention to at this stage, because this vehicle has been discreetly outfitted (by somebody) with an unsuspected range of motion, which seals the deal. There was Katzin, and nominal screenwriter, Harry Kleiner – neither being, for all their Ivy League background, a force for the ages. What they did have, however, was an association with Robert Aldrich and a predisposition to attend to dramas where there is someone who must (like *Kiss Me Deadly's* Mike Hammer) stand alone, for want of useful encouragement in the workplace and at home.

---

[241]   *The Doctrine of Awakening: The Attainment of Self-Mastery According to the Earliest Buddhist Texts* (Rochester, Vt.: Inner Traditions, 1995), "The Determination of the Vocations," p77. It should be noted that of the various psychological types or "races of the spirit" that Evola delineates, McQueen also shades into the "Nietzschean" who embraces impermanence in a spirit of *amor fati*. Asked by the interviewer "Would you do it all over again" he replies "Absolutely."

[242]   See my essay "Mike Hammer, Occult Dick: Kiss Me Deadly as Lovecraftian Tale," reprinted in *The Eldritch Evola ... & Others* (San Francisco: Counter-Currents, 2014).

The blogger doesn't spell out this "connection" but apparently,

Harvard-educated director Lee H. Katzin (1935–2002) was a protégé of filmmaker Robert Aldrich. Katzin's official directorial debut was the Aldrich-produced melodrama *Whatever Happened to Aunt Alice* (1969); in truth, a year or so earlier he had helmed the disastrous *The Phynx*, which had an extremely limited release in 1970. His big-budget break came when he replaced John Sturges as director for *Le Mans* (1971); Katzin's documentary approach in this film was at odds with his usual self-conscious, gimmicky visual style. The director's TV credits include "Movie of the Week" fare like *Along Came a Spider* (1970) and *Ordeal* (1973), pilot films like *Man From Atlantis* (1977), and several episodes of the British sci-fi series *Space: 1999* (1975–77). In 1988, Katzin directed *The World Gone Wild*, his first theatrical feature in years.[243]

That list of credits certainly puts Katzin in the B director league. The pro-McQueen doco presents Katzin as a nobody and never-was, forced on McQueen by the terms of his settlement with Cinema Center but totally dominated by McQueen, (after Katzin called for a second take on his first scene, McQueen told him that "I'll say when we need a fucking second take"[244]), but the Aldrich connection may have been just the alchemical element[245] McQueen needed to finally produce some kind of script that would synthesize a film out of hours of race footage:

The scenario McQueen had favored, for all its paucity of this-planet enthusiasms, did relate to the loneliness of a top-flight Grand-Prix celebrity, constantly exposed to nature-inflecting, life-changing motions. So between them, this unholy trinity did something that, if ever known, would break many hearts in the driving fraternity and render *Le Mans* even less marketable than generally understood. A

---

[243]   http://www.bentleypublishers.com/author.htm?who=Lee_H._Katzin.

[244]   In a pivotal scene in *Manhunter*, Will Graham, obsessively watching home movies of the murdered families to find a clue, shouts "I'll tell you when it's too fucking late" when Jack Crawford suggests time has run out; see my chapter on the film above, and watch the scene here: https://youtu.be/Kl62PvygKeA.

[245]   In my Mike Hammer essay, I emphasize the accidental emergence of Traditional themes when directors and screenwriters are not paying attention – i.e., consciously inflicting their modernist agendas.

storm-tossed voyage, no doubt; but notably having had its moment of brief, powerful (though unnoticed) buoyancy.

I suppose it should come as no surprise, then, that the ridiculously rare and expensive book on the making of *Le Mans* is called *A French Kiss with Death*.[246]

There's a Blu-Ray of *Le Mans* that you should buy.[247] The doco is quite good, and you should either buy it or rent it from Amazon or catch it on Showtime currently. It's masterfully cobbled together from archival footage, including never-before heard audio from McQueen, new interviews with survivors, and incredible amounts of film footage shot in, around, and for the production, which had been presumed lost.

The McQueen audio, which includes many great lines, such as the daydreaming one quoted earlier, seems to have been recorded while the actor was dying prematurely of lung cancer. They are captioned as "Mexico," and I recall that McQueen, like Steve Jobs much later, was much in the news as a celebrity pursuing an "alternative" cancer treatment; in his case, laetrile, a derivative of apricot pits that was banned in the USA but available down south. The filmmakers don't mention this, but instead insinuate that the disease was caused by the flame-retardant clothing he wore at Sebring and Le Mans. As a reviewer at IMDB notes:

---

[246] *A French Kiss with Death: The Story of Steve McQueen and Le Mans* by Michael Keyser. From the apocalyptic climax of *Kiss Me Deadly*: Lily Carver: "Kiss me, Mike. I want you to kiss me. Kiss me. The liar's kiss that says I love you and means something else." Cue, like Le Mans, explosion and flames. Neither Mike ever really connects, Hollywood style, with his femme fatale.

[247] For those who care, here's a technical review from DVD Verdict: "The sheer joy of watching *Le Mans* is amped up considerably by the stupendous high-definition transfer on this Blu-ray. The 1080p MPEG-4/AVC image offers sharp detail, superb depth, and perfect color reproduction. Print damage is minimal, as is any digital manipulation of the image. Audio is presented in a room-shaking DTS-HD Master Audio 7.1 surround expansion of the original analog monaural track. Dialogue is a bit flat at times, but the sounds of the race are surprisingly full-bodied and dynamic given the limited source. Purists can rest assured that a single-channel DTS-HD Master Audio presentation of the original audio is also available, as well as uncompressed dubs in French, German, and Spanish. In fact, most of the space on *Le Mans*' dual-layered platter is consumed by superb audio options. There are also 10 optional subtitle tracks. In addition to the feature, the disc offers a surprisingly substantive retrospective making-of documentary called *Filming at Speed: The Making of the Movie Le Mans*. The piece is hosted by McQueen's son, Chad, and includes contributions from Katzin. There's also a trailer for the movie."

One thing I took issue with was a prominently placed assertion that the asbestos caused cancer may have come from the flame proof driving suits. If that were the case, we would have likely seen this as a trend with drivers from that era. This was a sensational and reckless comment which ignored the fact that McQueen was in the Merchant Marine prior to acting and that the ships boilers and piping were wrapped in asbestos. This was the likely source of his issue as there are a number of former sailors and shipyard workers who had suffered from asbestosis.

I've seen this sort of asbestos panic before, from tenants forced to leave all their belongings behind when evacuated from damaged buildings (and subsequently looted by able-bodied thieves) to all these "home improvement" and "flipping" shows, even the restaurant rebuilding ones; asbestos is treated like plutonium, killing on contact rather than needing to build up over the years. This, like the similar panic over "secondhand smoke" (laws in NYC address the issue of smoke penetrating condo walls 80 stories away) seems part of the ongoing infantilization of the public, which I'm sure McQueen would sneer at.[248]

As would McQueen's son, Chad, who went along to Le Mans and returns there 40 years later. In between, he followed his father's racing lead, eventually breaking about every bone in his body, including a vaguely mumbled injury that apparently requires him to wear sunglasses when facing the camera (otherwise being the spitting image of his old man). He provides detail on what it was like to be at Le Mans with your dad driving, and reads pithy excerpts from his father's documents with gusto, such as this from a preliminary briefing for the cast and crew:

> [Grand Prix] is a prime example of a director playing with himself in public. .... OK gentlemen, battle stations!

Less useful are interviews with McQueen's widow, who (one is tempted to say "of course") is still around to complain about his infidelity and, no doubt, collect hefty residual checks. She's also part of a half-hearted attempt by the documentarians to link McQueen's lofty "don't give a shit"

---

[248]   No comments are made about David Piper, the stunt driver who lost a leg below the knee, and was known as "the Pirate" due to his ever-present pipe smoking. He looks almost unchanged today, pipe and all.

mentality to the "liberation" movements of the '60s.[249] Of course, no one could be less of a hippie than McQueen, except perhaps Frank Bullitt's contemporary San Francisco cop, Clint Eastwood's Harry Callaghan.[250]

The most annoying aspect is the captions or subtitles, which are absurdly and unnecessarily small, making them almost unreadable on the small screen, at least for those of us old enough to remember the phenomenon of Steve McQueen.

One final repetition, uncommented on in the doco or online as far as I can tell: at Sebring, the almost-winning McQueen greets the cheering crowds (his almost-victory and Hollywood fame eclipsing the actual winners) with the fashionable '60s "peace sign." At the end of *Le Mans*, the almost winning Michael/McQueen gives his rival, and the audience, the European "two-finger salute." Like so many outsider directors, in the final analysis, he really just didn't care; [251] and we are all the better for it.

---

[249]   The two themes collide when we learn that McQueen was to have attended the Hollywood party that was the target of the Manson Family murders; instead, he met some chick and had better things to do. Interestingly, one of the victims was Jay Sebring. All this comes up again in Tarantino's *Once Upon a Time in Hollywood*; the McQueen angle is explored here: https://screenrant.com/once-time-hollywood-steve-mcqueen-actor-damian-lewis-true-story/.

[250]   *Bullitt* adds the cool jazz and easy sex of *Play Misty for Me* to Dirty Harry's Callaghan. What Tarantino might call "The Jessica Walter Problem" illustrates McQueen's mantra, both the danger of casual involvement with even the most seemingly accommodating women and the willingness, if pushed, to fucking kill you.

[251]   A trope, coined by MST3k, defined as "This is when the production values of a work are just so far below what should be expected that you can't help but figure that They Just Didn't Care." For example: "I see the movie has finally thrown up its hands and said, 'I just don't know!'"— Tom Servo, MST3k, Episode 619, *Red Zone Cuba*. See TVTropes under "They Just Didn't Care."

Passing the Buck

Spy, Dandy, Übermensch

"In the Land of The Blind, the one eyed-man is in a circus."[252]
– Alexander Eberlin

THE AMAZON PAGE FOR the Kindle version actually lists this book as "A Dandy in Aspic: The greatest of all the Cold War spy thrillers." I don't really know enough about the genre to argue the point,[253] but it certainly is my favorite, endlessly re-readable in a way that the Fleming and Le Carré books certainly aren't; in fact, it's one of my favorite books, period – or full stop, as the Brits would say.[254]

While this 50th anniversary reprinting is indeed welcome,[255] the publisher's publicity is a bit ... off. Here's their blurb, with a bit of plot to start you off:

Alexander Eberlin is a small, faceless civil servant working for the Government at the height of the Cold War. As he nears middle age, he allows himself one luxury – to dress like a Dandy. His superiors send

---

[252] The Circus, of course, is British Intelligence (MI6) in John le Carré's George Smiley novels. This, by the way, is one of the "dandyish" epigrams that decorate the chapter titles in the US version of the novel, as we shall see.

[253] The Guardian called it one of the ten best first novels of all time and add that "It's baffling that a writer of Marlowe's quality, his style and sensibility setting him apart from all competition, has been out of print for so long." "Nicholas Royle's top 10 first novels," 27 February 2013. FWIW, I've never heard of any of the other nine authors or books.

[254] We'll soon see that the experience of the book will differ from one side of the pond to the other.

[255] Long out of print, it's been reasonably available on the second-hand market; I've acquired, in my obsessive fashion, the original US and UK hardcovers for about a dollar each, and a British move tie-in paperback. The film is available on DVD.

him on a mission to hunt down and destroy a cold-blooded and vicious Russian assassin named Krasnevin, who is responsible for a number of British agents' deaths. But Eberlin has a secret – he is Krasnevin. This is the story of what happens when Eberlin is sent to destroy himself. Now back in print fifty years after it was written, The Times says A Dandy in Aspic is 'A well groomed anecdote to today's fast-paced thrillers with gym-buffed heroes. Eberlin is the real deal.'

Where to begin? Perhaps with that quote from *The Times*; did they really say "anecdote" for "antidote"? They won't let me know unless I pay them twelve pounds, so let it stand, the bastards.[256] Why on Earth is "Dandy" capitalized?

More problematic is that "small, faceless civil servant" bit. It makes it sound as if Eberlin is one of those grey, mousey little spy-bureaucrats that Le Carré and Deighton began to produce as if to offer a more "realistic" alternative to the Bond fantasy,[257] and that he takes up his one indulgence — fancy duds — as part of some mid-life crisis.[258]

In fact, Eberlin does not "dress like a Dandy," he is one. It permeates all aspects of his life, such as it is, and, as we'll see, his existential problem is far more serious, and interesting, than any midlife crisis.

---

[256]   "Classic read: *A Dandy in Aspic* by Derek Marlowe" by Fiona Wilson; April 25, 2015.

[257]   Thus missing the whole point of the Bond appeal. It's the kind of "grey is real" miserablism that the Left usually traffics in, preferring "folk" ditty about mining disasters to pop hits, or, in the UK context, creating the dismal *East Enders* series to counter the popular *Coronation Street* (guess which one is on PBS in the States). The Right, in its Beautiful Losers mode, indulges in it too; see my "Hard Men vs. Wild Boys," reprinted in *The Homo & the Negro: Masculinist Meditations on Politics & Popular Culture*; Second, Embiggened Edition, edited by Greg Johnson (San Francisco: Counter-Currents, 2017). Kingsley Amis has a better understanding of Bond in his invaluable *The James Bond Dossier* (London: Cape, 1965), finding the appeal of Bond to be precisely his ordinariness; one feels one could do the same, if only one had the time and money. (In American terms, Batman rather than Superman). Amis points out that Bond, though a "secret agent," is in fact no grander than any of le Carré's grey men; he's not a spy, but though more accurate, a title like The Middle-level Civil Servant Who Loved Me lacks the right amount of pizazz. In typically fashion, Bond co-producer Harry Salzman optioned Len Deighton's *Ipcress File* for film to create an anti-Bond franchise, covering the markets for both snobs and slobs.

[258]   As for "gym-buffed heroes," again, Bond, in his book and classic film mode, is fit but hardly Superman-like. Amis, in his typical fashion, simply details all the injuries and weaknesses that Fleming assigns him — even, in Thunderball, consigning him to a health sanitarium! I explore the obsession with super-heroic musculature in "The Ponderous Weight of the Dark Knight," reprinted in *Dark Right: Batman Viewed from the Right*; ed. Greg Johnson and Gregory Hood (San Francisco: Counter-Currents, 2018).

The publisher's blurb is presumably a botched version of this key passage:

Obliged, by a quirk of fate long since regretted, to play out his role, he blundered on into the dawn of middle age, a hermetic dandy, surrounding himself only with the fetish of himself — predominantly his clothes, which he chose with exquisite and envied care, his books, his three double-barreled fowling pieces by Manton, and his collection of old Sèvres porcelain locked in a vault in the V and A — and an utter lack of envy for his fellow man. He had that noble selflessness of a man who cares for no one but himself. Brummell, a man he admired unashamedly, had that. Until he went mad.

A hermetic dandy, then, not a metrosexual clotheshorse. And what is a hermetic dandy? Marlowe tells us elsewhere, in an essay published around the time of his first — only — taste of best-sellerdom:

Dandyism ... is a state of mind as well as a state of dress. ... The dandy strives, above all, for self-discipline, and a discipline that denies friends, sex and ostentation; his goal is to achieve the super-ego via a rigid set of rules based on utmost restraint, naturalness, and simplicity.[259]

This, I think, is the reason behind the almost over-the-top praise for the novel and author –

"Graceful and brilliant." - Sir Tom Stoppard

"Derek Marlowe writes like John Le Carré at the top of his form." – *Yorkshire Post*

As well as accounting for both being almost entirely forgotten today.[260] At least one of the publisher's blurbs gets it:

"A classic of the cold war spy stories – one of the earliest and one of the best. Marlowe's Eberlin/Krasnevin is on the run from himself on

---

[259] Derek Marlowe, in *The London Observer.* I have long ago lost my blurry Photostat of this fine essay on The Dandy; this is taken from "Wit and Wisdom" on Dandyism.net.

[260] "If it wasn't for the internet, Marlowe's genius as a writer may have been lost, as none of his novels are currently in print." - *Dangerous Minds*, "A Dandy in Aspic: A Letter from Derek Marlowe," http://dangerousminds.net/comments/a_dandy_in_aspic_letter _from_derek_marlowe.

different levels and in different places: the evocations of London and Berlin in the 1960s are superb." – Piers Paul Read

In this essay, I intend to explore those different levels and different places. But to do so presents some perhaps unique challenges – and opportunities for paranoiac-critical fun.[261]

Apart from the usual postmodern folderol about fragmenting master narratives and the capitalistic ego, etc., it's often a situation calling for what Kaspar Gutman would call "the most delicate judgment"[262] to keep distinct such topoi as the novel versus the film, and the actor versus the role.

Take *Touch of Evil*: Is that Orson Welles we remember onscreen or Welles' brilliant portrayal of the character Hank Quinlan? How relevant is anything we know (if we do know) from the forgotten book it's based on?[263] I myself have been known to blithely amalgamate (not confuse!) actors and roles, books and films.

But there's nothing like *A Dandy in Aspic*. We are more than familiar with the re-writing of Ian Fleming's Bond books, including films that use only the title (*A View to a Kill, The Spy Who Loved Me*). What is unique is that not only does the film[264] differ from the book, it appears that Marlowe

---

[261]   I've discussed Dali's invaluable paranoiac-critical method several times on Counter-Currents. For a more sedate precedent, consider … Walter Pater. "Pater was not entirely without gumption; only he tended to hoard it for his imagination. … 'Facts' and historical accuracy are not the coin in which Pater traded. For him, history was a mine to be worked for the frisson of insight; a certain amount of poetic license only aided the process." See the review of *Walter Pater: Lover of Strange Souls*, by Denis Donoghue (New York: Knopf, 1994), "Art vs. Aestheticism: the case of Walter Pater," by Roger Kimball; The New Criterion, May 1995, http://www.newcriterion.com/articles.cfm/Art-vs—aestheticism—the-case-of-Walter-Pater-5150.

[262]   Kasper Gutman: "That's an attitude, sir, that calls for the most delicate judgment on both sides. 'Cause as you know, sir, in the heat of action men are likely to forget where their best interests lie and let their emotions carry them away." *The Maltese Falcon*. Marlowe, as you might imagine, had Raymond Chandler as a favorite writer ("A Letter," loc. cit.)

[263]   See my "Breaking Badge: *Touch of Evil* through the Lens of *Breaking Bad*," above, for the use of multiple media and a consideration of, for example, how audiences respond sympathetically to what Welles intended as a portrayal of fascist evil. Speaking of which: "Scanner Darkly and Laurence Harvey in the same story makes me have to point out that there exists an Orson Welles version of *Dead Calm* all but completed but abandoned when Laurence Harvey died of a heart attack before the final scenes were shot. Wouldn't it be great if we could see this with animated scenes where filmed ones do not exist à la Scanner Darkly?" The significance of P. K. Dick's *A Scanner Darkly* will soon become clear.

[264]   *A Dandy in Aspic* (1968); directed by Anthony Mann (and, uncredited, Laurence

136

not only wrote the original screenplay (which in turn was drastically modified by events, as we'll see) but re-wrote the book itself for American publication.

It exists in two print versions by Marlowe, one the UK original and the other, US version, apparently reflecting changes Marlowe made while writing the screenplay for the film. The film, of course, is itself a new version, and to make matters worse — or, for our purposes, more interesting — as IMDB says,

> More accurate than usual to discuss this film as by Laurence Harvey/ Derek Marlowe since this was Anthony Mann's final film; he died before it was finished and actor Laurence Harvey completed the film including the ending. Despite the credits, the film was not directed by Anthony Mann[265] but by ... Laurence Harvey ... Mann died of heart attack in Berlin on 29 April 1967 after directing only a few location shots. Harvey gallantly picked up the reins, finished the German scenes and then did all the British location and studio shots, accounting for at least 99% of the film, which premiered in April, 1968, almost a year after Mann's death.

Though others reverse the proportions:

> The film's ending was directed by the Laurence Harvey[266] who also directed some scenes shot in Berlin. Anthony Mann directed all of the scenes in Surrey and London as well as some of the Berlin scenes.

In any event, Marlowe was not happy:

> The director, Anthony Mann died during the filming (a superb man and great director[267]) and it was taken over by Laurence Harvey, the

---

Harvey); screenplay by Derek Marlowe; starring Laurence Harvey, Tom Courtney, Mia Farrow, Peter Cook, Harry Andrews, Calvin Lockheart.

[265] Not be confused with Michael Mann, director of our favorite and much referenced *Manhunter* (1986), although the latter, under that title or the novel — *Red Dragon* (again, ambiguity!) — has obvious parallels to Eberlin's mission. "You want the scent? Smell yourself."

[266] An important point, as we shall see; there are in total three distinct "endings."

[267] Counter-Currents readers might like, if they haven't seen it already, his 1961 *El Cid*, with Charlton Heston.

badly cast Eberlin. He directed his own mis-talent, changed it and the script – which is rather like Mona Lisa touching up the portrait while Leonardo is out of the room.[268]

So here we are with an unprecedented number of versions, media and authors (auteurs would seem to be singularly inapplicable here). And so, again, where to begin?

Perhaps it's best to begin at the beginning — or rather, how the book begins in 2015! — with Sir Tom's Foreword, which begins with Tom, his future wife, Piers Paul Read and Marlowe all sharing a flat in London, 1965. As we read elsewhere,

One day, as they watched Mick Jagger on *Top of the Pops*, the three wagered a bet on who would make a million first. It was decided Stoppard would, but Marlowe pipped him to it, with his first novel, *A Dandy in Aspic*.

In light of their subsequent careers, be careful what you wish for! Any, back to Tom:

We were skeptical. Surely that bandwagon had passed by? *The Spy Who Came in from the Cold* had been published years ago.[269] What I do remember is that when Derek told me the basic premise for his novel (a spy with two identities who is ordered to kill his other self) I thought: now, that is an absolutely brilliant idea.

Indeed. Those are what Read in his blurb above spells out as "different levels and places." Though simple to state, it certainly raises the level of the novel above the usual pulp fare. Legendary sci/fi, perhaps?

Harvey, as bitter and hostile to our sympathies as he was in The Manchurian Candidate, plays Eberlin, a British agent entrusted with the job of killing Krasnevin, a Russian spy planted somewhere inside the British secret service who's been killing off high-ranking state employees. The trouble is, Eberlin is Krasnevin.

The plot hook smacks of Philip K. Dick and *A Scanner Darkly*, and indeed the film has a paranoid twitch balanced on the knife-edge

---

[268] "A Letter from Derek Marlowe," loc. cit.

[269] Not really.

of a bad trip. It's commendable that overt psychedelia is avoided, considering when the film was made.[270]

Well, there are a lot of drugs in Dick's work, true, and both are products of the Cold War, but I think the wider significance would be better expressed as: hermetic. Eberlin is on a hermetic quest.[271]

So, back to the beginning, or rather, before the beginning. I suggest that the key to understanding this work (to use a blanket term for all the versions, and of course suggesting the "hermetic work") is that Eberlin does not just sally forth to meet his death – he is already dead before the book/film starts.[272]

It's not such a crazy idea. After all, the climax of the narrative, the revelation to Eberlin/Krasnevin, the Russians, and the reader/viewer, that the British had already known his identity from the start, means he's already dead anyway; it's announced in with a triad of deaths:

His countryman answered, his voice cold and final:

"You're dead, Krasnevin. You're dead." The phone went dead.

This theme, however, can be found from the beginning.

I think the best way of handling the three versions, and keeping both the reader and myself sane, is to start with the original UK text — the Ur-Dandy, as it were — a go through it, noting along the way differences of content or context as they crop up.

Talk about the author as hermetic dandy – Dandy UK opens with a rather long Prologue (10 pages out of about 150) which moves in a slow and stately manner, as befits its subject: a funeral. It's a bit of a slog for

---

[270]   "The Forgotten: Cold Warrior" by David Cairns; *Notebook*, 12 August 2010, https://mubi.com/notebook/posts/the-forgotten-cold-warrior. As our protagonist is variously known as Eberlin, Krasnavin, and even George Dancer, I began to refer to him as EKD which, it occurs to me, does suggest PKD, does it not?

[271]   "About the novels. All characters are close or have been observed in some element of truth. One book went too far and I was sued for libel – but I shan't reveal which one it was. Loner and anti-hero? Loner, certainly — even though I am married with four stepchildren and one son of my own — but not anti-hero. I'm for heroes, though if not Lancelot or Tristan, heroes appear out of the mould of the time." – Marlowe, "Letter," loc. cit.

[272]   Pater, reviewing Wilde's *Dorian Gray*, refers to "the, from the first, suicidal hero." See "A Novel by Mr. Oscar Wilde," published in *The Bookman*, November 1891; quoted in Kimball, loc. cit.

the reader, who knows nothing of these people, including the dead man.[273] Here we perhaps see further damage done by Walter Pater's dictum that "all art aspires to the condition of music," in which the modernist or post-modernist author tries to "compose" a sort of "overture" rather than just write the beginning of a tale.

It does have some points, though. It is the only time we get to spend time — stuck in a luxury motor car — with Brogue, Eberlin's superior, and get a backstory for him.[274] Brogue — named Lucius-Pericles Brogue by his mother after a fortune-teller predicts he will be "a man of distinction"[275] — is quite interesting. He is, above all else, African, as the book tells us quite bluntly and frequently.[276]

Brogue was the head of some East African security service "until Kenyatta fired him for being for being pro-British." That the British would want his services is understandable, but "the toleration of the Negro by the top ranks constantly surprised him[277] ... He had reached his present status mostly through his own efforts, finding that as he progressed higher in the scale that his colour was more of a help than a hindrance," although he does receive "daily letters from anonymous fellow-Negroes who addressed him as 'Uncle Tom.'"

Coming right at the start of the "civil rights movement" this raises, surprisingly, many more recent issues, but nothing is made of it beyond that paragraph.

---

[273] Further hermetic obscurity: the Table of Contents tells us this section is titled "Prologue" but the actual first page is headed "Prologue" and then "Nightingale," giving it a title like all the other chapters, and one derived from a character's name, in this case the dead man, as most of them are.

[274] "And I can't help but think that the book the movie is adapted from must do a better job of explaining the twists and turns of the plot so they appear well thought out. It also likely gives the many characters who are but briefly introduced and then forgotten something worthwhile to do, like the black spy (surely an unusual sight at that time) and Eberlin's Moneypenny stand-in." Soliloquies under the influence of tulips, August 5, 2011, https://tulipclaymore.wordpress.com/2011/08/05/a-dandy-in-aspic-1968/#reffn2. Cairns (op.cit.) calls him "a surprising black British spymaster."

[275] "Gypsy woman told my momma, before I was born/You got a boy-child comin', gonna be a son-of-a-gun." Willie Dixon, "Hootchie Cootchie Man."

[276] In the first chapter, Eberlin's Russian contacts seek clarification when Eberlin mentions Brogue: "'The Negro?' 'Yes.' 'Important?' 'To a degree.'"

[277] It's not clear if it's Brogue himself who thinks of himself as "the Negro" or thinks about the problem of "the Negro" in general, or the omniscient narrator.

We also learn Brogue is a man of "strict, regular habits" and "shuns all social involvements, both public and private" for 46 weeks of the year; for the rest, he vacations in East Africa — back to the Motherland! — under an assumed name, where he drinks Bondian quantities of alcohol and has "three secret affairs with three carefully chosen Ethiopian boys who were preferably above the age of puberty and below the age of consent."

Again, rather close to today's issues.

I think this is the key to Brogue's role as a kind of anti-Eberlin. He is not merely Eberlin's boss — and hence the man who will order his death if Eberlin's secret is revealed — but a competitor in the Dandy sweepstakes. Eberlin is a "hermetic dandy" who eschews all social involvements, public and private," full stop; a kind of "purity" of purpose Brogue falls short of with his secret life of occasional indulgence.[278]

Eberlin's sexlessness is essential to his dandified self-control as well as an asset to his undercover (as it were) role.[279] I'm suggesting as well that he functions as literally an ascetic, an anchorite, if you will. Of course, Eberlin's real secret life will soon be revealed, and the first step is his decision to actually attend a direly "swinging" drinks party in Bloomsbury.

All this, as I say, is dropped from Dandy US and the movie;[280] what

[278] We learn Eberlin has had one affair, producing both a son and a respect for the dangers of women; neither are ever seen by him again.

[279] "You let the wrong word slip/While kissing persuasive lips" from the contemporary "Secret Agent Man" (Johnny Rivers).

[280] What remains of Brogues aberrant sexuality seems to be dog-whistled by casting Calvin Lockheart in the role. There's no evidence of homosexuality in his biography, but this early role in England would lead him to star in Joanna by Michael Sarne, who would eventually put him as the effete Irving Amadeus in *Myra Breckenridge*, which can't help but color, as it were, one's perception of his performance; starring on *Dynasty* doesn't help either. Cairns, however, thinks it bleeds over into the whole film: "Maybe it's Mann's response to the perceived effete decadence of British culture, but in this movie it seems a long time before we meet any straight men at all. (Harry Andrews, with his weathered granite face, seems like the first hetero presence, though his auto-erotic asphyxiation death scene, while wearing a tutu, in 1972's *The Ruling Class* might cast even this certainty into question.) The bizarrely variegated cast appear to have been instructed to camp it up for all they're worth, with the ever-ambiguous Harvey a relatively mild offender. Peter Cook, a surprising presence in the first place, whose entire characterization is based around rampant womanizing ("She's eine kleine raver!") nevertheless flicks his hair and ponces about with the best of them. Tom Courtenay and Calvin Lockhart (a surprising black British spymaster) play their confrontations with Harvey in the hissiest way imaginable (in a shooting gallery scene, they fire at images of naked men), and there's a strong implication that Per Oscarsson's Swedish-accented Russian operative is or has been Harvey's lover." I'll

remains is a later scene where Brogue attempts to one-up Eberlin with the purchase of a snuff box supposedly given to Beau Brummel by Prince George, which claim Eberlin smoothly and arrogantly eviscerates.[281] In the movie, as a reviewer notes,

> Many things remain unspoken, and yet come through in the pauses, in tone of voice, in body language (such as the apparent racism of Eberlin towards a black colleague).

But it's not really "racism" but Brogue and Eberlin seeing each other as opposites; hence, Brogue's unusual blackness.[282]

The Prologue UK ends with a quick flash forward to the installation of the "plain, unfancy, rectangular headstone," inscribed with the name of the deceased and "nothing else but the two words carved underneath: CIVIL SERVANT."

Apart from giving a thunderously morbid END to the prologue, and reminding us of the funereal theme, I can't help but be reminded of Ananda Coomaraswamy's summation of the Path of Enlightenment:

> Blessed is the man on whose tomb can be written *Hic jacet nemo*.[283]

This "avowed intention to be nothing," this very "self-willed effacement,"[284] is the key to Eberlin's transcendental identity. The clue that the UK Prologue is giving us is, Eberlin is already dead, though he has yet to effect his final exit from the material world.[285]

---

comment on some of this later, but the last point is definitely all in Cairns' head.

[281]   In the UK Prologue, Brogue dictates a letter to Sotheby's inquiring about the provenance of the box.

[282]   "Tired with LALAland, Marlowe planned to return to England to finish his tenth novel, *Black and White*, but he contracted leukemia and tragically died of a brain hemorrhage at the age of fifty-eight, in 1996"; *Dangerous Minds*, op. cit.

[283]   [Here lies no one]. A. K. Coomaraswamy, *Hinduism and Buddhism*, p.30.

[284]   "WHO was—or what was—Ananda Coomaraswamy? The man is of no help here, as he discouraged biographical 'curiosity' in his avowed intention to be 'nothing.' And yet this very self-willed effacement affords a key to the answer. *Hic Jacet Nemo* was the epitaph he most desired, and 'Here lies no one' is already a clue to the response we are seeking." – Whitall N. Perry, "Coomaraswamy – The Man, Myth and History," *Studies in Comparative Religion*, vol. 11, no. 3 (Summer 1977).

[285]   Presumably, when his car cracks up in Tripoli, an event in the recent past of which people keep reminding him and us.

Perhaps it would be good to sketch out the difference in the arrangement of the texts of UK and US Dandy. UK Dandy, after the Prologue (aka "Nightingale") gives us seven chapters, thus:

Copperfield (UK colleague who may or may not be a double agent)

Gatiss (UK assassin, sent along with Eberlin to kill "Krasnevin")

Pavel (Krasnevin's Russian control in London)

Dancer (Eberlin's alias on his mission to kill "Krasnevin")

Krasnevin (aka Eberlin)

Mistrale (Eberlin's car, the significance of which will be dealt with)

Endgame

US Dandy abandons this structure entirely. It starts with a long quote from *Alice in Wonderland*[286] rather than the Prologue, and has two sections, APOGEE and PERIGEE,[287] with 16 chapters, some sharing names with UK ("Pavel," "Gatiss") the rest rather pretentiously opaque ("Friedrichstrasse Nein," "Amontillado Caroline," etc.) although the latter pretension is somewhat redeemed by the last, "The Passing of the Buck," which will attract our attention soon. Each chapter is now headed by one or more epigraphs, either supposedly from Eberlin, illustrating some kind of Wildean wit, I suppose, or from Nietzsche, Voltaire and the like, no doubt drawn from his dandified reading.

As I said, I'm going through the UK novel, noting interesting variants that provide us with clues. So, Chapter One, "Copperfield," give us Eberlin at last; indeed, a veritable day in the life of Eberlin; although the phrase is not used, it seems we are to take this as a specimen day.[288]

---

[286] John le Carré published *The Looking Glass War* the previous year, 1965. Was the quote the idea of the author or the publisher?

[287] "1. Astronomy. the point in the orbit of a heavenly body, especially the moon, or of a man-made satellite at which it is farthest from the earth. Compare perigee. 2. the highest or most distant point; climax." (Dictionary.com). Note the apparent inversion of the climax.

[288] One might think, perhaps, of the Lennon/McCartney "A Day in the Life" (1967), but that was in the future. More likely in the author's mind would be *One Day in the Life of Ivan Denisovich*, the novel written by Aleksandr Solzhenitsyn, first published in November 1962

The most likely literary connection here is Huysmans' *Against Nature*, whose Prologue and first chapter also give us an account of the origins and daily life of the self-sufficient dandy at home in his "snug little ark, his refined Thebaid."[289]

It's all summed up in that passage quoted above, which deserves a second look:

> Obliged, by a quirk of fate long since regretted, to play out his role, he blundered on into the dawn of middle age, a hermetic dandy, surrounding himself only with the fetish of himself — predominantly his clothes, which he chose with exquisite and envied care, his books, his three double-barreled fowling pieces by Manton, and his collection of old Sèvres porcelain locked in a vault in the V and A — and an utter lack of envy for his fellow man. He had that noble selflessness of a man who cares for no one but himself. Brummell, a man he admired unashamedly, had that. Until he went mad.[290]

I'm suggesting that Eberlin doesn't go mad, like Brummell, but achieves that rather similar state, enlightenment, which in the context of a spy novel is death.

Hermetic refers in the first instance to his isolation, partly due to his mission, but mostly due to himself (how many spies live like this?). This pedestrian sense of hermetic arises from the original and more profound sense of being on the path of the Hermetic tradition.[291]

---

in the Soviet literary magazine *Novy Mir* (New World) and translated into English almost immediately and several times over.

[289]   Eberlin, however, lacks Huysmans' dandy's palate; he is "apathetic about the acquired bigotry of wines and bouquets," preferring wine "bought ... cheap from the supermarket" which "came out of the decanter like sludge." As for food, "he never pruned his taste buds, considering food nothing more than a basic necessity to be completed as painlessly and quickly as possible." There's also his self-admonishment in "Copperfield," "Smoking too much, Eberlin," a very un-Bondian note. US Dandy gives us a wonderful passage about Eberlin's endurance of the "ceremony" of coffee preparation by some bore. Film Dandy drops all of this, leaving everything up to Lawrence Harvey's unmatched ability to portrait a bored, supercilious prick; "as bitter and hostile to our sympathies as he was in The Manchurian Candidate" (Cairns).

[290]   The next paragraph also introduces us to the Maserati Mistrale 3700, "at present disemboweled and eight feet in the air at Cutcher's Garage, twenty kilometres from Lyons." I will suggest that Eberlin is already in a similar postmortem state.

[291]   Dandy US describes him in the corresponding chapter as "a frivolous monk."

Eberlin is a realized man, but still held back in this phenomenal world, presumably due to his karma. His mission is to kill Krasnevin – i.e., himself; to finally kill off the last of his earthly ties: here lies nobody.[292]

In "Copperfield" Eberlin is forced out of his hermitic retreat by a coded summons to a boring drinks party where he is surprised to meet fellow agent Copperfield, who either is on to him or, being a double agent, is the reason for the invitation. During their cat and mouse encounters around the party they have this key exchange.

"But you – always surprised me ... you sticking it there. No ties or anything ... have you?

"No."

"No. I thought that. No ties."

Eberlin is already bored — to death? — with his solitary life and the "infantile absurdity" of spycraft; the ambiguous meeting with Copperfield leads him to seek out contact with his Russian control, Pavel, to demand he be returned to the Soviet Union.[293]

Here we get another clue; Eberlin is insulted by the crude goons sent to escort him:

"I at least should be worth something more than a couple of zombies like you."

They, and the author, make quite a thing of this remark:

[292]   "One year ago he had written 'Ex Libris' on the flyleaf of his passport and burned his suitcase." The former makes more sense if one recalls that British passports of the time looked more like little books than, say, US passports did.

[293]   Eberlin, real name Krasnevin, was born in Russia and raised to pass for an English schoolboy, part of a program supposedly created by Stalin to implant sleeper agents with impeccable backgrounds. "On paper it looked fallible. In practice, it was without error. Eberlin himself knew of a Troy M.P. of a Northern Constituency, whose loyalties ranged much further that the Houses of Parliament [and a schoolmate] whom he knew now to be a Democrat general in the U.S. Army." He met the latter at a White House cocktail party, which leads one to think there may be something to this Birther business after all, especially when Brogue says to Eberlin "I must admit your references are excellent."

The men laughed. Eberlin had said the world 'zombies' in English, which amused the men, they laughed again and repeated the word.

Get it? Zombies and repetition, repeated. "Zombie" of course strikes the contemporary note, today, but was much less common back then. If the word was even less common in Russian, I like to imagine a similar scene in Hollywood as Ayn Rand first hears the word, which will later turn up in John Galt's speech.[294] Anyway, I suggest the laughter arises from Eberlin's failure to realize that it is he who is the real zombie.

After taxi-ing around to evade any tails, we get another reminder: "God how he missed having a car."

The next morning, having decided on a plan "of utter selfishness and therefore of the utmost integrity," Eberlin is phoned by Copperfield, who relays a message from Brogue, to meet with him at 10. Still waiting for Pavel to relay his own message from Moscow, Eberlin stalls him till 11, and as he prepares for the day we meet with a truly remarkable image.

[Eberlin] showered in ice cold water, in a shower built to a design he had seen in Berlin. The bather sealed himself into a glass coffin and was impaled by bolts of water thrust at him, at infinite velocity, from every angle. After three minutes, one felt fit for anything.

Well, the coffin is pretty obvious, but the bolts of water from every angle, of infinite velocity, suggests not only the "caught" metaphor, but also, at a deeper level, the very opposite: Eberlin is the Realized Man, the Chakravartin, who has reached the Center, from which he stands upright at the meeting point of all the warp and woof of the strands of existence.[295]

---

[294] "The purpose of man's life, say both [the mystics of muscle and mystics of spirit], is to become an abject zombie who serves a purpose he does not know, for reasons he is not to question." As reprinted in *For the New Intellectual*, p. 171. *British Film Character Actors: Great Names and Memorable Moments* by Terence Pettigrew (Rowman & Littlefield, 1982) describes Laurence Harvey's performance in *The Manchurian Candidate* (1962) as "zombie-like" but "excusable for once" given his role.

[295] For more on this Traditional image, see my essays "The Corner at the Center of the World: Traditional Metaphysics in a Late Tale of Henry James," reprinted in *The Eldritch Evola ... & Others: Traditionalist Meditations on Literature, Art, & Culture*; ed. Greg Johnson (San Francisco: Counter-Currents, 2014), "The Babysitting Bachelor as Avatar: Clifton Webb in *Sitting Pretty*," above, and with particular reference to the secret agent motif, "The Baker Street Männerbund: Some Thoughts on Holmes, Watson, Bond, & Bonding," reprinted in *The Homo & the Negro: Masculinist Meditations on Politics & Popular Culture*;

146

The image is reinforced when we proceed to Eberlin's meeting with Brogue, in whose office, painted green,

Eberlin could see the small square outside filled with trees and no people ... He stood in the center of the room looking down at Brogue who was sitting, swiveling gently from side to side, in the mahogany chair and toying with a bone cigar-holder.

"I'd rather stand," replied Eberlin, "it would help you come to the point."

Eberlin remained standing, like a fulcrum, in the centre of the room.

Brogue smiled and puffed a column of smoke on to Eberlin's shoulder, so that it hung on the weave of the jacket then circled, dispersed and floated to the ceiling.[296]

Trees (including a mahogany chair) and green walls suggest the Garden, whose central tree is the *Axis Mundi*. Eberlin, like the world tree, stands upright, while his opposite, Brogue (like Satan, the ape of God/Eberlin), sits below, swiveling around the Axis in the material world, toying, like an ape in 2001, with a bone.[297]

The whole symbolism, Eberlin's life in the phenomenal world, his enlightened indifference and immobility, the center vs. the circling weave, is condensed in one movement:

[Brogue] picked up a red file from the desk, marked CONFIDENTIAL. EX. F3, and held it over his head like a banner.

"This is you in my hand, Eberlin. Ninety-six pages all dedicated to you. Catch!"

Second, Embiggened Edition, edited by Greg Johnson (San Francisco: Counter-Currents, 2017).

[296] The center pole of the *teepee*, for example, and other traditional designs where a hole is left at the top, to let smoke, and so the sprits, escape. See, for example, Ananda Coomaraswamy, *The Door in the Sky: Coomaraswamy on Myth and Meaning*, ed. by Rama P Coomaraswamy (Princeton, 1999).

[297] See *Julius Evola, The Hermetic Tradition* (Rochester, Vt.: Inner Traditions, 1995), Chapter 1, "The Tree, The Serpent and the Titans."

He suddenly pretended to throw the file across the room, but held his hand. Eberlin made no attempt whatsoever to receive it, but kept his arms to his side, and then turned to [his secretary] and said in a bored voice: "Let's go back."

Let's go back will indeed be the ultimate theme. Eberlin is dead, dead to the world, but keeps coming back, and will continue to do so, until he finally can kill himself.

And so Eberlin is given a mission: to kill Krasnevin, who is himself.[298] But first, before he even knows that's on the agenda, he is to attend a briefing on the following Monday.[299]

At this point, Chapter Two, we meet Emmanuel Gatiss, but not before the Center symbolism is driven home. Eberlin spends "the following two days of the weekend in planned despair" over the Russian refusal to repatriate him and what appears to be the British plan to, unknowingly, "promote" him to the active branch; from Q to oo, as it were.[300]

He goes to the V and A to sit alone in a vault with his Sèvres, "surrounded by the sample of his extroversion and his taste, piled high around him," and then bolts out, telling them to sell it all.

Once he spent one hour trying on every shirt he had, until he tired and stood with the discarded shirts lying round his feet. "My failures," he said, echoing Brummell, and left the room.[301]

---

[298]   Willard: "Everyone gets everything he wants. I wanted a mission, and for my sins, they gave me one. Brought it up to me like room service. It was a real choice mission, and when it was over, I never wanted another." *Apocalypse Now* (Coppola, 1979; script by John Milius).

[299]   We also get another hint: Nightingale had been killed "with a minimum of difficulty, apart from decapitating the Mistrale on the Route Nationale." And a reminder as he takes the train to the meeting: "Trees really are greener in England."

[300]   Though "trained to kill the secret enemies of the Soviet Union," "Eberlin" is a committed desk jockey, unlike Bond or, in le Carré's Spy who comes in from the cold, both of whom are driven nearly mad by paperwork and bureaucracy. In fact, since it's "frightfully probably that he would be asked to continue Nightingale's operation" despite having, as Krasnevin, assassinated him, it's rather as if one could obtain a oo license by killing one's predecessor. "Arm yourself because no-one else here will save you/The odds will betray you/And I will replace you." Chris Cornell, *Casino Royale* main title theme.

[301]   An American might recall the scene in *The Great Gatsby* where Daisy is overwhelmed by Gatsby's shirt collection: "They're such beautiful shirts, she sobbed, her face muffled in the folds. It makes me sad because I've never seen such beautiful shirts." Gatsby is another fake person, but Eberlin would no doubt consider him as another crude arriviste, like

So then, Selvers, some kind of country house where the spooks and secret government officials (the "Deep State," if you will) like to hang out in these kinds of books. Here, it looks like "a small exclusive school for the rich," which highlights the point brought out by Amis,[302] that the trope of Bond's uncomfortable meetings with 'M' (at least once, at his country house, Quarterdeck) as well as his more torturous meetings with various super-villains in their lairs, all recall — to a certain sort of reader — shamefaced meetings with parents or headmasters, in well-padded but stern rooms filled with adult indulgences, such as sherry and old leather books, which you can't really understand. The first Bond book, *Casino Royale*, established the trope:

> "My dear boy," Le Chiffre spoke like a father, "the game of Red Indians is over, quite over. You have stumbled by mischance into a game for grown-ups and you have already found it a painful experience. You are not equipped, my dear boy, to play games with adults and it was very foolish of your nanny in London to have sent you out here with your spade and bucket."

The "kitchen sink" or "Angry Young Man" movement (of which Amis was a peripheral member[303]), which rose up in the midst of the early Bond phenomenon, really picked up on that element, since the public school and the country house epitomized the stuffy, stratified, dead and deadening British Establishment they loathed.[304]

Brogue. Or, in the terms we're discussing here, Gatsby is destroyed because he actually believes in materialism, in wealth and women as the goal of life, and hence his avarice has no end, being a futile attempt to capture the infinite in finite goods — the green light will always recede.

[302] *The James Bond Dossier*, op. cit.

[303] See Colin Wilson, *The Angry Years: A Literary Chronicle* (Avova Books, 2007), and Jonathan Bowden's lecture "Bill Hopkins & the Angry Young Men," http://www.counter-currents.com/2013/07/bill-hopkins-and-he-angry-young-men/.

[304] Lawrence Harvey's breakout role, of course, was as Joe Lampton in the iconic AYM film, *Room at the Top* (1959) from John Braine's 1957 novel. For more on Braine, see my "Lovecraft in a Northern Town: John Braine's *The Vodi*," http://www.counter-currents.com/2014/06/john-braines-the-vodi/. The ultimate expression of the "dead" theme is the ending of *The Ruling Class*, where the Establishment is depicted as a roomful of rotting corpses; Harry Andrews, as noted above, starts off the film with a bang, and he's here in Movie Dandy as well.

Both angles suggest that there's more than a little resemblance between the British Establishment and, say, SPECTRE than you might think, which thus plays into the next big British fad, the "all cats are grey" world of le Carré; both are typified by their shadowy meetings, here what Eberlin sneers at as a "barely visible cabal."

Armed with Amis insight, we might then suspect that things are not as they may appear, and the real twist in the story is hiding in plain sight.

Here, the Mean Girls and public school angle appears in various childish tricks, such as apologizing for "forgetting" to offer the lunch that everyone has already eaten, or pretending not to notice that Eberlin, unlike them, hasn't got a brandy or a cigar.[305] Like SPECTRE, they enjoy playing with their victims, although not with electrified chairs. An attendee of the lower ranks advises Eberlin:

> "They always make their victims walk around for half an hour to decide. It's part of their routine."

There's a Uriah Heepish character named Quince who offers obsequious advice, all "may I suggest" and "If I may, sir" as he attempts to ingratiate himself with the big boys.[306] Here, even Brogue is subdued: "He had learned how to act among his superiors."

Speaking of cabals, and Brogue, who I suggested was Eberlin's dandy double, we meet another double, Emmanuel Gatiss. While Brogue is a double for the desk-bound Eberlin, Gatiss is Krasnevin's double in the field, an assassin. So, obviously, he must be sent out to accompany Eberlin on his mission to kill himself.

Like Brogue, Gatiss is an unusual character; in this case, a Jew. I really have no idea how common that would have been in the British Secret Service (it is, after, somewhat secret) but it seems unlikely that many would be there. However, it surely would have been more common in the grotty

---

[305]   It's a demonic version of the dandified Oxford youth of *Brideshead Revisited*: "… it seemed as though I was being given a brief spell of what I had never known, a happy childhood, and though its toys were silk shirts and liqueurs and cigars and its naughtiness high in the catalogue of grave sins, there was something of nursery freshness about us that fell little short of the joy of innocence."

[306]   Typically, the movie adds a line crudely informing him, and us, "Don't worry, you'll get your promotion."

little areas like sitting around decoding stuff, or, as here, doing the dirty field work of an assassin.[307]

Anyway, Gatiss is unusual because he's not just a Jewish assassin but a rather crude, vulgar, in-your-face what'yer gonna do about it mate? kind of agent; he has a chip on his shoulder about being a Jew in the post-WWII world, and he doesn't care who knows it; no worries about letters calling him an Uncle Tom for him. He's "self-coded EPSILON/32/Y."

Putting his job and his attitude together, what's remarkable is that he foreshadows both the social rise of the uncouth and proud of it Jew,[308] as well as films such as *Inglourious Basterds*, sort of combining Brad Pitt and Eli Roth. He particularly loathes Germany, of course, despite (or because) he operates out of Munich, and at the conclusion says "Well, I hope I never have to come back to this damn country again."

As Eberlin's counterpart — at the briefing Gatiss sits but "straight-backed" and unmoving, like Eberlin, and the two are frequently positioned next to each other, or across a lawn — he's a bit of a dandy himself; he disdains tie clips and cufflinks and such like,[309] but does have a gold Star of David on a chain around his neck. "Strongly built," with his "blond hair cut stylistically short," I can't help but imagine Daniel Craig in the role.[310] Unlike both Craig's Bond and Eberlin, he is neither chivalrous nor ascetic, merely unbelievably crude: "People say I only sleep with whores. That's not true. All women are whores."[311]

---

[307]   Q: "It has not been perfected, out of years of patient research, ENTIRELY for that purpose, 007. And incidentally, we'd appreciate its return, along with all your other equipment, INTACT for once, when you return from the field." (*Goldfinger*). James Bond: "Well, you'd be surprised the amount of wear and tear that goes on out there in the field." Here Bond is channeling his inner Upper Class Twit. As commentators from Amis on have noted, Bond sits uneasily between the upper and working classes; his devotion to Queen and Country in the novels is part of a forelock-pulling obsequiousness that makes him a sucker for powerful men like Goldfinger (in the novel he becomes his secretary, along with Tillie Masterson!) and above all, Sir Hugo Drax, much to 'M's disgust — or jealousy.

308   See, for instance, my collection *End of an Era: Mad Men and the Ordeal of Civility* (San Francisco: Counter-Currents, 2016).

309   "Edina: "Darling, even Amanda de Cadenet would remember the word "accessories." *Absolutely Fabulous*: "Magazine" (#1.6)" (1992). The Germans have a handy word for such male accessories: Schmuck.

310   Tom Courtney in the Movie, not so much, though he does establish another AYM connection through *Billy Liar* (1963) and *The Loneliness of the Long-Distance Runner* (1962).

311   Well, all shiksas, at least. Not for the first time we see that contemporary Pick Up Artist culture has only a dubious connection to traditional Western culture.

And, he just doesn't "get" how "the game" is played, either socially or metaphysically:

"I think even if he had known he was only a bait and that we'd been aware of his identity for months, he'd have done just the same, don't you?"

Gatiss laughed loudly and replied:

"You're just as big a fool as he was."[312]

Although he does, in his blunt way, have a sense of what's going on:

"You've got no past and he's got no future."

So Eberlin and Gatiss are not just opponents but counterparts; Eberlin embodies the true Western response to the material world, a haughty indifference or hauteur; Gatiss has a "telluric" identification with these forces, which he hopes to control or at least get some benefit from.[313]

Anyway, the Brits for some reason have decided to promote Eberlin to the field, to locate Krasnevin (who, we know, at least, is Eberlin). "So damned ironic and in such bad taste" thinks Everlin, yet a kind of reprieve.

Then they reveal who they think Krasnevin is: Pavel, Eberlin's control and the closest thing to a friend, such as he is, that he has. Some reprieve.

We get one last clue: he's given the perk of a chauffeur for the trip back to London, in starting which "the chauffeur turned the car smartly into the centre of the gravel square."

Whoa Nellie, we're only halfway through! No matter. The whole point of what follows in Berlin is sheer futility and repetition. As one "tulip" says:

---

[312] The Gospel is foolishness in the eyes of the world. Gatiss needs to learn the lesson of Mark 8:34ff. "The only way to attain 'life' — true life, the life of the age to come — ... is by behaving in a way which seems to unredeemed man unintelligent and self-defeating: willingly accepting loss and injury in the cause of Christ and his gospel, and refusing to bend all one's energies, as other men do, to preserving, securing, and enriching one's life in this world." D. E. Nineham, *The Gospel of St. Mark, The Pelican New Testament Commentaries* (Harmondsworth, Middlesex, England: Penguin Books, 1969), p. 226.

[313] See Julius Evola, *The Doctrine of Awakening: The Attainment of Self-Mastery According to the Earliest Buddhist Texts* (Rochester, Vt: Inner Traditions, 1995), pp. 76-77.

In an interesting subversion of audience expectations, the British spies who go to Eberlin for the job as mole-hunter receive numerous clues that something is fishy about him, and yet they do nothing. This is frustrating, because as it turns out, Eberlin really isn't all that good of a spy, or at least a good field agent. Like [Gatiss] says in the film, he manages to get precisely nothing done. Without wanting to spoil the ending outright: this conundrum does get addressed. It's just a bit questionable how well.[314]

Boredom, repetition, and futility ... Well, Constant Readers know I just love that kinda thing!

But it's not quite true. The Brits are doing something: they've figured out Eberlin is Krasnevin (although it's never clear exactly when – presumably after he's killed Nightingale and before the briefing; this may be what Brogue is talking about, obliquely, at the funeral) and by sending him to Berlin I suppose they assume he'll try to escape to the East and thus lead them to various Russian agents in the West.

Even so, it's a pretty lazy plot, especially since they presumably don't know that Eberlin is already desperate to be repatriated. It also leads to either a brilliant plot twist or an unfair trick by the author. Before he even leaves London Eberlin skedaddles right over to Pavel's place to again demand repatriation; as he leaves, he sees Pavel being shoved into a big black Buick and spirited away as fast as Hillary at the 9/11 Memorial. He thinks it's the Russians, cutting off his line of escape, but in the end realizes that it was the Brits, who therefore must have known about him all along; that triggers the "Dead ... dead ... dead" conversation we started with. [315]

Anyway, from the point of view of Eberlin's official mission, he does indeed accomplish nothing; and there's a peculiar kind of nothing or futility in the way what he actually does is hidden from him and thus largely accidental: as a "secret agent" his real secret is that he has no more agency than a puppet. And there's the way he goes back and forth across

---

[314] https://tulipclaymore.wordpress.com/2011/08/05/a-dandy-in-aspic-1968/#reffn2.

[315] This is actually the US version, which adds this layer of complexity to the plot. In the UK novel, it's clearly the Russians: Eberlin sees and is even spoken to by the agent Rotopkin; Rotopkin is killed by a racecar at the Gran Prix as he is running from Gatiss at the end. In the US version, it's Eberlin who thinks the Buick is "no doubt" driven by the Russians. A different Russian, Sobaevick, is killed at the Gran Prix by Gatiss (and a policeman is killed on the track, since Marlowe apparently liked the scene), and when Eberlin later calls Rotopkin, he learns the truth. The movie keeps this version, but with additional changes.

the border, always being sent back, always trying to find some way to cross over again.

What's really going on here, at the symbolic level, is the Eberlin is cutting his "ties," burning his bridges in and to the phenomenal world, reaching the limit of frustration and disgust, so as to be free enough to ascend to the (or at least a) higher realm. As the mid-century mystic Neville Goddard put it:

> I remember when I had so much wealth. I did not have one home, but many, each fully staffed from secretaries to gardeners. That was a life of sheer decadence. I recall walking out of it and not returning. Whether they ever found the body I do not know, but I do know I deliberately walked away ... So I do believe that one must completely saturate himself with the things of Caesar before he is hungry for the Word of God.[316]

Eberlin is dead, already, but until all this karma has been exhausted, he is stuck here, in endless repetitions.[317]

He could turn neither to the East nor the west now, both rejected him, and even if they didn't, Eberlin didn't much care.[318] Politics were over, ideologies were of no further consequence. He didn't belong any more on any front, and in the final analysis, he was glad. It had come to this. The Eberlin Trinity [Eberlin/Krasnevin/Dancer] was on its own.[319]

---

[316]   A frequent story in his last lectures, here for instance: "A Lesson in Scripture," (10/23/67), online at http://realneville.com/txt/a_lesson_in_scripture.htm.

[317]   The idea of needing to perform every possible action, good or bad, so as to exhaust all experience, was promoted by the Gnostic sect of Carpocrates; see my review of the work of Luis Varady, "Lords of the Visible World: A Modern Reconstruction of an Ancient Heresy," in my *Mysticism After Modernism: Crowley, Evola, Neville, Watts, Colin Wilson & Other Populist Gurus* (Melbourne, Australia: Manticore Press, 2020).

[318]   In Coleman Francis' *The Beast of Yucca Flats* (1962), the narrator informs us that "Vacation time. People travel East. West. North. Or South," to which MST3k's Mike Nelson responds "Some people just burrow straight down." (Episode 621). "Dancer" is officially on vacation, and in this case his choice is straight up the World Tree.

[319]   This literal apotheosis takes place at a German Gran Prix track, a reminder of the time when Gran Prix racing was the sport of kings. Gran Prix tracks, no less than NASCAR or ancient chariot races, epitomize the motif of man vs. circular futility. See my review of a similar man and a similar movie of futility, Steve McQueen's *Le Mans* (1971), "St. Steven of Le Mans: The Man Who Just Didn't Care," above.

So, let's get to the end ourselves, shall we? Again, we have a few variants to choose from, like a Gospel manuscript or a video game set up.

In both versions, someone has been set-up to take the fall for Krasnevin: in UK, the Brits (they tell Eberlin) decide it's the dead Pavel, in US, the Russians plan to offer the hapless Copperfield to get Krasnevin off the hook. The switch to Copperfield is needed because, as we've seen, in the US version the Brits have already got Pavel; Eberlin receives his "dead" verdict from Rotopkin, and the book just sort of peters out, in true grey, le Carré fashion.

The UK version is more interesting. As you'll recall, the penultimate chapter is "Mistrale" and indeed the car finally makes its (re)appearance.

> The Mistrale seemed just like new. Eberlin walked around it five times, prodded it, stroked it, then actually sat inside and held the wheel without starting the engine. It felt wrong but it was definitely the same car.

Indeed, the *Chakravartin* "holds the wheel without staring the engine."

Then, after Eberlin (thinks) he's blown his cover by trying to save Rotopkin from Gatiss (in this version, Gatiss kills Rotopkin), he attempts to escape to "Spain or Africa" and instead drives into a wall at 80 miles an hour.

And then there's Caroline. Now, Caroline was the hostess of the drinks party at the beginning. She doesn't get a chapter title in UK, but remember, US has "Amontillado Caroline," which is the code Eberlin receives to instruct him to attend the party. She claims to have met Eberlin in Tripoli (where he was to kill Nightingale, and where he cracked up the Mistrale). Later, she turns up in Berlin. Now, she's driving the car that Eberlin hits on the way to the wall. Later still, she'll buy Eberlin's house and its dandified contents at the postmortem auction.[320]

---

[320]   The reappearance of Eberlin's house and racing car surely recalls the ending of *The Prisoner* (1967); was there any influence here? The eponymous Prisoner is definitely an ascetic dandy in his lifestyle, especially if he is indeed the John Drake of Secret Agent/ Danger Man. He's given a new name, or at least number, and set on various tasks and mission while in the Village, all ending with his defeat or return, only to start up again next week. In the end, it is revealed (perhaps) that No. 6 and No. 1 are the same, with John Drake making an Eberlin Trilogy. And of course, the last scene has him drive up in his old racing car (a Lotus) to his old London house.

Is Caroline then a spy? An assassin? If either, for whom? It seems unlikely, since she's a kind of Twiggy/Marianne Faithfull sort of bird, an element of the contemporary "Swinging London" Marlowe was writing in. Her hysterical crying at the scene of the accident could be fake, of course.

I think she's not a spy at all – her connection to the cocktail party is likely through her parents, undoubtedly parlour pinks of the old Bloomsbury sort.[321] She's a perfectly ordinary person who for some reason — karma? — is constantly running into Eberlin at crisis moments. She is purely a symbol of repetition.

Only this time, the circle becomes a spiral; things are a little off. In Tripoli, Eberlin swerves to avoid a car and drove into a tree. The Ministry chaps at Selvers seem a bit obsessed with it, and interrogate him further.

"It was a question of expediency."

"Expediency? You deny it was your own fault?"

"Not exactly, but I could not have avoided the situation. I felt at the time that I did the correct thing."

"And now?"

"I beg your pardon?"

"Do you think you did the right thing now?"

"Yes."

And with that deterministic note, he's sent off on his Judas Mission, in the course of which I've suggested that he learns finally to cut his ties with the phenomenal world. This time — I wonder, was it Caroline driving what is only described as "a car" he swerves to avoid in Tripoli? — it is her Mini that is now "decapitated" but in the process Eberlin and the Mistrale are totaled.[322]

Gatiss arrives and telegrams a cryptic message to London:

---

[321] I imagine her in the big house with her mother, rather like Ab/Fab's Patsy growing up with her Isadore Duncanish mother.

[322] "A short paragraph details the anonymous ends of both, one to 'a large burial plot north of Spandau,' the other fetching 109 marks on the scrap market."

"HAVE JUST WITNESSED THE PASSING OF THE BUCK"

Though never decoded for us, it's important enough for US Dandy, which loses all of this action, to preserve the phrase as the title of the last chapter. If Caroline was not an assassin before, she is now; Krasnevin has made her responsible for his death, and passed his karma to her, freeing himself. It's not "fair" or "rational," of course, but who ever said the cosmos was fair or rational?[323]

What about Movie Dandy? As already noted, the film, perhaps necessarily, drops many of the dandy elements, making the title all the more obscure; it also drops the opening funeral, mostly. What it does that's interesting lies in the beginning and end.

The opening credits play over a dancing puppet. Now, the very mobile puppet is at first glance the very opposite of the stuck in aspic metaphor,[324] but then you realize that being controlled by various strings in essentially the same. And then you remember that Eberlin's new alias is Dancer, and it all fits beautifully; dandy becomes dancer, stuckness becomes illusory self-control.[325] It's a nice way to make a literary image "cinematic."[326] But

---

[323] "The only real reason something should come into being in the course of human events is that 'someone wishes it to be here.' To expect that the universe should somehow 'make sense' in itself, as if isolation from human actions that shape our world of meaning is a false expectation – and so horror in the face of an illogical or insane universe is misplaced. The abyssal lack of an inherent and immutable order can be seen as the free space for us to make the world meaningful in one way or another." Jason Reza Jorjani, *Prometheus and Atlas* (London: Arktos, 2016), "Being Bound for Freedom"; quoting and explicating William James. The idea is not unknown to those with considerable experience with the mysterious East: commenting on the final settlement of the Apple/Capitol/EMI litigation in 1989, George Harrison commented: "the funny thing is most of the people who were involved with the reason that lawsuit came about aren't even in the companies any more. So the people at Capitol and EMI had to take on the *karma* of their predecessors, and I'm sure that they're relieved too." Peter Doggett, *You Never Give Me Your Money: The Beatles After the Breakup* (HarperStudio, 2009; UK subtitle: The Battle for the Soul of the Beatles), p. 297.

[324] "I feel caged in" is the only way Eberlin can express his reasons for wanting out to Pavel, which really combines the stuck in a viscous solid and string/wire metaphors. During the Selvers briefing, an apology is offered for having "to have kept you hanging about for so long in the dark."

[325] While in Berlin, "Dancer" stays at the Kleist Hotel, which surely must connect him to Heinrich von Kleist and his "Essay on the Marionette Theater," which discusses, pessimistically, the consequences of our encounter with the Tree of Knowledge in the Garden of Eden.

[326] "Remember, this is a *motion* picture!" MST3k, Episode 603, *The Dead Talk Back*.

ironically — or not, as all Traditional symbols resonate with what appears to be their opposites on the phenomenal plane — the dancing puppet is also the Dancer, Krishna.[327]

There follows an abbreviated version of the funeral, this time with Eberlin in attendance, for no particular reason. Eberlin's metaphorical duel with Brogue is set in a basement firing range at London HQ, which again is a nice transposition from page to screen.

The only reference to Eberlin as a dandy occurs when Pavel admires his suit, which is odd since it's mostly hidden under his overcoat at that point; moreover, we've just come from the briefing scene, where Eberlin wears a ghastly light brown suit, presumably to highlight his "not being one of" his well-dressed superiors. He also gets a chance to use some of those "witty" epigrams that decorate the chapter titles in US Dandy ("What do I do? I collect noses off statues"). Otherwise, bit players are assigned to tell us "he's a snob" and "he's completely sexless" (the latter seems account for Caroline following him around as some kind of challenge).

We're left with Eberlin's stated motivation as "I'd give it all up for an identity, just to belong somewhere," which sounds a little too much like a bow to '60s clichés about alienation etc. But basically, as noted, Lawrence Harvey just plays his usual bored prick.

Other changes are not so welcome: Gatiss loses all trace of Jewishness, aside perhaps from Tom Courtney's dark hair, which misses the point — he isn't dark-haired Eberlin's double, he's his counterpart;[328] Eberlin's Moneypenny, Miss Vogler, is now Eberlin's casual bedmate, not one of Gatiss' castoffs; Caroline's role is expanded, as played by Mia Farrow, but not further explained.[329]

Worst of all is Lionel Stander as Sobakevitch. While it's always fun to have Stander's side of brisket face and Merchant Marine growl, he plays the Russian operative like a "comical" taxi driver from his hometown, the Bronx.[330]

---

[327]   As Eberlin calls himself, the Eberlin Trinity (Eberlin, Krasnevin, Dancer).

[328]   He also now carries around, from his first scene on, a "sitting stick," as an MST3k robot calls the similar Schmuck carried around by Ed Platt — later Get Smart's "Chief" — in the late '50s caper The Rebel Set (episode 419). In both cases, it's a Chekov's Gun, in Gatiss' case literally so.

[329]   She's a swinging London photographer, here, with an actor partner named Neville, which I appreciated for obvious reasons.

[330]   One has to wonder if his attempt to portray a Russian Communist spymaster as a

Now, finally, about that ending. As noted, US Dandy, the basis of the screenplay, just gives us the downbeat ending of Eberlin being hustled onto the plane to London, having just learned that the Brits have known the truth all along. But again, this is a motion picture, and even something as dreary as *The Spy Who Came in From the Cold* ends with a big shoot 'em up.

As also noted, Lawrence Harvey himself seems to have been responsible for not just directing but writing, or at least dreaming up, the final sequence. Now, at the end of his Berlin stay Eberlin does get his car back, but since nothing has been made of it until now, it seems rather pointless. Nor is it a racing car, just some kind of American muscle car with a garish Chinese red paintjob. He drives it around frantically for a while and I think we're supposed to think he's going to race through a checkpoint but nothing doing; this seems to be all that remains of the death/crash motif.

Instead, on the tarmac, Eberlin notices Gatiss in a car at some distance. Is Gatiss (who, we are casually told just now, was the only Brit who didn't know Eberlin was Krasnevin until the end) supposed to sneak up at 60 miles an hour and run him over?[331]

In any event, Eberlin/Krasnevin breaks away and runs toward the car, while Gatiss starts up (was he waiting for Eberlin to make the first move, so as to make running him down "self-defense"?) and bears down on him. Eberlin fires his pistol (which for some reason the Brits still let him carry) point-blank[332] at the windshield ... and freeze-frame on Eberlin's face as he

---

crusty but benign father figure is a function of this being one of the films he made during a longtime exile from the USA, as a result of being one of the most obvious and obstreperous members of the Hollywood rat pack. Wikipedia adds that "After 15 years abroad, Stander moved back to the U.S. for the role he is now most famous for: Max, the loyal butler, cook, and chauffeur to the wealthy, amateur detectives played by Robert Wagner and Stefanie Powers on the 1979–1984 television series Hart to Hart." Indeed, his Sobakevitch definitely recalls his "Max," whose "My boss" line and gravelly voice often crops up on MST3k, including the same Episode 419 that gave us the "sitting stick."

[331] The same year, 1968, brought us Ted Mikels' *The Astro-Zombies*, where that very scenario is played out, with equal unlikeliness. Jabootu comments: "This isn't as exaggerated as tying Batman up in a giant popsicle-making machine, but it still seems a pointlessly exaggerated way to kack the guy. And that's even assuming you could build up a fatal amount of speed in the at best twenty-foot distance between Sergio and where the car was parked. Perhaps Sergio actually died choking on the ketchup packet that he was apparently carrying in his mouth for some reason." (http://jabootu.net/?p=1183). After all, Gatiss still has his sitting/shooting stick.

[332] Earlier, when Eberlin resolves to kill Pavel and returns to his apartment — Pavel

turns away, or perhaps is hit aside by the car; who knows? Cut to puppet tangled up in strings and lifted up out of sight.

Marlowe may have hated the ending, but at least someone sensed there needed to finally be some kind of climactic action (which the UK novel, ironically, does have), and remembered that Eberlin and Gatiss were supposed to be opposing forces of some kind. But since all that has been dropped, and we are simply told that Eberlin is "such a snob" and that Gatiss "Hates you, hates me, hates everybody," one has no sense of a metaphysical resolution, one only wishes to see the last of these two jerkasses.

In any event, we have reached the end of our epic traversal of three versions of the passing of the buck, which I have suggested many a time is one of, if not the most basic, metaphysical theme of film and fiction.

It's good to have at least the US version of the novel back in print, and the movie is a nice way to spend a couple hours of time (there's a DVD which is so bare-bones it not only has no "special features" it doesn't even have chapter stops!), but you really should get on the intertubes and find a second-hand copy of the UK original.[333]

As for myself, time for a break from all this reading and viewing. That coffin-shower thing sounds like just the ticket ...

having already been spirited away — "Harvey pumps his bed full of bullets, just like Lee Marvin in Point Blank the same year." (Cairns, op. cit.).

[333] Now I admit I have been known to harbor perhaps idiosyncratic preferences for UK versions of LPs (although I have recently come to admit the US Beatles LPs are better sequenced, despite their atrocious covers), but comparing the UK and US versions of Dandy is not so much like comparing the UK and US versions of, say, *Aftermath* but comparing *Aftermath* to, say, a Bill Wyman solo album.

Coffee? I Like Coffee!

The Metaphysical Cinema of Coleman Francis

Wherefore Bad Film?

NOT LONG AGO I devoted a pair of reviews to two books on Ed Wood, one good,[334] one bad.[335] I noted that the creation of the "so bad it's good" cult, and the resurrection of Ed Wood as its icon, was a veritable *"Plan Nine"* from the culture-distorters.[336]

The one book is part of the Medved cult: digging up the alcohol-soused cross-dressed corpse of Ed Wood for another round of mockery, while Judaically insisting "Hey, we kid because we love!"

The other reflects the genuine fascination and, yes, affection that really bad movies, of a certain sort, can exert on even the most hardened filmgoer. We must distinguish not only "good" and 'bad" films, however those terms are defined, but also the interesting and the uninteresting, or as I've called them, the unwatchable and the compulsively watchable.[337]

---

[334] "Getting Wood: Closely Watching the Cinematic Alchemy of Edward D. Wood, Jr.," https://counter-currents.com/2014/10/getting-wood/, reviewing Rob Craig's *Ed Wood, Mad Genius: A Critical Study of the Films* (Jefferson, N.C.: McFarland, 2009).

[335] From Bozo to Bertolucci: How Not to Watch the Films of Ed Wood, Jr.," https://counter-currents.com/2015/07/from-bozo-to-bertolucci/, reviewing Andrew J. Rausch and Charles E. Pratt, Jr., *The Cinematic Misadventures of Ed Wood* (Albany, Georgia: Bear Manor Media, 2015).

[336] The maestro, Michael Medved, went on to become something of a fixture of the neo-con commentariat and Christian radio, though the cult continued to prosper among smug, self-styled "hipsters" who would be horrified to be associated with such a retrograde figure; a lovely example of the way some individuals always control both sides of any debate.

[337] See "Essential Films … and others," https://counter-currents.com/2015/02/essential-films-and-others/, where some films are good, some bad, but all are compulsively watchable. "If, like me, you're amongst the very few who found the disastrous Hammersmith Is

Schopenhauer, I believe, can be our guide here, in the contrast he makes in literature between beauty and mere "interest":

The beauty of a work of art consists in the fact that it holds up a clear mirror to certain ideas inherent in the world in general; the beauty of a work of poetic art in particular is that it renders the ideas inherent in mankind, and thereby leads it to a knowledge of these ideas. ...

On the other hand, we call drama or descriptive poetry interesting when it represents events and actions of a kind which necessarily arouse concern or sympathy, like that which we feel in real events involving our own person. The fate of the person represented in them is felt in just the same fashion as our own: we await the development of events with anxiety; we eagerly follow their course; our hearts quicken when the hero is threatened; our pulse falters as the danger reaches its acme, and throbs again when he is suddenly rescued. ...

[I]nterest does not necessarily involve beauty; and, conversely, it is true that beauty does not necessarily involve interest. Significant characters may be represented, that open up the depths of human nature, and it may all be expressed in actions and sufferings of an exceptional kind, so that the real nature of humanity and the world may stand forth in the picture in the clearest and most forcible lines; and yet no high degree of interest may be excited in the course of events by the continued progress of the action, or by the complexity and unexpected solution of the plot. The immortal masterpieces of Shakespeare contain little that excites interest; the action does not go forward in one straight line, but falters, as in *Hamlet*, all through the play; or else it spreads out in breadth, as in *The Merchant of Venice*, ... or the scenes hang loosely together, as in *Henry IV*. ...

Father Homer lays the world and humanity before us in its true nature, but he takes no trouble to attract our sympathy by a complexity of circumstance, or to surprise us by unexpected entanglements. His pace is lingering; he stops at every scene; he puts one picture after

Out fascinating despite the million things very obviously wrong with it, and [Richard] Burton's performance therein to be outstanding, then a visit to *The Medusa Touch* is in order, as it offers the rare spectacle of an actor getting a second chance at something which flopped first time round." http://parallax-view.org/2010/02/16/review-the-medusa-touch/.

another tranquilly before us, elaborating it with care. We experience no passionate emotion in reading him; our demeanour is one of pure perceptive intelligence; he does not arouse our will, but sings it to rest; and it costs us no effort to break off in our reading, for we are not in condition of eager curiosity. This is all still more true of Dante, whose work is not, in the proper sense of the word, an epic, but a descriptive poem. The same thing may be said of the four immortal romances: *Don Quixote, Tristram Shandy, La Nouvelle Heloïse,* and *Wilhelm Meister.* To arouse our interest is by no means the chief aim of these works.... [*Art of Controversy,* Ch. 4]

By the way, it's no coincidence that all four of those "immortal masterpieces" are stylistically shambles — the "loose, baggy monsters" that Henry James sneered at[338] — and, to most honest readers, utterly boring.[339]

And so, a film may be a complete failure, in technical or narrative terms, and yet hold, maintain and even demand our continued attention, due to the ideas it presents.

As Rob Craig showed, the films of Ed Wood are such. Yet, not always; his attempt to read the whole Wood canon like that yields fascinating yet fitful results. Paradoxically, I think that's because Ed Wood wasn't actually, or always, a bad director.[340]

---

[338] "A picture without composition slights its most precious chance for beauty, and is moreover not composed at all unless the painter knows how that principle of health and safety, working as an absolutely premeditated art, has prevailed. There may in its absence be life, incontestably, as *The Newcomes* has life, as *Les trois mousquetaires,* as Tolstoi's *Peace and War,* have it; but what do such large loose baggy monsters, with their queer elements of the accidental and the arbitrary, artistically mean?" Henry James, "Preface" to volume 7 of The New York Edition, 1908.

[339] You'll note Schopenhauer's selection encompasses, likely on purpose, the "great" nations of Europe, Spain, England, France and Germany. He was not unfamiliar or contemptuous of American literature, although he recommends the reading of Franklin's Autobiography to the young as an antidote — or rather a substitute — for filling their heads with romantic nonsense. Anyway, if he drew up the list today sure *Moby Dick* would find a place.

[340] "Ed Wood was a good director," Bob Burns insists during "No Dialogue Necessary: The Making of an Off-Camera Masterpiece," a special feature on the Mystery Science Theater DVD of *The Beast of Yucca Flats.* "I don't think of them as junk." "If Ed Wood had the money and backing behind him, he would have been a top-notch producer-director." – Tony Cardoza, B-Monster Profile.com interview talking about *The Beast of Yucca Flats,* http://www.bmonster.com/profile37.html.

The reader may have intuited by now that the truly bad director creates a kind of Zen-like absence of intent (or failure of intent) that, like the well-swept soul, forms the perfect home for a host of perhaps unwelcome ideas.[341]

By contrast, the modernist aesthetic is indeed swept clean and boarded up against the intrusion of ideas; as T. S. Eliot said in praise of Henry James, "He had a mind so fine that no idea could violate it."[342]

Mary McCarthy quotes that at the beginning of an essay, "Ideas and the Novel," that explores how the tradition Schopenhauer alludes to, the "novel of ideas," has been displaced by the modernist novel. Yet, she goes on to specifically exempt the "moving-picture" art form:

> But, unlike the novel, the moving-picture, at least in my belief, cannot be an idea-spreader; it's images are too enigmatic, e.g., Eisenstein's baby carriage bouncing down those stairs in Potemkin. A film cannot have a spokesman or chorus character to point the moral as in a stage play; that function is assumed by the camera, which is inarticulate… [W]ith the cinema, for the first time, humanity has found a narrative medium that is incapable of thought.[343]

While Ms. McCarthy is right, that the traditional novel of ideas did tend to rely on a spokesman to articulate the author's point, I don't see why a film can't, or even needs to. In fact, we're more than familiar with film makers trying to drive home some moral, whether it's Hollywood piety or Communist subversion. It is, though, a tricky business; due, perhaps, to the collaborative nature of film making and audience reception.

As a case in point, consider a film I review elsewhere, Robert Aldrich's *Kiss Me Deadly*.[344] Here the film makers set out, by their own admission, to destroy the popular, but to their minds dangerously sadistic and fascistic,

---

[341] Luke 11:24-26: "Jesus said, When an evil spirit comes out of a man, it goes through arid places seeking rest and does not find it. Then it says, "I will return to the house I left." When it arrives, it finds the house swept clean and put in order. Then it goes and takes seven other spirits more wicked than itself, and they go in and live there. And the final condition of that man is worse than the first."

[342] T.S. Eliot writing of Henry James in the *Little Review* of August 1918.

[343] Reprinted as the first chapter of *Ideas and the Novel* (Houghton Mifflin, 1980); loc. 610-615 of the 2013 Open Road Media kindle.

[344] Reprinted in *The Eldritch Evola* (San Francisco: Counter-Currents, 2014); see also my "A Hero Despite Himself: Bringing Mike Hammer to the Screen," http://www.counter-currents.com/2016/06/bringing-mike-hammer-to-the-screen/.

Mike Hammer character; instead, they wound up making a film so violent and nihilistic, that it horrified audiences and critics more than Hammer himself, and went on to become the definitive portrayal of Hammer onscreen.

Moreover, since the film makers "had contempt for the material" and were "working on auto-pilot," they were not able to prevent, or even notice, Traditionalist metaphysics and symbols taking shape within their production. While the camera itself may be "inarticulate" as Ms. McCarthy insists, all it takes is a viewer in the right frame of mind to decode the message, as I do in my reviews.

I would argue, then, that the same holds true for the "bad" film maker, and the "bad" film audience; in the right combination, magic happens.

Enter Coleman Francis

Mystery Science Theater was not part of the So Bad It's Good cult. They were not assholes.[345] And, appropriately, with their love and affection for the true art of the cinema, it was they who uncovered the man who would prove to be the most iconic of all truly bad film makers, Coleman Francis.[346] As Frank Conniff ("TV's Frank") reminisces:

Of all of the film makers we did he was sort of the one we discovered. You know, Ed Wood gets all this attention, shouldn't Coleman Francis be getting some attention, as someone who made these Grade-Z movies.

I'm proud in a way, because everybody knows Ed Wood, but Coleman Francis was our big filmmaking discovery.[347]

---

[345] "[Joel] Hodgson: Our riffs were never too negative. We were the audience's companions, and people don't want to spend time with assholes. If you're negative, it may be funny, but it's not sustainable. So we had a lot of respect for the movies, because we had to work with them. Trace once said a really clever thing: 'The movies are Margaret Dumont, and we're the Marx Brothers.'" Brian Rafferty, "Mystery Science Theater 3000: The Definitive Oral History of a TV Masterpiece." *Wired*, 4/22/2014.

[346] An example of what TVTropes calls a Colbert Bump: "Honestly, would anyone have known anything about some of the films riffed? The biggest beneficiary is *"Manos" The Hands of Fate* (a documentary, two sequels, some videogame adaptations), but ... [i]t also led to new awareness of the oeuvre of Coleman Francis, turning him into a serious challenger for Ed Wood's 'Worst Director Ever' crown."

[347] "No Dialogue Necessary."

You want to talk about film making genius? OK, I'll show you genius. Take your guy, whoever; Welles, Truffaut, Kurosawa, Fellini, Scorsese, Tarantino. Now, imagine that every single one of their films, no matter how diverse the plots and characters, climaxed exactly the same way.

And: that particular way, that tied up all the narrative arcs and character developments, was a guy flying in on an airplane with a rifle, shooting the entire cast.

Well, I cheated a little. Sometimes it's a helicopter, and maybe not exactly all the main characters. Still, it's a pretty amazing feat of negative cinematic imagination. And sure, there's only three films, but still, consider the diversity of theme: a defecting Russian scientist is hit by an A-bomb and becomes a prehistoric monster; love and jealousy in the cut-throat world of sport parachuting; and two hoboes and an escaped con join the anti-Castro forces at the Bay of Pigs and ride a freight train all the way to Hell – and they all get resolved the same way! Genius![348]

The reader has probably already intuited — perhaps not by the writer's design — what the theme will be here: repetition, and its subjective counterpart, boredom. Watching — and nowhere else in cinema is the passive term "watching" more relevant — the films of Coleman Francis presents a perfect storm of repetitive film making producing a boredom in the watcher so acute and unaccustomed in cinema — truly unheimlich — as to put the watcher in a trance state, perfect for the assimilation of the Traditionalist teachings on the very topic of endless repetition.

Footprints on the Wasteland: The Storylines

The Coleman Francis trilogy: for convenience, I will refer to them as B, S, and R. Also for convenience, let's start by looking at the "storylines" provided by IMDB. Inconveniently, they prove almost insultingly bare and uninformative, yet this is precisely due to the nature of the material on offer.

---

[348] "Probability dictates that every now and then, a totally clueless director like Hal Warren or Tony Malanowski might punch through and end up making one of the worst movies ever just by pure chance, but to make three of them clearly requires active hatred towards paying audiences." – Albert Walker's epic, nine-part recap of *Red Zone Cuba* at *The Agony Booth*; alas, access to this now requires a $5/month Patreon donation.

B: A defecting Russian scientist is transformed by an atomic test into a hulking monster, Tor Johnson, of course. Not much else except some people are killed, boys get lost, and a rabbit sniffs Tor's corpse. It looks like we don't have any Synopsis for this title yet.

S: A couple own an airfield which makes its money on skydiving in the middle of New Mexico. They are having marital problems because the man is cheating on his wife, but she tries to remain true to him. The woman he is cheating with is jealous of the man's wife, so she seduces another guy to conspire with her to kill him. Meanwhile, the wife is cheating on the cheating husband with the husband's old Army buddy... and they all enjoy coffee all the while.[349] [There is actually a fairly detailed Synopsis for this one]

R: A trio of convicts joins up for an assault on a Cuban stronghold. After they are captured, they plan to escape before they face the firing squad. They eventually make it back to the American Southwest, where they go from town to town, robbing and killing. It looks like we don't have any Synopsis for this title yet.

The Trilogy

Three movies, which for convenience, as well as to emphasize, as we shall see, their interchangeability, I shall call B, S and R.[350] Three algebraic re-combinations of a handful of themes.

---

[349] At the beginning of the episode TV's Frank describes the movie as like "*Manos* without the lucid plot."

[350] "Hello. I'm Crow T. Robot of the Satellite of Love. You know, *The Beast of Yucca Flats, Skydivers*, and *Red Zone Cuba* are just three examples of the many, many god-awful films made during this century. Tragically, films like these are not deteriorating fast enough. That's why I urge you to support F.A.P.S.: The Film Anti-Preservation Society. At F.A.P.S., we're devoted to allowing the films of Coleman Francis and countless others to die a gentle natural death. We'll use your donations to transfer these films to fragile, volatile silver nitrate stock, so they'll rot quickly into nature's compost. (Mike passes behind Crow, comes back, looks into the camera because of what Crow is saying) Now here's how you can help: if you find a copy of a film as bad as ohhh, Aspen Extreme, please store it in a warm, moist, salty place such as a cheese factory or your mouth." MST3k, Episode 621: *The Beast of Yucca Flats*.

The Time(s)

While *Mad Men* presents the illusion that people lived by in the post-War world — that "everything was sunny and perfect"[351] — Francis reveals that the apocalypse had already happened.[352]

Despite surface differences, caused by the illusory "passage of time," each movie takes place at the same, post-Apocalyptic moment as the others.

Crow: I thought they portrayed 1961 quite well.

Tom Servo: Not too hard since they made it in '65!

Crow: D'oh![353]

B clearly "takes place" in a world post-Hiroshima and already references a space race with Russia, years before Kennedy, but we are clearly meant to understand this is only to set up the real plot point, atomic scientists facing the consequences of their work in their own persons, as if the Los Alamos experiments had gone horribly wrong.[354] Men like Joseph Jaworsky, a Russian physicist (played by Ed Wood's Tor Johnson[355]) transmuted into a monster by his own science.[356] As the narrator (Coleman) intones:

---

[351] MST3K, Episode 612, *The Starfighters*. As the posse closes in on Griffin at the conclusion of R, MST3k notices the dark suited FBI agents and snarks that "The cast of How to *Succeed in Business* moves in." That film was Robert Morse's breakout role, and 40 years later he returns to that era as the iconic Bert Cooper of *Mad Men*; no doubt that would have been the cultural reference had MST3k been filming at that time.

[352] That the worst has already happened, long ago, is the theme shared by both Lovecraftian horror and the Traditionalism of Guénon and Evola, as I suggest in the title essay of *The Eldritch Evola ... & Others* (San Francisco: Counter-Currents, 2014).

[353] MST3k, over the end credits of R.

[354] "Though they are masters of the atomic bomb, yet it is created only to destroy them." Simone de Beauvoir, *The Ethics of Ambiguity*; translated from the French by Bernard Frechtman (Citadel Press, 1948; Open Road Media, 2011); p. 9.

[355] "When I think of Russian scientists, I think of Tor Johnson." (Crow, MST3k). "That's just smart casting." Larry Blamire, interview in "No Dialogue Necessary."

[356] For a different and profound perspective on the Hiroshima event, see Jason Reza Jorjani: *Prometheus and Atlas* (London: Arktos, 2016), Chapter 12, "Kill A Buddha On The Way."

"Shockwaves of an A-Bomb. A once powerful, humble man. Reduced to ... nothing."[357]

Or, in S, reduced to ... drinking — and discussing — coffee. The titular skydivers are products of the Korean War, where they learned their "skills" which they now "teach" to other losers. Hunter S. Thompson's *Hell's Angels*, written around this time, has an opening chapter that summarizes the sociological research on the origins of the motorcycle subculture in returning 'white trash' veterans who had nothing to live for and so took out "on the road" astride their cheap bikes; one of the characters in S rides a motorcycle — badly — and for no particular reason — we never see it, or him riding it, again; he makes his futile "escape" being driven in his "girlfriend's" — quotes because there are no real "friends", girl or otherwise, among these no-longer human sad sacks — Thunderbird convertible, like Dean Moriarty driving Jack Kerouac — prompting the 'bots to make lots of "Born to be Wild" and "Wild One" references during his scene.

The skydivers occasionally stop to muse on their existential situation:

Beth: "Why do you think we jump?"

Pete: "I feel real free up there in that high blue sky. Nobody to tell you what to do, you just have to please yourself up there."[358]

Further suggesting the Beats, they don't fly but "drive" the planes; they say things like "drive me up there" or "I'll drive." In R, Coleman will revert back to the more normal — or sane — "fly": "My friend here can fly."

As for *Red Zone Cuba*, for once we have a clear time period; not just the Bay of Pigs fiasco, but actually taking place in the Bay of Pigs;[359] they seem to be some kind of advance unit for the "main invasion force" which if true could explain a lot about what happened.

---

[357] "He was brilliant. He was outstanding in every way. And he was a good man, too. A humanitarian man. A man of wit and humor. He joined the Special Forces. And after that, his ideas, methods, became unsound." *Apocalypse Now* (Coppola, 1979) at 00:14:40 in the DVD version of the movie.

[358] The line, and the delivery by Coleman's son (?) are very Beat; "The man can't touch me up there" add Mike and the 'bots.

[359] "Bay of Pigs," Griffin mutters as he squats in a Cuban jail, to which Mike Nelson adds "That's what they say when I get in the pool."

169

Hiroshima. Korea. Bay of Pigs. Three traumatic moments in post-War Western consciousness.

"Now listen, Mike. Listen carefully. I'm going to pronounce a few words. They're harmless words. Just a bunch of letters scrambled together. But their meaning is very important. Try to understand what they mean. Manhattan Project, Los Alamos, Trinity."[360]

"Guard ... Water ... Sick man." (R)

And what is the "meaning" of these places? Michael A. Hoffman II suggests:

Fabled alchemy had at least three goals to accomplish before the total decay of matter, the total breakdown we are witnessing all around us today, was fulfilled. These are:

1) The "Creation and Destruction of Primordial Matter" (was accomplished) ... at the White Head ("Ancient of Days") at White Sands, New Mexico, at the Trinity Site. [B]

2) The "Killing of the Divine King" was accomplished (by the public, occult execution of JFK) at another Trinity site located approximately ten miles south of the 33rd degree of north parallel latitude between the Trinity River and the Triple Underpass at the Dealy Plaza in Dallas, Texas. [Result of the Cuban events of R]

3) The "Bringing of Prima Materia to Prima Terra" was accomplished in the 1969 Apollo moon flights and the returning to earth of the moon rocks. Some of these rocks have been "stolen" for use in occult rituals of no mean significance (what astounding Masonic "ashlars" these make). [The flights up and down of the Skydivers][361]

---

[360] Lt. Pat Murphy to the irradiated Mike Hammer in *Kiss Me Deadly* (Aldrich, 1955). For more on the irradiated landscape of the film, see my review "Mike Hammer, Occult Dick" reprinted in *The Eldritch Evola*, op. cit.

[361] Michael A. Hoffman II's *Secret Societies and Psychological Warfare* (2001).

The Place(s)

Like each act of Beckett's *Godot*, each of his films takes place in the same place, mostly depicted by some blasted piece of godforsaken desert, known to aficionados as "Coleman Francis country" but lacking any of the majesty of John Ford's Monument Valley.

"Is that the mountain?" (R, a voice, likely Griffin, typically from off screen)

"Let's kill that mountain" (the MST3k 'bots' sarcastic reply)

Something of an exaggeration, if taken literally; there are various locations, apparently in the Southwest, but all are pretty low-key to begin with, and thanks to Coleman's negative-magic with cinematography, they all take on a flat, grey, sameness that could have been filmed anywhere; anywhere in Hell.

Crow T. Robot: I think the location scout was a spaz! (R)

A typically crude, hand-lettered sign (a Coleman motif!) tells us we're in the titular Yucca Flats; an even briefer shot of a hand-written envelope address tells us S takes place in "Half Moon Bay, Ca." By the time of R, there's really no attempt made to identify locations, other than half-assed Southern accents, reference to "up north" and "down south," and the presence of Castro hats (and Castro himself[362]), cigars, and a woman in "native" dress to suggest that we really, really are in Cuba.[363]

Yucca Flats is, well, Yucca Flats, I suppose, although it could be any barren desert or blasted heath; there's also a highway (where the vacationers break down and from which the kids stray) and a large butte or plateau of some kind,[364] so as to require the "desert patrol" to take to the air for the "shoot from the sky" sequence that will recur in every film.

---

[362] Played by Tony Cardoza in a ridiculous beard; the reuse of actors will be commented on in the next section.

[363] There is, however, another crude, this time wildly illiterate, sign, advertising Cherokee Jack's air services; typically, after spending the time to write it up, it flashes on screen for only a split second, too fast to read.

[364] "I get the Yucca part, but why is it called Flat?" muses Crow T. Robot.

That small airport (military? Civilian? CIA, like Clinton's Mena AR?) just happens to be in driving distance of a nuclear test site (B); it's also a small civilian airport giving "parachute lessons" to local drifters and losers, mostly played by the director's family and "friends" (S).

"There is no landscape bleaker than the rural airport" (Crow, S)

The only other business is a bar ... called "The Skydiver."[365]

The main characters, a married couple that run the sport parachuting facility, have a 'home' that looks, on film, like the inside of a refrigerator crate or a basement crawlspace; they throw a "dance party" that takes place ... on a runway. The band, of course, is "The Night Jumpers."[366]

In R, it's a small, broken-down plane for-hire business (how sound is that business model?) run by Cherokee "I'm Cherokee Jack" Jack, which is near enough to a prison for an escapee (Coleman) to run to it, at least after hitching a ride with two hoboes (played by actors we recognize from S, a point we'll return to) in a broken down truck, and close enough to fly "the boys" (as he calls Coleman and the hoboes, like the lost children from B whose mother refers to them as "the boys" or the "Boys, boys" that Beth calls Harry and Joe in S) to a "secret" camp (which indeed looks like the same area of Arizona or Utah or Texas) where someone is training somebody to overthrow Castro; close enough to water to "shove off" by boat (actually, clearly a marina, perhaps the same "artificial bass environment" that Frankie and Suzy were "frolicking" in during S) for a "Bay of Pigs" that, again, looks like the same area, from which the Three Amigos are captured and stowed away in a makeshift "prison" (again!) which is (again!) near an airport (fortunately, "my friend [Landis] here can fly" just like Cherokee "I'm Cherokee Jack" Jack, and why not, since it's the same actor who played the skydiving instructor in S) from which they can "fly" to what looks like the same area and then, after senselessly killing an old man by throwing him down a well and raping his blind daughter, hitch another ride, this time on a train, to what looks like the same area from which they will buy a car and drive to what looks like the same area, meet

---

[365] "How sound is a skydiving-based economy?" (Crow, S)

[366] In "reality," Jimmy Bryant, a rather good and interesting guitarist, whose hit single, "Stratosphere Boogie" is featured. Yes, actual good music in a Coleman Francis movie. Again, Coleman cocks a snook at "reality" by not only having him perform with a fictitious, skydiving-oriented band, but also having him mime to the song using a regular guitar, not the specially built one the track was intended to show off.

up with an unsuspecting widow of a dead "comrade" and drive to what looks like the same area, overlooked by the iconic Coleman Mountain…

Crow: "This movie has the courage to unabashedly repeat itself."

Mike: "Is it a good idea to invade the Bay of Pigs again so soon after the last time?"

Mike: "Did they even need to GO to Cuba?"

In the name of God, where are we? If we didn't hear it the first time when John Carradine told us at the beginning:

"Griffin … he ran all the way to Hell."

Then the voiceover — Francis, over his own corpse! — tells us again at the very end:

"Griffin! … ran all the way to Hell … with a penny … and a broken cigarette."

The People

Tom: "Is the film grainy or are these guys just kinda grainy?" (R)[367]

In this world men wander, scarred forever by the blast, the same people doing the same things, over and over.

B: Tor just wanders, boys get lost, cops shoot people at random, Jim does what he did in Korea: shoot people and jump out of a plane. The narrator laconically observes from time to time:

"A man runs. Someone shoots at him."

---

[367]   The dissolution of matter Michael A. Hoffman II talked of in the wake of Trinity; the elementary particles of Houllebecq; the atoms into which Buddhism dissolves all apparently stable "things."

"Kill. Kill just to be killing."[368]

S: Joe and Tony also do what they did in Korea: jump from planes. Here, they teach others, who go up, and then down again. Except when someone goes down ... and stays down.[369]

Crow: "A stranger comes to town, touches no one's life, then leaves."

Joe the Coffee Guy: "Did I have a kind of brooding intensity?"

Mike: "No, goodbye!"

R: our protagonists no longer have any fixed abode: an escaped convict on the run, and two hoboes who claim to be migrant workers:

"We follow the harvest. Crops froze up North, we head South."

Griffin's crime? "Sold a buncha cotton one day, moved his trucks in and stole it right back."

Both hoboes and Griffin try to change:

"Me and Landis got busted back in '58! Liquor store! Two years of hard labor! Now we grab at a job anywhere we can find it! No more iron cages!"[370]

---

[368] Said by the narrator of Tor's Beast, but just as appropriate if directed at Jim and Joe, the trigger-happy deputies, or any other "lawman" is later films. "Tor is described as a cave man" notes film historian Larry Blamire, "but I think that's an insult to cave men. He just suddenly becomes a homicidal maniac." Interview in "No Dialogue Necessary."

[369] "Maybe ... won't be over." Tony Cardoza, now playing a hobo in R, who dives to his death in S.

[370] "In sociology, the iron cage is a term coined by Max Weber for the increased rationalization inherent in social life, particularly in Western capitalist societies. The 'iron cage' thus traps individuals in systems based purely on teleological efficiency, rational calculation and control. Weber also described the bureaucratization of social order as 'the polar night of icy darkness'." – Wikipedia. It also suggests, as we shall see, the vertical and horizontal, warp and woof of the material universe that revolves around the Pole. As Jay Dyer says in discussing Kubrick's 2001, "This is the middle stage of man's gradual ascent out of the cage — the box — of time and space, which is precisely what the monolith signifies in part." *Esoteric Hollywood: Sex, Cults and Symbols in Film* (Walterville, Or.: Trine Day, 2016). We'll later comment on Cook's monkey-like appearance, when he dances around, excited by Griffin's beating of Landis, like the apes at the beginning of Kubrick's film.

Griffin, towards the end, suggests he's finally "goin' legit." But we know he's doomed – we already heard it in the flashback and title music.

Their journey takes them from prison to … trapped in contra training camp, then … Cuban prison. Then back to the Southwestern USA, and, at lease for Cook and Landis, re-arrest, and back to prison.

Mike: "Did they even have to go to Cuba!"[371]

Tom Servo: "Their lives haven't changed a bit!"

Crow: "This movie is a Moebius Strip!"[372]

Emphasizing the sense of futile repetition is Coleman's habit of working with a small company of regulars. The only apparent exception is S, where a large cast of unknowns, presumably local eccentrics and members of the regulars' families,[373] is pressed into service for the last act's dance party; however, the extreme eccentricity of the group inevitably suggests comparison with Ed Wood,[374] Fellini or Welles, thus reinforcing the very idea of a company of regulars.

> The entire contingent of Frandoza Freaks™ is here *en masse*. You see, all the little vignettes of the Freaks we've been getting so far have really only been a preparation for this. The scene begins with a guy jumping off the nose of a plane, which cues a thug on a motorcycle to pop a wheelie through the dance area.
>
> And here Coleman must've said, "It would be impossible to train any of you weirdoes to perform, so just do whatever you would naturally do." So it's up to the heroin addict to get the party going. Crazed out of his gourd, he dances by himself for a while, then one of the pretty girls goes out to join him. They dance, then another girl cuts in (more about

---

[371] "The title was changed to "*Red Zone Cuba*" for release, which gives the impression that this movie is about the Bay of Pigs invasion, but the movie is supposed to be about fugitives on the run, and the Bay of Pigs invasion is just one of the many incidents that the characters become involved with along the way." MST3k Wiki. "Many incidents" gives a false impression of the hopeless, pointless slog we see on screen.

[372] A phrase that has also applied to *Mulholland Drive* and *Donnie Darko*.

[373] As the opening credits appear Servo observes that: "This is an 'I can't pay you, but I'll put your name in the credits' cast list."

[374] "Well, I see the usual gang of misfits and drug addicts is here." Ed's wife, Dolores Fuller, in *Ed Wood* (Burton, 1989).

her in a second) and starts dancing with him. What does it say for your town when the heroin addict is the one the girls fight over?

But if they had all paired off already, we'd have missed one of the most bizarre people to be cast in this film. That would be the girl who cuts in, who appears to be a champion lady wrestler, because she's wearing nothing but a black, strapless swimsuit (even though they're in the desert) and heels. And when she cuts in on the cute girl dancing with Heroin Addict, she literally shoves the girl out of the way.

There's a grown man in a cowboy suit, one lone black girl in a polka dot bikini (diversity!), the ever-present Lady Wrestler, and a Scotsman in a kilt and tam-o'-shanter. They're like Village People rejects. I can only imagine Coleman, with Checkbook Cardoza in tow, heading into Ed Wood's Lightly Used Costume Rentals and saying, "We'll take one of each."[375]

Coleman plays several bit parts in B; in S he appears in a speaking role as a cigar chomping Southern *pater familias* (with his real family) and then at the climax reappears, inexplicably, as a FAA official (?) who jumps in a plane and attempt shoot down the fleeing killers[376] (thus assuming the role of Joe in B and prefiguring his fate as Griffin in R). Producer Tony Cardoza is in all three films, while Harold Saunders, the other hobo in R, is another "FAA man" in S.

Re-doubling the effect, many actors "appear" as voice-overs, sometimes dubbing parts by different actors. Most infamously: a Cuban contra is shot by firing squad, and then the actor reappears, as a Cuban guard, in the very next scene. Politics is no more "real" than life and death.

And such is the contempt and loathing with which Francis directs and shoots his actors, especially women, that it comes as a genuine shock to realize or learn later, as I did, that the same "actress" appearing as the anonymous wife of one of the cops in B, apparently only so that Coleman can show her décolletage. ...

Tom : "Yes, we get it, breasts."

... also plays the small town rich girl/slut in S...

---

[375]   *The Agony Booth* review, Part Six and Part Seven. Really, this makes it sound far more interesting than what's actually on the screen.

[376]   Mike Nelson: "It's Pat Buchanan ... with a gun!"

Tom: "Oh, this hotsie-totsie"

Crow: "Oh, the femmy-fatahly"

...where her pasty charms are far more dubious

Crow: "Lumpy butt!"

Mike: "Stop calling me 'Lumpy Butt.'"

And that the anonymous woman strangled and raped by Tor Johnson in the first, shockingly disconnected moments of B is in fact the same actress — same character? — as Chastain's wife, Ruby, killed, shot this time, by hulking Tor-like Francis, just before he is shot and killed ... from a plane.[377]

As Tor dies in the dirt at the end of B, he (in a shot entirely accidental) is approached by a small rabbit, which he cuddles as he expires. (Being a Coleman Francis film, we assumed he would break its neck). As Tor-Coleman dies in the dirt at the end of R ("The intercutting is just like The Godfather!") Chastain's wife is picked up by an actor strongly resembling Phil Silvers whom the 'bots give an Elmer Fudd voice and line: "I killed a poor little rabbit!"

The ends, *se touchent*!

Excursus: Children and Animals

Animals: There's a steady decline of animals, in keeping with the apocalyptic bleakness. B, for all its mind-scorching barrenness, is fairly bustling with livestock: the gas station attendant [Coleman!] lazily feeds

---

[377] The use of the same actors in similar roles suggests a useful comparison with Bill Rebane, a truly bad, that is, simply untalented director. His *Monster A Go Go* is infamous for having been shelved half-way through when financing fell through – like Orson Welles! Unlike Welles, he gave up. Unfortunately for us, it was bought and then "completed" by sleaze tycoon Hershel Gordon Lewis, to serve as the bottom of a double bill. The willingness of both Lewis and Rebane to treat his film as raw material for a cinematic sausage is almost refreshingly honest, and quite accurate in its evaluation of the material. Another way he differs from Welles — apart from the lack of talent — and even Francis is that he was not able to reassemble the same Fellini-esque company of actors; some had disappeared – the rest were noticeably older, of course, requiring plot changes, including one balding actor who was "killed" in the first version and now suddenly reappears as "his brother"!

a sandwich to a dog; there's the pigs the boys famously "feed soda pop" to, as the narrator intones, along with a coyote who gets a shout out as well: "Missile bases run 'em off their hunting grounds." and of course the famous final rabbit that snuggles up to the dying Beast (who I guess counts an animal himself).

S simply contains no animals at all that I can see; no pets, no wild critters (not even a bird in the endless skydiving sequences!); it's not even clear what Beth and Harry are having for dinner.[378]

R has bloodhounds at the opening (one poor guy gets hung up in the barbed wire; thanks, Coleman/Griffin) and some dogs are being fed towards the end.

Why? As we'll see, Coleman is concerned with Liberation, and Liberation only occurs from the human station; sorry, PETA.

Same with families. In B, Jawarsky's wife and children are killed before the movie, but at least he had them. There's one patrolman's wife; a couple with a flat tire that get killed right away; but there's also a whole subplot about a vacationing family and their "lost boys" that ends happily for Francis: the father shot from a plane but alive, the boys rescued from the Beast.

S has the whole Francis and Cardoza clans in bit parts, along with a collection of airport gawking freaks and weirdoes that makes Ed Wood's crew look like the Algonquin Roundtable; but the plot, such as it is, revolves around Harry and Beth's barren marriage and their ugly affairs; it's as constricted as the refrigerator crate they seem to live in, by contrast with the free-wheeling ecstasy of skydiving. Though reconciled — presented with typical Francis autism as quick and unmotivated as their squalid affairs — he's immediately killed; the last shot is widowed Beth in black, looking vaguely around the empty, desolate airport.

In R, Griffin's wife "become a streetwalker", Chastain is left to die in Cuba and his widow is shot by Griffin, Griffin kills the old man and rapes his blind, widowed daughter.

R does present us with three Männerbunde, or what I have elsewhere called "false Männerbunds"[379] which work only for evil under the guise of

---

[378] Monitor lizard is Mike's helpful suggestion.

[379] See "'God, I'm with a heathen.' The Rebirth of the Männerbund in Brian De Palma's *The Untouchables*," in *The Homo & the Negro: Masculinist Meditations on Politics & Popular Culture*; Second, Embiggened Edition, edited by Greg Johnson (San Francisco:

camaraderie: our three "heroes," the CIA contras (either of which must be the "Devil's band" or "men" referenced in the theme song) and the law enforcement posse (which the 'bots disparage as "the gay high school Secret Service" and "the cast of How to Succeed in Business."

No Dialogue Necessary: The Vision of Coleman Francis

"Coleman Francis had a vision. A dark vision. With cars."[380]

It's always the same place;
It's always the same time;[381]
It's always the same people;
It's always the same "actions."[382]

Obviously the three films instantiate this vision in different ways and to different extents.

B is the shortest, crudest — but for all that, not the ugliest — version.[383] But what else would we expect from a first-time director's first outing? As Tom Servo ironically observes at the start of B: "Typical of young directors: too many good ideas. Or in this case, no ideas."

And yet the vision is already complete. As B-filmmaker and historian Larry Blamire notes:

"If you took out the MST3k jokes, and removed the music, which is just re-cycled, it would be an incredibly deadening experience."[384]

One almost cliché problem is that rather than embracing the lack of available sound and going full silent movie, Coleman instead set up shots

---

Counter-Currents, 2017).

[380] Mike Nelson, MST3k, B.

[381] "The mythical narrative is of timeless and placeless validity." Coomaraswamy, *Hinduism and Buddhism* (Philosophical Library/Open Road Media, 2014) p. 6.

[382] Or, as the 'bots suggest, the Beckett-like "action ... less ... ness."

[383] Even Tor Johnson covered in "wrinkled toilet tissue" can't match Coleman's Griffin for sheer ugliness, at least of spirit. "Where does his face end and his pillow begin?" – Tom Servo.

[384] Larry Blamire, "No Dialogue Necessary."

to avoid the actors' mouths and wrote and dubbed the extensive and infamous narration himself.[385]

"I thought I was listening to Spoon River Anthology performed by atomic mutants."[386]

Yes, it's the dreaded "telling not showing."[387] Yet arguably B gives us a key visual clue: the atomic blast that precedes Tor, the deputies, and the family all wandering in the desert.[388] As we take in, compulsively, the extraordinarily bleak black & white photography, here and in the following two films, we may realize that we've seen this before: the famous footage of atomic tests blowing apart mock buildings.

Although ex-industrial film cameraman Lee Strosnider provided the cinematography, he recalls balking at Coleman's idea of depicting the atomic blast by simply opening up the camera iris; yet he admits, it worked.[389]

B was originally titled, at the start of production, *The Angry Sun*, which of course suggests The Angry Son: the Savior in his second coming, bringing his righteous wrath. I suggest that fundamentally all three films take place in a post-apocalyptic wasteland: the film merely records the "footprints on the wasteland" left by the wandering survivors.

That our post-Cold War experience tells us retrospectively that no such holocaust "actually" occurred is irrelevant; it is the existential landscape of the post-Atomic Age, where the worst has already happened, long ago,[390] and cannot be prevented or repaired; where only a god can save us.[391]

---

[385] Lee Strosnider – who should know, being the cameraman and sometime editor, says he hired "some radio announcer" for the job, but I and most listeners assume it's Coleman himself.

[386] Larry Blamire, loc. cit.

[387] As Tom Servo exclaims during an especially talky scene in the wholly abominable *The Dead Talk Back* (Gould, 1957; released 1996): "We could use a flashback here, this is a motion picture."

[388] The father eventually stumbles across a "Test Site" warning sign, but seems to take it with a shrug and neither he nor anyone else mentions it again.

[389] Interview, "No Dialogue Necessary."

[390] In the title essay of *The Eldritch Evola* I suggested that both Evola and Lovecraft share the same concept of horror: the worst that can happen — the primal Fall — has already happened.

[391] Martin Heidegger, "Nur noch ein Gott kann uns retten," *Der Spiegel* 30 (Mai, 1976):

This disjunction between powerful visual symbol and wordy message would be corrected, ironically enough, in his next outing, *Skydivers*, his first with synchronized sound, where — although neither he nor we are interested in the conventional romantic plot — Coleman digs into his own, small bag of personal interests and drags out … sport parachuting.[392]

It's an absolutely brilliant metaphor for the human condition: the parachutists go up, then come down, and then repeat the process, until death intervenes.[393] Moreover, during the cycle, the eponymous skydivers are hanging from the various tethers attaching them to the chute, an obvious allusion to the "puppet" metaphor of total determinism as revealed by mystical experience brought about by enthogenic substances.[394]

Southern pater familias (Coleman & family!): "When are those fools going to jump?"

Joe the Coffee Guy: "Who? Oh, the fools."

This is especially brought out by Coleman's primitive method of splicing aerial shots of the skydivers with inserts of the actors' faces, apparently shot while hanging in a studio or warehouse.[395]

193-219. Trans. by W. Richardson as "Only a God Can Save Us" in *Heidegger: The Man and the Thinker* (1981), ed. T. Sheehan, pp. 45-67.

[392] "Coleman Francis evidently thought plotless skydiving segments were much more important than story, so skydiving is to this film what refueling was to *The Starfighters*." "The 10 Most Unwatchable Films Featured on MST3K" by Jim Vorel; *Paste Magazine*, November 15, 2013.

[393] In this context, even the ill-fated romance plotline could be defended: "Reinhold Merkelbach suggested that the Hellenistic romance novels were secularizations of the ancient Mystery myths (the novels perhaps still being understood by the initiated as religious allegories). The separation of the lovers, their arduous search and final reunion reflect the death of Attis, Tammuz, Adonis, Osiris, the pursuit into the underworld by Cybele, Ishtar, Aphrodite, Isis, and their glorious reunion after the resurrection of the beloved." Robert H. Price, "The Christ Myth and the Christian Goddess," http://www.robertmprice.mindvendor.com/art_christgoddess.htm.

[394] See the research gathered by Michael Hoffman at his egodeath.com site; for more on the puppet in film, see my review of *A Dandy in Aspic*, "Passing the Buck: Spy, Dandy, Übermensch."

[395] The ever-present danger of becoming entangled in puppet strings or parachute ropes recalls the repeated (of course) reference to being "caught in the wheels of progress" in B.

He'll fly his astral plane.

He'll take you trips around the bay.[396]

He'll bring you back the same day.

He'll take you up, he'll bring you down,

He'll plant your feet back firmly on the ground.

He flies so high, he swoops so low,

He knows exactly which way he's gonna go.[397]

Coleman did know which way: Cuba; and *Red Zone Cuba* (also known by the more profound title *Night Train to Mundo Fine*) would prove to be his fine-st achievement. And appropriately enough, Coleman would drop the narrating — "until the end" as the theme song says[398] — and little bit parts, and instead take center stage: "Full Metal [Coleman]," as Crow T. Robot intones.[399]

---

[396] According to Wikipedia, "*The Skydivers* is also known as *Fiend from Half Moon Bay* and *Panic at Half Moon Bay*," and IMDB agrees, but unlike R, I've have never seen it referred to by either title, and won't start here. Presumably, it alludes to Eddie Andreini Sr. Airfield (formerly Half Moon Bay Airport) which Wikipedia says "is a public airport in San Mateo County, six miles (9 km) northwest of Half Moon Bay, California. The airport is on the Pacific Coast, south of San Francisco." Freezing the film at 10:07 shows that Joe's letter to Harry is being delivered to RRI, Half Moon [Something]; the futility of shooting a whole scene, addressing the envelope and zooming in on it but not allowing the viewer to clearly make it out will be echoed in R when Cherokee Jack's sign is carefully written out, illiteracies and all, but flashed only for a split second; the *Agony Booth* review helpfully transcribes it. The bay referred to in the lyric is obviously San Francisco Bay, since "he" is Timothy Leary. According to IMDB as well, the movie was shot at several California locations, including several airports, but not Half Moon Bay or airport.

[397] "'Legend of a Mind' is a song by the British progressive rock band The Moody Blues, and was written by the band's flautist Ray Thomas, who provides the lead vocals. "Legend of a Mind" was recorded in January 1968 and was first released on the Moody Blues' album In Search of the Lost Chord." (Wikipedia). Suzy's bizarre plan to kill Harry involves dumping acid into his parachute back, an idea that is discussed at length with special emphasis on the world 'acid.' The connection to Leary is obvious.

[398] Which also suggest another, darker 60s hit, Jim Morrison's "The End" in whose chorus Jim Morrison repeatedly intones "until the end."

[399] An online reviewer notes that "*Red Zone Cuba* dispenses with any clear narration. In fact, it doesn't bother to show or tell how the characters get from one place to another. Half of the time, the viewer isn't sure where the characters in the story are," then adding "Coleman Francis is possibly the worst, ugliest, stupidest, most violent piece of sh*t director ever to walk this earth and I hope he burns in some very hot place for producing this rubbish."

Like sport parachuting, Coleman has found another objective correlative: the Bay of Pigs invasion,[400] where official history seems to have been written by Coleman himself:[401]

But we didn't have to invade Cuba, because it was already ours. You don't need to invade an island where you already have a large military base. The story couldn't be any stupider if it included clowns on tricycles. [402]

Stupid, and futilely repetitive.[403] But even in R, the Bay of Pigs is only an irrelevant epicycle.[404]

Excursus Diagnostic

"Someone with Attention Deficit Disorder edited this film." – Crow T. Robot, S

We have to ask, what's eating Coleman Francis? By all accounts, such as they are, he was a good guy, a nice chap. He drank, but no more than anyone else in this Mad Man era, and though he began drinking heavily as he went into a sudden, steep decline in his last years, there's no reason to think one was any more the cause than the other.

Yet what accounts for the unique vision projected by his films?[405]

"A kind of dark lyricism."[406]

---

[400]   "Bay of Pigs," mutters Coleman as Griffin, and Mike Nelson gruffly adds "That's what they say when go in the pool."

[401]   As the narrator of B drones "Coyotes. Once a menace to travelers. Missile bases run them off their hunting grounds" Mike takes on Coleman's voice and concludes "That's another script I'm working on."

[402]   Miles W. Mathis, "Fidel Castro: CIA Agent," http://mileswmathis.com/castro.pdf.

[403]   Tri-cycles indeed; the Coleman Francis trilogy of repetition.

[404]   "Did they even have to go to Cuba?" rants Mike Nelson.

[405]   "Coleman Francis had a vision. A dark vision. With cars." – Mike Nelson, B.

[406]   TV's Frank, "No Dialogue Necessary." Frank adds that "Some people on the staff would disagree." For example, Mike Nelson: "I had to go to him and say, 'The Coleman Francis movies are actually crushing me and destroying my health." "Mystery Science Theater 3000 turns 20" by Kate Ward; EW.com, Nov. 21, 2008. Even Frank admits that B "was a particularly painful experience, … I think B would fall under the category of "Well, we have to fill our order …"

"The shots of the mother looking for her children are so bleak ... If you took away the Mystery Science Theater comments, and the music, which is just library music, it would be an incredibly deadening experience."[407]

"There was no such thing as clinical depression until this film"[408]

I suggest that autism would explain much; yes, our auteur was an autiste.[409]

Now of course, I'm no kind of doctor,[410] and I even if I were I would not try to diagnose a long dead man on the basis of some movies. But contrariwise, perhaps the diagnosis can help us understand the movies themselves.

To aid our man in the street idea of autism, let's look at some recent research, helpfully summarized by a recent article from the Right On blog.[411]

Cambridge university autism researcher Simon Baron-Cohen, the cousin of comedian Sacha Baron-Cohen, advances the idea that Autism Spectrum Conditions (ASC) including Asperger's syndrome can be at least partially explained as being the expression of an "extreme male brain" (EMB) that results from unusually high concentrations of testosterone during fetal development.

This would certainly seem to fit Coleman, with his large, hulking presence, and evident ease at portraying murderous brutes.[412]

---

[407] Larry Blamire, ibid.

[408] Tom Servo, B.

[409] "Our auteur, ladies and gentlemen!" – Mike Nelson as Coleman sits on the ground and spreads his legs wide in R.

[410] I do, however, has a Master's degree ... in Science! See TV Tropes on "Not that kind of doctor." For example, "Dr. Charles B. Pierce from Boggy Creek 2 The Legend Continues is mistaken for a medical doctor when asked to treat the mountain man Crenshaw's captive baby Boggy Creek Creature. Turns out Dr. Pierce only has a doctorate in Boggy Creek Studies." Crenshaw muses "Ah thought all doctors wuz good at fixin' up folks." See MST3k Episode 1006.

[411] Roderick Kaine, "Autism and the Extreme Male Brain" Right On, December 22, 2016.

[412] Most notably Griffin, of course, but in S he portrays the government official (the FAA?) who jumps in a plane and tries to shoot down the fleeing Frankie and Suzy, and earlier a buffoonish pater familias who orders around his family and even bystanders. In B he's a lazy gas jockey and an early morning drunk buying a newspaper (a part all too close to home). A comparison of Coleman with the chap in the photo illustrating the article is engaging; the later could be his son, Paul (seen in S as the doomed Beat diver "Pete"), cleaned up and with

Although in the past autist were often assumed to have low IQ's, this is like a case of selection bias (those with low IQ's are more likely to be subjected to testing). In fact,

> It is well-known that some autists, despite having social problems and difficulty functioning independently, often display some remarkable intellectual talents; especially when it comes to detailed memory of their favorite topic. The subset of autists with uncanny intellectual abilities used to be widely referred to as idiot savants to indicate both their lower level of overall functioning and their above average excellence in a particular narrow domain.

Again, we can well imagine Coleman as a highly talented individual whose "difficulty functioning independently" easily explains his attraction to filmmaking, the collaborative art par excellence.

The precise nature of Coleman's cinematic vision becomes recognizable when we look at the two dimensions of intelligence that Baron-Cohen postulates:

> The first dimension, empathizing reasoning, involves interpreting the goals of conscious agents and general theory of mind. Empathizing reasoning allows efficient inference of mental and emotional states in others and promotes the drive to respond with appropriate emotion and physical actions to those states. ... The major thrust of this form of reasoning is understanding the emotional states of others and responding to those states well; whether this knowledge is used to sympathize with others or pursue raw self interest is secondary.

> The second dimension, systemizing reasoning, is defined as the drive and ability to analyze and construct rules for a particular system that can produce consistently predictable outputs from given inputs as a result of operational rules. It is especially effective at interpretation of non-agentative lawful systems such as are common in the natural world. Lawful systems are characterized by being highly predictable. Given a specific input, a lawful system can be expected to repeatedly have a consistent output after some operation takes place. Examples of highly lawful systems, approaching 100% lawfulness, would be things such as mathematical formulas, the functioning of engines, and the

a degree from DeVry.

movement of celestial bodies. Given a perturbation of such systems, the resulting change or output can be predicted with the real-world results varying minimally from predication. Moderately lawful systems, such as meteorology, are also amenable to systemizing reasoning.

The functioning of engines, now keep that in mind. Basically, we can see that the autist will be relative lousy at understanding human interaction, based as it is on agency, and will compensate by a fixation on rule-based systems.

Autists can be thought of as hyper-systemizers who attempt to interpret all sensory input, including agentative action, through systemizing. Interpreting agents and high variance systems in terms of input-operation-output isn't feasible and as a result social situations tend to cause a lot of consternation for autists. To cope with the inability to successfully systemize unlawful environments or situations, autistic people develop preference for stable, unchanging environments or at least environments which change predictably. Unexpected change or a break from routine can commonly cause autists immense discomfort since it breaks the systemizing mental schemas on which they are reliant. As a result, they tend to form interests in topics and hobbies which are amenable to systemizing and also attempt to force the environment around them to conform to some rule set. For example, systematically recording the weather, repetitively watching certain TV shows or specific episodes, developing encyclopedic knowledge of important dates or train schedules, repetitively rocking or other stereotypical behaviors are all examples of hobbies with lawful properties taken up by autists. In the case of TV shows, even though a TV show has agents, the events, script and other aspects of the story never change from one viewing to another and thus it is highly lawful.

Repetition, eh? As we've seen, this is exactly the Coleman vision, a world of endless, futile repetition, extended even to human interaction, never changing from film to film, from actor to actor.

These elements can help us to understand both the sources of Coleman's cinematic vision, and its nature.

First, the inability to understand, and thus to portray, human motivation and psychological processes. This is most on display in S, where Coleman, in his sophomore outing, unwisely attempts to portray an intense love triangle (or quadrilateral, actually[413]) leading to murder. While Kevin (yes, Kevin) Casey seems to struggle heroically to get some emotion going between her and the other actors, the latter, along with the script, defeat her every time.[414] It's possible Tony Cardoza was cast precisely to play a stereotypically stoic, inexpressive "real guy" who resists and resents his wife as she tries to get them to "talk about our problems," but more likely he's here, as in all of Coleman's films, because he's the producer.[415]

And here is where coffee, "a Coleman Francis motif" (R), makes its first appearance, to be continued in R. Coffee — making, offering, accepting, enjoying — is Coleman's universal social lubricant, the chief means of getting his actors to interact, or even to get up and move or do something with their hands.

Thus, we have this moment, a key plot point[416] and a pivotal scene in the Coleman oeuvre, like Eisenstein's baby carriage, as described by the indefatigable reviewer at *The Agony Booth*:

---

[413]   One reviewer at IMBD.com explains the "sexual algebra" involved: "Just try and keep this straight: Harry is married to Beth (with whom he runs an airport/parachuting school), but catting around with Suzy, who also has a thing going with Frankie, who used to work for Harry. Frankie's place as mechanic has been taken by Harry's war buddy Joe, who would probably like to take Harry's place as Beth's husband as well. But when Harry leaves Suzy and calls her a "broad" in the bargain, well, she just has no other choice but to Do The Nasty with the local pharmacist in exchange for a little acid to pour all over Harry's parachute, which she does with the help(?) of Frankie (actually, she does the driving, the planning, gets the acid, and actually applies it to said parachute – while he stands and/or sits around looking stupid and/or nervous)." The over-ambitious plot is itself an indication of an unawareness of how complicated human interactions are. "It's a typical mistake of new filmmakers. Too many good ideas. Or, in this case, no ideas." Tom Servo, B.

[414]   After one typically stuttering encounter with Cardoza, she turns to the camera with a puzzled look and Crow muses "Now what did he mean by that?" The *Agony Booth* review describes another marital stalemate thus: "Harry chews on his lips and looks in Beth's general vicinity as she says, "Harry, I'm scared." But she insists it's not the FAA man that scares her. Harry looks at her and angrily asks, "Well, what does scare you?" Coleman Francis nude scenes? She looks him in the eye, then shakes her head and walks out of the scene, making it look like it would have been just as natural for her to turn straight to the camera and go, "Line?"

[415]   The MST3k cast discusses how "Tony Cardoza really gets into his role. Yeah, he gets right in and just sits." When his name appears in the credits of R, Crow exclaims "Oh, he's good in everything!"

[416]   As the bots summarize the film at the end, "A stranger comes to town, touches nobody's life, and leaves."

187

Here we get some truly terrible stage business as Suitcase Guy walks up, stops, looks at Beth, obtrusively puts down his suitcase, stands back up, stares at Beth a while longer, then speaks. (I promise you, it's even more stilted than how I described it.) He says, "I know you. Beth, you're prettier than your picture." Beth continues to look at the guy in shock and horror, until it finally dawns on her this is Harry's war buddy, Joe Moss. Remember, Beth? The guy you said they should send for, and who therefore you should have been expecting? You really don't get a lot of customers, do you, Beth?

She grabs his hand and tells him it's great to finally meet him. As she gushes, she realizes she's held his hand a little too long, so she offers him coffee. Coleman Francis Rule #1: When in doubt, coffee out. This leads to Joe's immortal line, "Coffee? I like coffee!" For a Coleman Francis movie, that's the equivalent of a guy in a Western saying, "I like six-shooters!" Beth makes this elaborate and dorky right this way gesture, like she's revealing a speedboat in the Showcase Showdown. They leave the now suffocating confines of the Parachute Room for the bright, clean outdoors.

The two walk around. They look the place over by walking about a yard or two and tilting their heads like birds listening for worms. Joe then passes judgment: "I like this place." But do you like it as much as you like coffee?

Beth agrees, but says she'd like it better if it were paid for. Joe smiles and says, "Well?" Which sounds like he means, "Well, why isn't it paid for?" Frankly, I don't think that's any of your business, Joe. Beth's stymied for a reply, so she asks Joe to rephrase that in the form of an actual question.

Joe asks, "Where's the general?" This also stumps Beth. Geez. What is this, Obtuse Day? Finally, she realizes he's asking about Harry (who's a corporal, if there ever was one). This leads to her making the incredibly lame reply, "Oh! He had to go into the village and check the troops!" Hmm. Is that what he calls Suzy's butt? She says this very seriously at first, but then smiles. I'm guessing this is what passes for "deadpan humor" when you're Coleman Francis.

Joe totally blows off her stupid reply and asks, "Uhhh, weren't you saying something about some coffee?" Geez, no kidding. What a lousy hostess. Don't dangle the prospect of coffee before us and then just leave us hanging, woman! You know what? I'll bet the coffee's not paid for, either.

As they walk along, General Harry arrives in his land boat Cadillac and – rarest of rare sights! Tony Cardoza just smiled! I don't believe it. And the whole time he's greeting Joe he maintains this smile. Amazing stuff here!

They all decide nothing would cap this moment off better than a cup of that mythical coffee, so they head inside. Joe immediately makes trouble by joking about a native girl who tried to get Harry to marry her during the war. How is this guy a chick magnet? This movie makes no sense.

Was that tedious and puzzling? Well, imagine watching it slowly, painfully enacted on a screen in front of you.

But it would be wrong to leave the suggestion that Coleman was just inept.[417] There's an important second piece of the puzzle: he's really good, or at least interested, in one thing: flying small planes.

B opens with Jaworski landing in a small plane,[418] and the central "action" is that for no reason at all the "desert patrol" gets in a plane and parachutes on top of a mesa, after shooting down an innocent civilian (another Coleman motif, as we'll see).

S is entirely set at a "sport parachute" facility and excels in shots of planes taking off and landing, and the eponymous skydivers jumping out, sailing down and landing. It's no surprise that most people consider this to be his "best" film.[419] Here the human element again fails Coleman; it's not clear who did the quite convincing shots of the skydivers in the air,[420]

---

[417] "Coleman was extremely well prepared for someone who didn't know what he was doing." – Lee Strossnider, "No Dialogue Necessary."

[418] Why a civilian plane? Cover, I suppose. But of course, Tor Johnson looks absurd in the tiny cockpit; the door isn't even fully closed, presumably due to his bulk, and cameraman Strossnider adds that they had to "cheat" (i.e., cut away from) his exit, which must have been as inept as his exit from his grave in *Plan Nine*.

[419] "Skydivers, however, is the forgotten, neglected gem of the Coleman Francis trilogy. Perhaps that's because it's actually the best of the three, and almost verges on watchable. Is that saying a lot? No." *Agony Booth*, op. cit.

[420] At least some of it is not stock footage, since some minor actors are there; "Did the actors do their own skydiving? No, the skydivers did their own acting." – MST3k.

but Coleman then inter-cuts shots of the actors in close-up, presumably hanging in a warehouse somewhere against a blank background; it's as convincing as it sounds. And once more, the "climax" is a guy — Coleman himself this time — getting in a small — again, civilian — plane and shooting down some supposed bad guys.

R again reverts to B to give us a central episode where a civilian plane takes Coleman and pals to a CIA training camp; then later they steal another plane — again, a civilian plane though on a supposed Cuban military base — to fly back,[421] an entirely unnecessary detour.[422] And again, the climax is reached when an (FBI?) man gets in a — civilian, sigh — plane and this time shoots down Coleman.

A bad filmmaker who, like the Hedgehog, knows just one thing; this is what prevents Coleman's films from being entirely bad and thus slipping out of existence entirely. As a useful comparison consider Bill Rebane, a truly bad, that is, simply untalented director. His *Monster A Go Go*[423] is infamous for having been shelved half-way through when financing fell through – like Orson Welles! Unlike Welles, he gave up. Unfortunately for us, it was bought and then "completed" by sleaze tycoon Hershel Gordon Lewis, to serve as the bottom of a double bill – if one can imagine something on the bottom of a bill featuring a "film" by the Wizard of Gore. The willingness of both Lewis and Rebane to treat his film as raw material for a cinematic sausage is almost refreshingly honest, and quite accurate in its evaluation of the material.[424]

But the main difference is that while Rebane is utterly incompetent, like an inverted Fox,[425] Francis, like the Hedgehog, knows one big thing:

---

[421] As a Chekhov's Pistol, on the flight down Coleman grunts out to the pilot that "If you need help, my friend here (Tony Cardoza) can fly"; an unlikely skill for a hobo, but it sure comes in handy when escaping Castro's clutches!

[422] "Did they even have to go to Cuba?" demands Mike Nelson.

[423] Also MST'd, as Episode 421, as is his later *Giant Spider Invasion* (Episode 810); as a kind of trademark of stupidity, the later uses the same still shot of a galaxy for the opening background, but this time in color.

[424] "Nearly the entire cast of the show and Best Brains stated this was officially the worst movie they have ever seen up to this point." MST3k Wiki.

[425] His mistake, like Coleman's autism, is to try and make "science" fiction films without any concept of how actual science is conducted; not only is are the explanations typical B-movie "science," his "scientists" and "laboratories" show that he's never seen an actual one. "What do you expect from me" shouts one of them, "I don't have your precision mind." Yeah, he's only a scientist. This kind of "implied expertise" (suggested by, say, wearing a

flying planes. As we've seen, they play key roles in all his films, and his most conventionally successful, S, is entirely devoted to planes. There, Coleman can relax and present some cool, mechanical competence. Everywhere else, from setting up synchronized (or not) sound to depicting real human emotions and speech – Coleman, like Rebane, is entirely, pervasively incompetent.

"Coffee? I like coffee!" (S)

"I'm Cherokee Jack!"[426] (R)

"A corpse ... a woman's handbag ... and footprints on the wasteland." (B)

But then, have we not seen an alarming increase in the diagnosis of autism in our post-Apocalyptic society?

Excursus: Mr Arkadin (aka Confidential Report)

And speaking of Welles: if there is any "mainstream" cinema masterpiece that approaches the Coleman Trilogy, it would be *Mr. Arkadan* (aka *Confidential Report*) by Orson Welles. Made (mostly) in 1955, it slightly predates the Trilogy; is it possible Coleman was attempting a homage?[427]

Anyway, the parallels are striking. They start right at the start: what's this? A murky aerial shot of ... a single engine plane! Look out below! Over the drone of the engine, we suddenly hear a deep, sonorous voice – narration, by our auteur himself.[428]

---

lab coat) occurs in R when we are told that Griffin (Coleman) was "The Cotton King of the South"; TVTropes points out that it's hard to imaging Griffin as having been any kind of financial magnate, and Coleman wisely doesn't offer any financial advice or attempt anything more than robberies by brute force rather than Ocean's 11 style "capers."

[426] "In context, the character is a bit of fifth business, an okie who convinces the gang to fly to Cuba. M&TB are bowled over by his pie-eyed delivery of this introductory line. The riff is often repeated when a new character appears unannounced or says something unexpected." – MST3k Wiki.

[427] The only obvious homage in the Trilogy is the aerial chase in Beast, where some shots clearly mimic the cornfield chase in Hitchcock's recent *North by Northwest* (1959). Mike: "Coleman only steals from the best."

[428] Critic Gary Giddens actually calls it "worthy of Criswell in *Plan Nine*."

And among the pomposities, he predicts the plane will be involved in a murder. Now, having seen the film, we know that it's a suicide; bit of a difference, eh, Mr. Welles? However, Harry in S will indeed be murdered when an acid-sabotaged chute sends him plummeting to Earth. But no matter: the inaccuracy — itself a Colemanism — hides a deeper truth, as we've seen: the end of Griffin — the cotton king of the South, just as Arkadin is a global financier — is really a suicide (suicide by cop). Welles hammers this home by having Arkadan essentially just disappear, magically from the plane, no doubt due to budget constraints; yet if he had had Coleman's audacity, would he have bought some skydiving footage and supplemented it with close-ups of his actors hanging from hooks in a warehouse? Welles of course is doubled in Coleman, actor turned director, down on his luck, and rather fond of vino and carbohydrates, it would appear; and it indeed would have been a sight to see either one plunging from a plane.

We also have Robert Arden in the Tony Cardoza role of a non-acting, non-charismatic "romantic lead," involved in a romantic triangle (if we count Arkadin's love of his daughter). There's the long shooting schedule, interspersed by the repeated drying up of funds and the search for new donors, the bad dubbing,[429]the cast of weirdos and hopeful "guest stars," the "real" locations shot in a way that somehow seems entirely fake.

Is it any wonder it exists under two titles (like R) and in three versions (paralleling the Trilogy)?

All this makes the fictional encounter of Welles and Wood in Ed Wood even more ironically inappropriate. Coleman is Welles' true doppelganger.[430]

Is Griffin Enlightened?

Coleman Francis was found in his car, dead. His films were forgotten until rediscovered by MST3k. What is his legacy? What accounts for their terrible fascination?

I will suggest this: that a likely unique combination of ambition, autism and amateurism created a perfect storm that produced the most intense

---

[429]   After one bad sound effect, Mike Nelson comments dryly "Coleman Francis solves the problem of sound sync."

[430]   I've previously discussed Welles, Coleman and Traditional symbolism of falling bodies in "Breaking Badge."

cinematic vision of the nature of *samsara* and the path to *nirvana*. Once again Schopenhauer is our guide:

> Our life is like a journey on which, as we advance, the landscape takes a different view from that which it presented at first, and changes again, as we come nearer. This is just what happens – especially with our wishes. We often find something else, nay, something better than what we are looking for; and what we look for, we often find on a very different path from that on which we began a vain search. Instead of finding, as we expected, pleasure, happiness, joy, we get experience, insight, knowledge – a real and permanent blessing, instead of a fleeting and illusory one.

> This is the thought that runs through Wilhelm Meister, like the bass in a piece of music. In this work of Goethe's, we have a novel of the intellectual kind, and, therefore, superior to all others, even to Sir Walter Scott's, which are, one and all, ethical; in other words, they treat of human nature only from the side of the will. So, too, in the *Zauberflöte* — that grotesque, but still significant, and even hieroglyphic — the same thought is symbolized, but in great, coarse lines, much in the way in which scenery is painted. Here the symbol would be complete if Tamino were in the end to be cured of his desire to possess Tainina, and received, in her stead, initiation into the mysteries of the Temple of Wisdom. It is quite right for Papageno, his necessary contrast, to succeed in getting his Papagena.[431]

> Men of any worth or value soon come to see that they are in the hands of Fate, and gratefully submit to be moulded by its teachings. They recognize that the fruit of life is experience, and not happiness; they become accustomed and content to exchange hope for insight; ...

> It may even be that they to some extent still follow their old wishes and aims, trifling with them, as it were, for the sake of appearances; all the while really and seriously looking for nothing but instruction; a process which lends them an air of genius, a trait of something contemplative and sublime.

---

[431] Compare Bailey and Ruby in R.

In their search for gold, the alchemists discovered other things – gunpowder, china, medicines, the laws of nature. There is a sense in which we are all alchemists.[432]

Evola expands on the "journey" metaphor in a way that is extremely important for our considerations here:

An Eastern saying puts it as follows: "Life on earth is a journey in the night hours." One can explain its positive content by referring to the sensation of a "before" (with respect to human existence) and "after" (with respect to the same). In metaphysical terms, birth is a change of state and so is death; the human condition of earthly existence is only a restricted section in a continuum, in a current that traverses many other states.

In general, but particularly in a chaotic epoch in dissolution like the present one, it can be difficult to grasp the sense of this apparition of the being that one is, in the guise of a certain person, who lives in a given time and in a given place, who goes through these experiences, of whom this will be the end: it is like the confused sensation of a region traversed in a night journey where only a few scattered lights reveal some glimpses of the landscape. Nevertheless, one should maintain the sentiment, or presentiment, of one who when getting on a train knows he will get off it, and that when he gets off he will also see the entire course traveled, and will go further. This sentiment favors an immanent firmness and security, distinctly different from the state that arises in the soul facing death within the framework of a creationist theistic religion, in which whatever part of the being is superior and anterior to life, thus also metaphysically surviving the death that ends it, remains effectively hidden.[433]

We need only recall at this point that the original, now occluded title of R is *Night Train to Mundo Fine*. Suppressing the title, replacing it with the puzzling and irrelevant *Red Zone Cuba*,[434] is a masterstroke of subtle

---

[432]   *Counsels and Maxims*, Chapter One, Section 3

[433]   Julius Evola, *Ride the Tiger: A Survival Manual for the Aristocrats of the Soul*, trans. Jocelyn Godwin and Constance Fontana (Rochester, Vt.: Inner Traditions, 2003), pp. 220-21.

[434]   What is a "red zone" and how does it relate to Cuba? And as Mike Nelson says, "Did they even have to go to Cuba?"

genius. The film is Griffin's night journey to the end of the world; "end" meaning both the end of his entanglement in worldly desires and the end, or axis point of the world, from which escape is accomplished.[435]

But the title still hides in plain sight, in the opening prologue where "guest star" John Carradine makes his brief appearance as "the engineer on the train that night" when "it was dark" and Griffin "ran all the way to Hell."

And then immediately follows the theme song, sung (!) by Carradine himself. I've alluded to a few lines already, but now is the time to lay the whole thing out.[436]

"Night Train to Mundo Fine"
written by: Ray Gregory
"music played by": Ray Gregory and the Melmen
"sung by": John Carradine

Night train to Mundo Fine
Night train to the end
Running hard and running fast
To meet my future and away from my past
Taking that gamble that cannot last
Night train to the eeeeeend!

Hell's ride to Mundo Fine
Hell's ride to the end
Sold my soul to the devil's men
He draws me hard with a merciless hand
And all I bought is a handful of sand
Night train to the eeeeeend!

I'm on this ride 'cause I have no pride
In myself or in man or in God

---

[435] Anthony Kerrigan said that Unamuno seems like it must mean "one world," but in no known language. "Mundo fine" (fine is two syllables as sung here) seems to mean "end of the world," but also suggests the "fine" world of Samsaric attractions. It also appears to be a cocktail, also unknown, at least to me: http://cocktails.underthelabel.com/l/3865/Mundo-Fine.

[436] And you can listen to it here: http://media.agonybooth.com/sounds/articles/Red_Zone_Cuba_1966/John%20Carradine%20with%20Ray%20Gregory%20and%20the%20Melmen%20-%20Night%20Train%20to%20Mundo%20Fine.mp3.

Now if you want to share in the price of my fare
Then fill your mind with greed that is blind
And wander in its evil fog[437]

Night train to Mundo Fine
Night train to the end
Running hard and running fast
To meet my future and away from my past
Taking the gamble that cannot last
Night train to the eeeeeend!

Thus, it is inaccurate, to say the least, to characterize this prologue sequence as gratuitous or "never referred to again."[438] In fact, is a clear leitmotiv; no sooner does Griffin settle in the hoboes than he mutters contentedly "I'm gonna grab me a long freight train." At the CIA camp he again mutters that "There must be a highway or railroad somewhere around here." And, of course, they eventually do hop the night train out of Albuquerque,[439] though from that point on cars — driven by Landis — are the preferred mode of transport.[440]

What emerges from the para-competent and depressing vision of R (and to a lesser extent S) is a narrative that is true and compelling, because it is the narrative of all our lives, the metaphysical Truth behind the boring, depressing round of existence that can only be escaped by abandoning its attractions and heading straight up.

---

[437] This verse is sung during a sequence cut from the MST3k print, leading to a rather unfair joke about how poor editing (not Coleman's!) seems to have Griffin being chased twice over the same terrain; even so, from our point of view, it only adumbrates the Futile Repetition theme.

[438] "Hilariously, an ominous blare of horns is heard, as if this statement was somehow shocking or involving or intriguing or anything. The reporter looks up in shock, also for no reason. Mr. Wilson, having dropped this bombshell, takes a moment to suck on his cancer stick again and blow smoke, presumably right into the reporter's face. And that, my friends, is the extent of John Carradine's cameo in this movie. Sadly, you could almost call this the quintessential John Carradine cameo." *The Agony Booth*, op. cit.

[439] Walter White's stomping grounds, of course.

[440] There may be a symbolism here, but after all, it's hard to travel everywhere by train.

Pete: "I feel real free up there in that high blue sky. Nobody to tell you what to do, you just have to please yourself up there."[441]

In the final sequence, Griffin has come to the end of the line, announcing, bodhisattva-like:

Griffin: "No one's going back."

Not just cheated of his "thousand bucks when you join, and a thousand bucks when it's over" — another splendid metaphor for *samsara* — and the perhaps mythical uranium mine, he has been stripped of all possessions, still wearing some stolen clothes and carrying only, as we'll soon be told, "a penny[442] and a broken cigarette."

He's abandoned everyone (running from Cook and Landis and shooting Ruby) and run across a field (the Field of material existence). We switch to an aerial perspective on the Field as a whole as the helicopter closes in on him. We see Griffin standing, stock-still, as he shot and falls over, horizontally across the ground.

Is Griffin done for now, only to return to the endless round? No: unlike Rico in *Little Caesar*, this is not "the end."

We cut to Ruby, who also lies on the ground. An unknown man in a pickup truck stops by and, well, picks her up, shoving her onto the flatbed.[443] Ruby is returned to her house, where her husband, presumed dead, also shows up.[444] None of this is explained or even sensible. However, it shows that by shooting Ruby Griffin has transferred his karma to her, a process we've called "passing the buck."[445] Griffin is now free.

Griffin has followed as ascetic path; prison, breakout, old clothes, sharing food with hoboes, military training, combat, capture and escape, begging hospitality of Chastain's wife. Like a monk or priest, he has nothing, owns nothing.

---

[441] The words of "Pete", portrayed by Paul Francis (Coleman's son?) in S.

[442] Some have pointed out that Coleman could have at least had Griffin carrying the quarter that we see is all that's in the café cash register; but that kind of "mistake" actually just drives home the point about how ephemeral and interchangeable things are in *samsara*.

[443] "Why is Phil Silvers [whom the actor resembles] rounding up corpses?" – Crow.

[444] "Do not reveal the incredible secret of *Red Zone Cuba*!" – Tom Servo.

[445] See my review of *A Dandy in Aspic*, "Passing the Buck: Spy, Dandy, *Übermensch*," above. To see this, we need to recall that in "real life" Coleman was found dead, inexplicably, in the back of a station wagon.

"A once powerful, humble man ... reduced to ... nothing" (B)

As the posse searches Griffin's pockets, a narrator suddenly speaks up,[446] informing us that "Griffin ran all the way to Hell ... with a penny ... and a broken cigarette." Of course, we can see the penny and the cigarette; the narrator is needed to add the running to Hell part, thus linking this final shot to the prologue speech.

This time, however, the voice is not Carradine. Was he unavailable? If so, why not overdub his previous line reading – certainly not a technique Coleman was afraid to use.

No, this time the voice is Coleman's, as in B; the line circles back to the prologue, but the voice circles back to the narration of B. More deeply, it tells us Coleman has in some sense survived, his body is discarded on the Ground of Existence not in defeat but in triumph, in transcendence. The voice is disembodied, and the next shot returns to the aerial view. It must be Coleman's new, transcendent POV.

"Timothy Leary's dead / No, no, no, no he's outside looking in" – "Legend of a Mind"

"The Kingdom of Heaven is for none but the thoroughly dead." – Meister Eckhart

Meeting his final end, his is "arrested," he "gives up" the ghost, is "finished."[447] Missa est. The Knower withdraws up and circles around the Pole at the center of the Spiral.[448]

---

[446] Larry Blamire said of B, where the narration is constant, that due to the lack of sync'd sound "it's like someone next to you in the theatre started talking." Interview in "No Dialogue Necessary."

[447] Beckett was present once at a rehearsal of one of his plays at an American university. At the end, the puppet-like sole protagonist is lifted up off the stage and away. A student timidly asked if this meant he had been "saved". Beckett chuckled and said, with some glee, "No, he's finished."

[448] See the world-wide symbolism explicated by Coomaraswamy in *The Door in the Sky: Coomaraswamy on Myth and Meaning* (Princeton, 1997). For a survey of the primary Indo-European symbol of the center, and the *charkrvartin* (the Turner of the Wheels) see Boris Nad, "The Idea of the Center" in *Aristokratia IV*, ed. K. Deva (Manticore Press, 2017). "Today's uranian individual is alone, 'lost in the midst of hostility of the 'chthonic' mass. Novels such as ... *The Marble Cliffs* by Ernst Jünger [and, I would add, the films of Coleman Francis] can be read as a testimony to the passage of such heroes through the hell

Dead ... but in Hell? Well, of course, all symbols are inverted on the material plane; what deluded mortals call Hell may very well be the transcendent realm. After all, Judeo-Christianity, the sworn enemy of "prideful" search for gnosis,[449] condemns those who would strive for such knowledge to eternal punishment.[450] And as we've seen, death is only birth at another level of the spiral.[451]

But Isn't Griffin Evil?

But isn't Griffin evil? How can he be enlightened?

Although Walter White and Hank Quinlan are also large men who commit bad deeds and come to similar falls — even, as we've seen,[452] almost identical in cinematography — the comparison stops there. Unlike Walter White, Griffin is not a bland, good man who gradually discovers that, as Jack Donovan would say, he's not a good man, but good at being a man. Griffin is just a clumsy brute, roaming the countryside and pointlessly brutalizing[453] anyone who looks sideways at him. Although Hank Quinlan's "famous intuition" at crime scenes suggest the sort of shamanic powers that would make him Griffin's equal, Griffin is not led into a downward spiral of evil by grief over the loss of his wife; he was already a criminal when he was the "Cotton King of the South" and although his wife has "spent all the money and become a streetwalker" she is likely still alive, yet he makes no attempt to find her or even mention her.

---

of the modern world, through the very centre of the vortex of modern nihilism, in its most extreme and destructive form. Their stay there, in a world that has become truly monstrous, and which is the exact opposite to celestial order, is akin to actually staying in hell. Such a hero endures life as if it were a war. He lives in constant war, in the midst of a hostile environment, under siege. But the experience of nihilism is necessary. At the end of the road the light must be found; the light of Order, and the sacred principles of the cosmos."

[449] Griffin, of course, is "on this ride because I have no pride / in myself, or in men, or in God."

[450] See Julius Evola, *The Hermetic Tradition* (Rochester, Vt.: Inner Traditions, 1995), especially "Introduction to Part One: The Tree, the Serpent, and the Titans."

[451] "In either case death of the victim is also its birth, in accordance with the infallible rule that every birth must have been preceded by a death." Coomaraswamy, *Hinduism and Buddhism*, p. 12.

[452] See "Breaking Badge: *Touch of Evil* through the Lens of *Breaking Bad*."

[453] *The Agony Booth* suggests a new term: "I hereby decree that the act of brutally grabbing someone shall now be referred to as "Griffinizing.""

No, Griffin is just a thoroughly bad man, at least in conventional terms; in fact, that could be said to be his only "purity," his thoroughly and consistently evil behavior.[454] It shouldn't be surprising that our autistic filmmaker has given us a "protagonist" with no inner life or plausible motivation to "explain" his acts. The lugubrious yet lyrically profound theme song tells us all we need to know:

I'm on this ride 'cause I have no pride
In myself, or in men or in God.
So if you want to share in the price of my fare
Then feed your mind with greed that is blind
And wander in its evil fog.

So again, we must consider how an evil man can be enlightened, or an enlightened man be evil.

It may seem hard to fathom how Griffin could be an enlightened being, since apart from his Buddha-like bulk he is surely one of the ugliest and nastiest protagonists ever to sully the silver screen.[455]

And yet....

We are not to imagine that various events in a man's life are out of relationship with one another. A Barbados plantation, dramatic school, theatre, professional dancing, and teaching metaphysics – while these seemingly point to a discrepancy in the continuous line of his life, that appearance is only due to our lack of insight. It is one of the characteristics of our age that we see for superficial consistency, failing

---

[454] Appropriately, the only hint of morality about him is his desire to escape from the CIA camp and "get his hands around Cherokee's throat" for misleading them about getting cash money: "Nothing I hate more than a liar." Our autistic auteur can't understand, and hates, hypocrisy and deceit. Although something of a Trickster himself, it's interesting as well that Coleman never bothers to change his appearance or clothing throughout the entire film. See Jason Reza Jordani, *Prometheus and Atlas* (Arktos: 2016) for a discussion of Paul Feyerabend's observations on the inability of Homeric man to understand lying and hypocrisy, as well as for his own observations on the Trickster or con man motif.

[455] An online reviewer says that "The main character, played with greasy flabbiness by the auteur Mr. Francis himself, is perhaps THE most unlikable character I have ever seen, and that includes the guy from *Manos* and Francis's mentor Ray Dennis Steckler who played an amazingly unlikable character in his *Mixed Up Zombies* movie. This jerk is first seen escaping from prison, and for most of the rest of the movie all he does is smoke, threaten people, grouse, and of course pointlessly beat up and kill people [i.e., "Griffinizing"]."

to realize that there may be deeper levels of reality, hidden from view, where the true line of continuity may be seen. A man's life is in reality a continuum. Regardless of the number of breaks that may appear in the line of his life, a true continuity does exist. We must not imagine for one moment that growth and development persist anywhere in nature in a straight line. The process of growth involves the idea of a spiral, of an apparent occasional backward trend, of appearances and disappearances, of surges and retreats, of endeavors and new endeavors ... If we bear such a concept in mind, we will be enabled to understand far more readily the intelligent direction of our lives – and in particular, the work and life of Neville.[456]

Can we think of the Mage, the Realized Man, as a Dirty Trickster?

Uncomfortable as it may be, I think the answer may very well be "Yes." The Realized Man has by definition passed beyond the "pairs of opposites" and is no more bound by our notions of moral law than JHVH himself. I've discussed this many times before when discerning the notion of "passing the buck" — passing on one's karmic burden to a sucker and transcending the Wheel of Becoming — in various films.

To understand the deeper level that provides the continuity of Griffin's run "all the way to Hell" we must, as Baron Evola insists, distinguish and keep separate the religious/moral point of view from the mystical/ metaphysical. He writes that:

It is worth pointing out that, in the ancient tradition of the Mysteries (which the current history of religions often confuses with the religions of salvation, the so-called *Erlösungsreligionen*), the essential ontological aspect by which the Initiatory conception is opposed to the religious one is highlighted. From Diogenes Laertius we know of the scandal provoked in certain already 'illuminist' Greek circles by the Mystery doctrine according to which even a delinquent Initiate would have a privileged destiny after death, to which even men of such high moral intelligence as Agesilas or Epaminondas, as uninitiates, would not have access. In this connection, one can speak of a 'transcendental realism',

---

[456] Israel Regardie, *The Romance of Metaphysics: An Introduction to the History, Theory and Psychology of Modern Metaphysics* (1946); this chapter on Neville is reprinted in Mitch Horowitz's anthology, *The Power of Imagination: The Neville Goddard Treasury* (Penguin/ Tarcher, 2015). Regardie knows whereof he speaks: he was Aleister Crowley's personal secretary.

which is confirmed also in the conception of the objective effectiveness of the Initiatory rite: it is admitted that its power is, on the spiritual plane, as objective and impersonal, and as detached from morality, as, on the material plane, actions of a technical nature are. Like such actions, the rite only requires that certain objective conditions are satisfied; then the effect will follow of its own accord by necessity, whoever the subject. ...

[...]

This is how the relationship between Initiation and morality can be defined. In general and in every tradition, from the Initiatory point of view, it is necessary to distinguish a part which has an exclusively social and mundane value, acting as a factor to hold in check the human animal, and a part which is really turned upwards, towards transcendence. The relativity of moral precepts becomes clear in both of these areas. In the first case, moral precepts undergo, in the various traditions, ethnic and historical conditionalities which make it impossible to find anything really constant and invariable, and therefore intrinsically valid, in the numerous varieties of rule prescribed according to times and places. In the second case, when, that is, a purely instrumental value is attributed to moral precepts, the sole criterion is the extent to which the means — of whatever nature — allow the goal to be reached, so that, not only are very different Initiatory paths indicated, with a view to the predominant dispositions of this or that individual, but also the chosen means may be in complete contrast to the moral precepts which a tradition in its exoteric aspects prescribes for the life of the majority in the world. The most typical cases are the so-called 'Left-Hand Path' of the Tantric *vâmâcâra* (which has some points of contact with Dionysianism – for example, when it comes to the use of sex and the emphasis put on the orgiastic and destructive element), and the 'heroic path' (*vîra-mârga*), which, under the sign of pure transcendence, have as principle a true anomia, and a scorn for the common moral and religious rules, although the ultimate end is not different from that of the 'Right-Hand Path', which instead uses such rules as a support ("the rules which do not chain but sustain those who do not know how to go by themselves"). In general, the recurrence of 'antinomianism' (this word designates the rejection of the rules of the current religion), which almost always indicates connections with

202

the world of Initiation or of esotericism, is well-known in the history of religions.[457]

As we have seen, the violent course of Griffin's life, as we've seen in a condensed and concise form in the film, has succeeded, perhaps even inadvertently, of burning away the mundane desires that keep him, and us, chained to the wheel of *samsara* (the ironically named "Wheels of Progress" we are "caught in," according to the narration in B), thus freeing him to ascend to a higher, relatively enlightened state at the end of R.[458]

If this, and particularly the idea of "passing the buck," dropping ones' karma on another, seem immoral, well, that's just how it is.

> The only real reason something should come into being in the course of human events is that "someone wishes it to be here." To expect that the universe should somehow "make sense" in itself, as if isolation from human actions that shape our world of meaning is a false expectation – and so horror in the face of an illogical or insane universe is misplaced. The abyssal lack of an inherent and immutable order can be seen as the free space for us to make the world meaningful in one way or another.[459]

"Seems I read about a Griffin once …"

Griffin as Trickster

It may, however, be more comforting to assimilate Griffin to a well-known archetype, the Trickster.[460]

---

[457] "The Concept of Initiation," online at http://www.juliusevola.it/.

[458] In this way Parsifal, "animated by indignation and pride," "separated from God" and "avoiding churches," "eventually triumphs, achieving the glory of the king of the grail." Julius Evola, *The Mystery of the Grail: Initiation and Magic in the Quest for the Spirit* (Rochester, Vt.: Inner Traditions, 1996), p. 74. Unlike Parsifal, Griffin, according to the theme song, is "on this ride because I have no pride;" this illustrates the relativity of moral virtues, as well as the equivalence of inverted symbols, such as Griffin's goal being described in the same song as Hell rather than the conventional Heaven; the point being "anywhere out of this world" (Baudelaire).

[459] Jason Reza Jorjani, *Prometheus and Atlas* (London: Arktos, 2016), "Being Bound for Freedom"; quoting and explicating William James.

[460] See, of course, *Trickster Makes This World: Mischief, Myth and Art* by Lewis Hyde (New York: Farrar, Straus & Giroux, 1998).

The narrative gives us many instances of Griffin's tricky nature. As the "Cotton King of the South" he "sold a lot of cotton one day, then sent his trucks [tricks?] in steal it back," a rather obvious move that led to his imprisonment. He then escapes through a method he laconically describes as "Drain pipe. Dug up some dirt." He evades both dogs and a curious sheriff by jumping onto the back of Cook and Landis's truck – "You sure fooled that bull[461] last night," Cook says admiringly.

Although tricked himself into joining up "to fight for some peasants in Cuba" — a point we'll return to — it could be argued that his presence there is itself a trick played on the CIA: "Those men!" Chastain exclaims, "how much help can they be?" Captured (apparently by Castro himself, or at least his elite guards), he figures out the sentries' schedule and uses the old "Guard! Water! Thirsty man!" trick to escape again.[462]

Finally, after a few more Griffinizing episodes, he reverts to form, stealing a car (despite earlier assertions of "going legit"[463]) and tricking Chastain's widow into helping him and the hoboes to look for Chastain's fabled "mountain of pitchblende."

Over and above all this, there is Griffin's name.

In the Prologue, John Carradine intones the theme, muttering in vague reminiscence "Griffin … he ran all the way to Hell" before singing about it in the theme song. Griffin himself[464] will repeat this at the very end.[465]

As Griffin hides the second sheriff announces, "His name is Griffin" — ominous horns sound — "and the reward is $5,000."

At the CIA camp Griffin balks when ordered to sign his name (Cherokee had told them they'd get cash, as Cook helpfully exposits for the audience). Later, in their bunks, Landis recalls that it "seems I read about

---

[461] Another mythological hint?

[462] "Griffin tells Cook to go ask for more water, and specifically, he wants Cook to get the guard to lean in close. 'If I can get my hands on him,' a bored Griffin says, 'I'll snap his neck.' Or maybe I'll take a nap. Either one would work out just fine right about now." *The Agony Booth*, op. cit.

[463] MST3k and most reviewers seem to think this cryptic phrase means "becoming a good citizen" but I think it means simply "use a regular means of transportation rather than hopping trains and stealing cars." He immediately follows this line by forcing Cook to surrender his father's ring and uses it to trade for a used car.

[464] As noted, the voiceover seems to be Coleman Francis himself, as in B.

[465] Augmented thus: "with a penny [symbolizing the endless wheel of *samsara*] and a broken cigarette [the breaking of ties to material desires]."

a Griffin once" and insists on trying to draw out Griffin's past until Griffin jumps up and chokes him into silence.[466]

Quite a lot is made of the name, and we don't even know if it's his first or last name.[467] Nevertheless, it is a clear clue that we are dealing with no ordinary thug; as the Wikipedia article on "Griffin" states:

> The griffin, griffon, or gryphon (Greek: γρύφων, *grýphōn*, or γρύπων, *grýpōn*, early form γρύψ, grýps; Latin: *gryphus*) is a legendary creature with the body, tail, and back legs of a lion; the head and wings of an eagle; and an eagle's talons as its front feet. Because the lion was traditionally considered the king of the beasts and the eagle the king of birds, the griffin was thought to be an especially powerful and majestic creature. The griffin was also thought of as king of all creatures. Griffins are known for guarding treasure and priceless possession ... In antiquity, it was a symbol of divine power and a guardian of the divine.

And so Cook may very well have "read about a griffin once" who was the "[cotton] King of the South." Other literary sources quoted by Wikipedia confirm Griffin's transcendental nature:

> In Dante Alighieri's *Divine Comedy*, after Dante and Virgil's journey through Hell and Purgatory has concluded, Dante meets a chariot dragged by a Griffin in Earthly Paradise. Immediately afterwards, Dante is reunited with Beatrice. Dante and Beatrice then start their journey through Paradise.

While others relate Griffin to his Satanic, "all the way to Hell" aspect:

> John Milton, in *Paradise Lost* II, refers to the legend of the griffin in describing Satan:

---

[466] As always in myth, to know one's name is to have power over one. At various points in the Gospels Jesus encounters demons who announce that they know who he is (unlike the disciples) as a threat when he tries to exorcize them, and later others will cast out demons "in his name."

[467] Bourgeois critics may cite this as a typical "blunder" but actually it shows Coleman's (autistic?) concentration on symbolic import; what would be the point of dubbing him "Griffin Jones" or "Ed Griffin"?

As when a Gryfon through the Wilderness
With winged course ore Hill[468] or moarie Dale,
Pursues the ARIMASPIAN, who by stelth
Had from his wakeful custody purloind
The guarded Gold [...]

Truly, there may be deeper levels of reality, hidden from view, where the true line of continuity may be seen.

To flesh some of these out, let us again look at Jason Reza Jorjani's *Prometheus and Atlas*, this time chapter 12, "Mercurial Metaphysics," which draws some key characteristics of the "Trickster god" Hermes from Hyde's work. Although "in his capacity as liar and thief" (like Griffin, and the initiated thief Evola references) Hermes is the cultural source of slaughter and butchery, he does not eat this sacrificial meat, "which establishes a connection between self-denial of appetite and the rise of nous (intellect),"[469] just as we have suggested that Griffin's ride to Hell draws out and cauterizes his material desires (principally, greed[470]).

Indeed, lying for its own sake is, Hyde and Jorjani suggest, a key moment "when the child crosses over the boundaries set by others and, by means of the lie, proliferates meaning of her own making."[471] This relates us to the numerous crossings Griffin accomplishes by his lies, such as crawling under the barbed wire fence at the opening, the flights to and from Cuba, his (improbable) climb up the Cuba cliffs, the cross-country murder, rape and robbery spree, and the final run across the field pursued by sheriffs and FBI agents, when he achieves transcendence, i.e., new meaning.

Connected with crossings is Hermes as the god of roads and safe passage. We note that the section of barbed wire Griffin crawls under is led up to by what appear to be paper cups; did he mark it out for some reason, as part of the (never detailed or shown) escape plan?[472] Cook is sent to watch the highway alongside Cliff's Café for "cars coming," and eventually

---

[468] "Ore hill" = Chastain's "mountain of pitchblende"?

[469] Referencing Hyde, op. cit., p. 59.

[470] "I always wanted money," Griffin muses in the CIA camp, perhaps the only time he voluntarily refers to his past. The theme song asks us to join him on his ride and "fill your mind with greed that is blind, and wander in its evil fog," although this is of course the first step only, not the goal.

[471] Referencing Hyde, p. 65.

[472] "Those are the malt cups from his previous takes" suggests Mike Nelson.

the hoboes fool Chastain's widow into leading them to the supposed pitchblende mine in lieu of a treasure map.

There is also the "connection between hunger and telling lies,"[473] which clearly applies to Griffin, from his agonizing hunger he feels as he hides in the truck listening to the gas jockey describe the delights on sale by his wife inside,[474] to the surrealistic Cliff's Café where the entire menu is painted all over the building — SHRIMP SCALLOPS CHICKEN FROG LEGS TOP SIRLION STEAK TROUT CAT-FISH FRIED OYSTERS ABALONE — but nothing is offered inside but ... coffee,[475] to the final dinner (a Last Supper?) prepared by Chastain's widow.[476]

When there is nothing to digest, the stomach acid of hunger begins to break down illusory "truths" and to recollect things conveniently "forgotten."[477]

Road signs, crossings, lies and new meanings all lead us to the one counter-example, Griffin's fury over his deception by Cherokee Jack (he of the absurdly illiterate sign):

"There's nothing I hate more'n a liar."

Well, we needn't attribute much to that; despite the theme song, Griffin still has enough "pride in myself" to be piqued at being tricked by another roadside trickster, and this needn't lead us to attribute any real moral concern to him, just a bit of hypocrisy – and what's more Hermetic than that?

While at the café, Griffin engages in some hard-to-stomach Griffinizing

---

[473]   Referencing Hyde, p. 66.

[474]   "Cook goes to walk away, but the attendant stops him, giving him what sounds like a complete and annotated list of the entire inventory of his wife's store. I'm even originally from the South, and I have absolutely no idea what half of these foods are. It sounds like he says, 'Hog jaw, pickle pig feet, cy belly, rib in can syrup, anything.' Next, the attendant will try to con them into buying that old jar of pickled eggs that's been sitting on the shelf since the Great Depression. In the back of the truck, Griffin gets a truly pained expression on his face. He must really be jonesing for some hog jaw." *The Agony Booth*, op. cit.

[475]   "Ah, a Coleman Francis motif!" exclaims Tom Servo.

[476]   Even here, and in the next day's shopping trip, we hardly see Coleman touch his plate, while Cook (appropriately!) is stuffing his face like a true hobo. "You sure fix fine vittles," he sighs. The shopping trip is itself a blunder, leading to their identification and capture.

[477]   Jorjani, loc. cit.

which I think we can even squeeze into his Trickster role. He kills the old man, but he was obviously ripe for death.[478] and throwing him down the well is again a kind of inverted reference to the World Tree.

As for the daughter, well, MST3K does cut it out; but even then, her off-key hymn singing leads the 'bots to say "I heartily endorse throwing her down the well" and describe her as "the lure of the Siren", making Griffin the wily trickster Odysseus.

In line with his Hermetic Prometheanism and Nietzscheism, Griffin rejects the "siren" call of compassion. Both deaths then are somewhat mercy killings — the old man did say he wanted to "fold up and pull out" — and anyway, Griffin does immediately pay the price: the cash register is empty, the trickster tricked.[479]

Jorjani contrasts "the trickster and arch-comedian[480] who buzzes about mumbling lies"[481] to the pure, "Solar Oracle" of Zeus," and notes that it is the Semitic religions — Christianity and Islam — that trace their origins to Gabriel, the analogue of Hermes. How much more conventionally respectable an ancestor could Griffin be expected to have?[482]

---

[478]   "She's been blind since, y'know, her husband got killed in the war. Doctors have done everything for her. With no effect. Spent all my money. Since that freeway went in, I lost all my business. I guess there's not much use trying! May as well fold up and pull out."

[479]   "It is recognized that the sacrifice and dismemberment of the victim are acts of cruelty and even treachery and this is the original sin of the gods, in which all men participate." Coomaraswamy, *Hinduism and Buddhism*, p. 12.

[480]   Sally Jupiter: "Things are tough all over, cupcake. It rains on the just and unjust alike. The Comedian was a little bit of both." (*Watchmen*, Snyder, 2009). Coleman's oeuvre was revived on Comedy Central; his resemblance to Curly Howard is frequently pointed out by Mike and the 'bots when screening R, though in both Watchmen and R the "comedian" partakes in a graphic rape sequence. In fact, despite his more obviously "comical" appearance Griffin dispatches people as easily as The Comedian, using hands, guns (he reveals that he has a pistol strapped to his ankle in the Cuba jail — where did it come from? When did he get it? — and he's a master of the just turn and shoot school), and even dropping an old man down a well. The Comedian apparently assassinates JFK; this is often attributed to the CIA (e.g., Oliver Stone's 1991 *JFK*) in revenge for, among other things, the Bay of Pigs disaster Griffin participates in.

[481]   MST3k immediately notices the resemblance of Coleman to Curly Howard of the Three Stooges, and from the credits onward we are prepared for his lying and shapeshifting: "Coleman Francis is Curly Howard in … The Fugitive!" Coleman's subsequent performance is largely mumbled, perhaps due to his lingering problems with sound-sync.

[482]   Jorjani's main interest here is drawing a further analogy between the Semitic revelations and the trickery associated with UFO's and other alien visitors and communications. There might be a further parallel here with Griffin's shamanistic flights, including his final

Besides, if like Jorjani we reject the "One True God" yet must postulate some kind of god to render existence less futile, then we have been, as he concludes: "Gifted with a new world – but only if ... we can steal it." [483]

Or as Cook says,

If we stick together, maybe we can get money!

Excursus: Cook and Landis

Cook and Landis are the two hoboes Coleman hitches up with; there's a tendency, given Coleman's overall failure at characterization,[484] to treat them as the Rosencrantz and Guildenstern of R, and I confess that in writing this essay I may have on occasion confused the two names,[485] but I think they deserve some comment on their own, both singly and together.

Landis is played by Tony Cardoza, the only actor — I think — to appear in all three films, even "starring" in S as well as being the producer and financier of all three. Here he takes the backseat to Coleman, but I think he at least presents us with what a saga researcher would call a "secondary cycle," shadowing our Hero, Coleman; and that's some shadow.

"appearance" as narration to an overhead shot of his baffled pursuers — still trying to figure out the "penny and a broken cigarette" left behind — which recalls the ending of Rocky Horror Picture Show, whose connection to UFO and Alien Abductions accounts is explored in Bruce Rux's *Hollywood vs. The Aliens: The Motion Picture Industry's Participation in UFO Disinformation* (Berkeley, Cal.: Frog Limited, 1997).

[483] Jorjani, loc. cit., where he only italicized "we."

[484] "The "characters" are about as charming as my living room furniture. (And I live in a crack house.) The three main characters actually have negative personality. That is to say, as I watched this movie, personality was sucked out of me and I become a significantly less interesting person than I was before I saw it." *The Agony Booth*, op. cit. On negative personality, Coleman was ahead of his time; reviewing the Coen Bros' *Inside Llewyn Davis*, Miles W. Mathis starts off with "I hated Oscar Isaac (above) from the first scene. ... Like all modern-day movie people, Isaac has zero or negative charisma. All he has is nice hair, but that isn't really enough, is it? Plus, his hair is actually too good. Under the circumstances, it always looks about three steps better than it should, which makes you hate him and the directors just that much more." See "The Folk Scene was Totally Manufactured", http://mileswmathis.com/folk.pdf.

[485] The muddy sound recording and poor dubbing by perhaps random actors (a Wellesian touch!) doesn't help. Also, for some reason, the edits in the MST3k version, perhaps based on an existing television print, remove some key lines, as I'll indicate in what follows.

Initially, he is the driver of the truck that Coleman jumps onto to escape the bloodhounds, riding hidden on the truck bed. Actually, he's not very well hidden; he never bothers to lift up the tailgate (a "goof" or deliberate) and the gas station attendant clearly sees him but though puzzled, does nothing.[486] Anyway, when flying to Cuba he takes the backseat to Coleman, but the latter, as we've seen, observes "My friend here can fly" which he proves by later taking the wheel of the stolen plane to escape from Cuba. When on the trips to and from Ruby Chastain's house, it's Landis at the wheel.

When we first meet Cook and Landis, the latter is holding a tire iron which is clearly shot so as to resemble a cross or crucifix;[487] the investigating deputy tells him to "Get rid of it" and he does so immediately. The abandonment of Christianity, and the ability "to fly" clue us in to Landis as a fellow shaman, perhaps a neophyte in training, still tied to the Wheel of Progress (Coleman's ironic name for *samsara*).

And so, it is given to Landis to announce the theme: told they'll get "a thousand bucks [to pass?] when it's over," he mumbles: "Maybe won't be over."[488]

Landis is the one of the pair who seems ready to give up Coleman to the cop until restrained by Cook — "Griffin'll kill you!" he stage-whispers — so perhaps he might have been able to escape the Wheel if he'd had more courage and handed over Griffin. "I'll be watching you" threatens Griffin; why not just kill him now? I guess the same reason Bond villains never just kill Bond: he is a potential successor.[489]

It's Landis whose questioning of the gas jockey yields the knowledge of a job available at a camp where they "send men to fight in Cuba,"[490] while Cook's negotiations with Cherokee Jack seem to leave them with the short

---

[486]   "I thought I heard something last night" Landis mumbles, to which one of the 'bots adds "But I was too lazy to turn my head and look."

[487]   "The Lord be with you!" mumbles Crow.

[488]   "Oooh, Tony, you're deep!" snarks Crow, reminding us of how Cardoza's acting in B was sneered at as "Tony Cardoza gets deep into character and then just sits there."

[489]   One of the lines cut from the MST3k version. "There are always two" as George Lucas tells us. "Inherit my mantle and surpass my achievements" says Dr. Lecktor to the Tooth Fairy. I address the Bond/Villain dynamic, first outlined by Kingsley Amis, in "Passing the Buck," above.

[490]   Another scene cut from MST3k, leaving the question of how they found out about the camp a mystery unfairly chalked up to Coleman's incompetence,

end of the stick. Landis accompanies Griffin to the café and helps him throw the owner down the well (an inversion of the scaling the Tree motif of metaphysical escape), while Cook is sent to watch the road. Griffin, however, sends Landis to fix/steal the owner's Buick and returns to the café to rape the blind daughter alone.[491]

The parent/child, guru/chela role is apparent when Griffin demands that Landis "give up" a ring given to him by his father. "I don't care if Moses gave it to you" — having dropped the Christian cross, he must also "give up on" the Torah — sneers Griffin, who then whips off his belt and beats Landis like a red-headed stepchild.[492]

During the beating[493] Cook is grinning and jumping around like a monkey. Cook is "played" by Harold Saunders, who was briefly in S. He makes no attempt to hide or alter his thick Brooklyn accent, which puzzles reviewers who wonder how he can be a Southern migrant laborer. I think, however, that it is the key to his role here. He's a typical New York "wise guy" or "schmarty" who thinks he knows more than anyone else in any given situation. He takes it upon himself to introduce the pair to the deputy at the beginning, and later to Griffin.[494] In the first case, he enunciates the theme:

"We follow the harvest. Crops froze up North, we come down South."

Cyclical repetition; and futile as well: the gas jockey will comment that the "crops are all froze … fruit pickers on relief" before revealing that the CIA is apparently the biggest employer now.

---

[491] MST3k cuts the rape scene, and consequently we never see, or rather, hear, Cook shouting a warning from the road. Is Griffin exercising *droit de seigneur* or assigning an ascetic trial to Landis? The whole scene of the deserted café, "where everything dried up" when the new highway went in, the menu is bizarrely painted all over the walls but only coffee — of course! —is available inside, the blind damsel, the well, etc. simply screams Grail Legend.

[492] Given the framing of the shot, one of the 'bots says he "hopes that's his belt he's whipping out!"

[493] The ring, and the mountain they are seeking, containing a mine of treasure, suggests *Lord of the Rings*, but the staging here, on a slag heap, recalls the confrontation of Anakin and Obi Wan at the climax of *Revenge of the Sith*, continuing the "chosen one/there are always two" motif.

[494] Again, the framing and dubbing make the latter scene confusing as to who's talking, a typical Colman motif.

In the second case, he exposits that "we've been up the river" but now they are looking for "honest work" and "no more iron cages," a rather Weberian phrase that suggests the imprisonment of the soul in the warp and woof (iron bars) of material existence.

Cook's smug self-assurance leads to the film's pivotal moment. Lying horizontally on their cots in the CIA camp, trying to sleep, motor-mouth Cook says that Griffin never told them "how you busted out." With evidently great reluctance, Griffin grunts out:

"Drain pipe. Dug up some dirt. I worked three long months."

Somehow, this rings a bell for Cook, and he starts to speak in an oddly dissociated voice (a bigger budget might insert a flashback here), recalling that

"Seems like I read about a Griffin once. Called him The Cotton King of the South."

This Cotton King's business strategy was simple: sell a bunch of cotton, then steal it back. Surprisingly, this did not work in the long run: "They sent him up for a long stretch. Seems like … a thousand years ago."

Cook, apparently eager to show off his newspaper reading ability, and, as *The Agony Booth* puts it,

[O]bviously not very good at determining the right moment to shut up, … then says that the Cotton King's wife has "spent all the money and become a street walker!" He then remarks that the newspapers all had pictures of her, and calls her "a beautiful broad!" Ah, those hoboes, so refreshingly un-PC.

Suddenly, and quite hilariously, all this "your wife's a whore" talk boils over, and Griffin jumps out of nowhere and starts strangling Cook. Unfortunately, he doesn't finish the job — the bastard! — and he just gets up off of him and goes back to his cot to lie down. Cook lifts his head up for a second to silently stare at Griffin, but then just lowers his head back down and goes to sleep. Sure, Griffin just tried to kill him, but that's nothing to get all riled-up over. Anyway, we fade to black.[495]

---

[495] *Agony Booth* review, op. cit. The 'bot later suggest he should ask the camp commander "Are your roommates supposed to strangle you?"

Cook is clearly trying to drag Griffin back to the past, which Griffin clearly wants to forget or overcome.[496] He insists Griffin tell the story of how he made his escape, then further back, to his life of riches, fame, and a beautiful wife, all of which have proven ephemeral.

Griffin responds by leaping up, out of the horizontal position, and standing vertically over Cook, strangling him into silence.

Saunder's rather simian features — one reviewer calls him "a living cartoon character" — and especially his laughing and hopping around as Landis is being beaten, clue us into his role as the idiot sidekick, often literally a monkey, who serves as an illustrative foil for the Hero, reminding him of the joys of a full belly and a warm bed, just as often mocking those who have them (here, he mocks the happily married, mine-owning Chastain) as those who have lost it all, such as Griffin.

At end, Cook and Landis are standing still, as we saw them in the beginning. Their lives haven't changed at all: it's back to the "iron cages" as another deputy arrests them. They are oddly standing stock still (another Coleman "goof"), but this serves to emphasize the paradoxical immobility of endless repetition; simultaneously, we intercut to Griffin, also standing, but he is in the middle of a field which he has run across to the center – the Primal Man standing at the World Pole in the center of the phenomenal field.[497]

Ground Zero. Yucca Flats. Trinity.

There, he is not arrested[498] but instead (in the usual Coleman Francis nod to vigilante justice) shot down, falling stiffly onto the field.[499] But as we've seen, this is immediately subverted by the voice of Coleman/Griffin voicing over, apparently from Above, speaking "Griffin's" epitaph in the third person. No more iron cages.

---

[496]   "Hearing my name from out of the mouths of others is like being caught in a prison break." Jarrad Ackert, "Do Not Believe in Yourself," *Aristokratia IV*, ed. K. Deva (Manticore Press, 2017).

[497]   See Boris Nad, op. cit.

[498]   "Our conscious "life" is a process, subject to corruption and death. It is this life that must be "arrested" if we are to live immortally." Coomaraswamy, *Hinduism and Buddhism*, p87.

[499]   "Glad did I live and gladly die / And I laid me down with a will." Robert Louis Stevenson, "Requiem."

"Goodbye horses/ I'm flying over you."[500]

Shock Waves of an A-bomb. A Once powerful and Humble man. Reduced to ... Nothing

What happened to Coleman Francis? He seems, appropriately enough, to have simply disappeared, along with his film legacy. Cinematographer and friend Lee Strosnider says he "went down drastically." Backer, producer and "actor" Tony Cardoza recalls:

Q: When was your last encounter with Coleman Francis?

ANTHONY: The last time I saw him, he was about Tor's weight. After being only like 200 pounds, he went up to about 350. He was on a bus bench with an overcoat, and he looked like he was gone ... three sheets to the wind. I don't know what happened to him. I was driving by and I saw him on the bench and I couldn't believe my eyes. I felt sorry for him, but at the same time ... you know ... you gotta take care of yourself and your family.

Q: I was told that he later died under strange circumstances.

ANTHONY: Coleman Francis' body was found in the back of a station wagon at the Vine Street Ranch Market.

Q: Was it natural causes, or ...?

ANTHONY: Nobody knows. I don't know, he doesn't know – he's dead! [Laughs] Nobody seems to know. There was a plastic bag over his head and a tube going into his mouth or around his throat. I don't know if he committed suicide, or ... I have no idea. Never looked it up because we were on the outs at the time.

As the mock-narration of "No Dialogue Necessary" intones in an imitation of the inimitable Francis narration style:

---

[500] "Goodbye Horses" by Psyche, as featured during Buffalo Bill's mirror dance in *The Silence of the Lambs* (Demme, 1990). Horses are a traditional symbol of worldly desires.

Coleman Francis, forgotten filmmaker. Spent his days filming moving vehicles. Mysteriously found in his own vehicle, not moving. A victim of man's inhumanity to man.

Like Ruby, shoved into the back of the pickup truck (just as Griffin hides in the back of the hoboes' truck at the beginning), or Griffin himself lying horizontal in the field (symbolized by the "ranch market").

That last bit about "inhumanity," of course, is just another mocking quote from the original B narration. Rather, I think Coleman was the "victim" if you will of his inhumanity to ... himself. That is, as we said about the ending of R, Coleman achieved the shamanic transcendence of self — note the references to extreme body modification and unrecognizability — and simply disappeared from the range of three-dimension vision – "like he was gone."[501]

"Blessed is the man on whose tomb can be written *Hic jacet nemo*." [Here lies no one].[502]

Filmography

Like the cast of *Citizen Kane*, the work of Coleman Francis may be new to many of you. If you feel a desire to expose yourself to them – and for once, the bacteriological or radiological metaphor is apt – I highly recommend viewing the MST3K versions rather than the "uncut" originals, which can be found on YouTube ... if you must.

Only B has a commercial DVD release, but as you can imagine, copies of various degrees of legality are floating of the other two. The MST version benefits from two fine though somewhat overlapping documentaries about Francis's filmmaking career. About this 'uncut' business: MST usually cuts films to fit the timeslot and to make room for various bits. B is short enough already to actually need not one but two shorts to pad out the episode; S shortens some of the innumerable, interminable skydiving "action" sequences and some of the antics of the gang of weirdos but otherwise nothing is lost; moreover, the MST disc includes the "uncut" version on the flipside.

---

[501] Rene Guénon speculates on the similar fate of one who has transcended the conditions of our temporal plane in *Man and His Becoming According to the Vedanta*.

[502] A. K. Coomaraswamy, *Hinduism and Buddhism*, p. 30.

Z is the most effected; the rape of the blind woman is cut due to its lack of comedic value, but otherwise there are a dozen or more pointless quick cuts, some in mid shot or sentence, that are likely to have already been made in an old TV print. Most of the loss is at the beginning, allowing for the 'bots to make plenty of somewhat unfair jokes about the herky-jerky narrative. Above all, we never see how the hoboes find out about Cuba, and the important bridge section is cut from the theme song.

Nevertheless, I would advise not viewing either B or Z unless you feel a powerful need to experience Full Metal Coleman. R actually has a bit of zip and "action" to it, what with invading Cuba and all, but B, although short, can seem like a whole lifetime, and S is one of the most deadening, depressing, suicide-inducing experiences available in the cinema. (Personally, like TV's Frank, I love it).

If you insist on the uncut experience, perhaps the easiest and safest way thing would be to avoid actually watching them and instead consult the incredibly detailed and amusingly snarky "recaps" of "The Coleman Francis Trilogy" over at *The Agony Booth*, with extensive screenshots and transcripts. Enjoy!

Manos Redivivus

"Why is he sleeping on a pile of dirt?"

"This movie has deep philosophical significance."

"What about the beer bottles?"

"Oh ...."[503]

W ell, here it is: the bottom of the bottomless barrel,[504] the worst of the worst – the loathed[505] and legendary Worst Movie of All Time: *Manos, the Hands of Fate.*[506] Comes now this two disc version, on DVD and Blu-Ray, that surely must be considered definitive.[507] And there's nothing in all this restoration and commentary that comes close to in any way challenging the film's reputation.[508]

---

[503] Jackey and Tom Neyman, commentary track.

[504] "Coleman Francis is at the bottom of the barrel that's beneath the one Ed Wood is in." — Larry Blamire, interviewed in "No Dialogue Necessary: The Making of an Off-Camera Masterpiece," a featurette on the DVD version of the MST3k episode *Beast of Yucca Flats.*

[505] "Oh Joel, there's a plethora of loathsomeness" says Crow T. Robot as the end credits begin to roll.

[506] According to Wikipedia: "*Manos* holds a 0% rating on Rotten Tomatoes based on 11 reviews. The book *Hollywood's Most Wanted* lists *Manos* as the #2 in the list of "The Worst Movies Ever Made," following *Plan 9 from Outer Space. Entertainment Weekly* proclaimed *Manos* "The Worst Movie Ever Made." The scene in which the seven-year-old Debbie is dressed as one of the Master's wives was included in a list of "The Most Disgusting Things We've Ever Seen" by the Mystery Science Theater 3000 crew."

[507] New 2K restoration; audio commentary; *Hands: The Fate of MANOS* Featurette; Restoring the Hands of Fate Featurette; FELT: The Puppet Hands of Fate Featurette; *Manos: The Hands of Fate*: Grindhouse Edition (Blu-ray only).

[508] "Will I have a bad rep?" is a line suggested by Tom Servo as the teenage girl in *Manos* confronts the highway cops.

But why? Why this film of all films?[509] Other films certainly have their own urgent, unique claims.

It's not like there are no other candidates, even within the somewhat arbitrary universe of "movies I saw on MST3k." For example,[510] *The Creeping Terror* shares *Manos*' origins in a bet (that the director could make a scary movie just like those guys in Hollywood), casting of the director in a starring role (though under the pseudonym, "Vic Savage"), entirely overdubbed soundtrack (the original having been lost, supposedly, in Lake Mead), and above all, arguably the worst cinematography in history – some shots are so over-exposed that the screen is almost entirely white, making *Manos*, even in its unrestored state, seem like a Technicolor blockbuster.

Other films share the incompetent filmmaking but go one better in post-production. *Monster A Go-Go* and *The Dead Talk Back* also dispense, for whatever reason, with sound sync, in favor of narrators; but the first was never even finished (Bill Rebane sold the remains to schlockmeister Herschel Gordon Lewis, who patched in new scenes, using some but not all of the original actors[511]), while *Dead*, finished, sat on a film lab shelf from 1957 to 1997 when it was discovered and shipped directly to Mystery Science Theater. Both movies also share the supremely irritating trait of cheating the ending: "There was no monster," the narrator sternly informs us, and, as Tom Servo exclaims, "Hey, the dead never talked back!"

The attentive reader will have noted that so far all these movies (one doesn't have to be Pauline Kael to hesitate calling them "films") are of the sci-fi/horror genres. It's true that these genres, much to the chagrin of their fans, do tend to produce a lot of junk.[512] Or it may be, that their fans are seriously devoted enough[513] to demand a high level of performance

---

509   "But why? What's the difference between 17 and 20?" demands the teenage boy in the educational short "Are You Ready for Marriage?"

510   I discuss these films, briefly, at the end of my "Essential Films ... & Others," http://www.counter-currents.com/2015/02/essential-films-and-others/#more-53076.

511   "This is like an entirely different movie" Joel says in stunned amazement during Episode 421; unfortunately, the new movie is just as bad.

512   Lovecraft, of course, was a frequent and rigorous critic of this fellow "authors," while for sci-fi, the legendary Theodore Sturgeon defensively formulated his well-known Law, or Revelation, that "90% of everything is crap."

513   The stereotypical "nerd," demanding to know why dome detail was changed, and proclaiming, like the *Simpsons*' Comic Book Guy, "worst [blank] ever."

to match the seriousness of the theme, making the gap between aim and achievement more visible, and risible, than in, say, a failed Hollywood rom-com like *Gigli*.[514]

But it can happen elsewhere: take *The Wild World of Batwoman*, where the sci-fi elements (a superheroine with no particular abilities or fashion sense, a mad scientist whose role is realized mainly through splicing in scenes from *The Mole People* and an Mexican wrestling movie) are combined with an apparently[515] deliberate attempt at "comedy" or satire of some kind; the gap here produces 80 minutes of continuous douche chills.[516]

Douche chills, however, will keep you awake. Just as its craggy non-actors have "broken the face barrier," *The Starfighters* is easily the most boring, sleep-inducing movie ever made.[517] Designed, apparently (more research is needed on this), to convince NATO that the F-104 Starfighter was worthy of purchase, despite a comically deadly accident record,[518] its

---

[514] Patton Oswald, apparently an MST3k fan (he moderates a couple of Comic Con MST3k panels that appear on the DVDs) has a bit where he fills in the blanks on the typical movie preview "From the director of BLANK and the star of BLANK, comes BLANK" with various flatulent noises. See Gregory Hood's Counter-Currents review of Oswald's "black comedy" *Big Fan* at http://www.counter-currents.com/2011/10/big-fan/.

[515] Directors frequently insist, like Martin Short's Nathan Thurm character, that of course, they were actually trying to be funny, why would you think otherwise? For example, Lewis insisted that whatever Rebane thought he was doing, he, Lewis, at least knew it was crap and tried to turn it into a *Twilight Zone* parody. As *Mad* magazine told us long ago (to the tune of "The Rain in Spain"), "An ad that's bad will wind up spoofed in *Mad*." As a further turn of the screw, directors began sending their own recent but unknown films to MST3k in hopes of generating enough "so bad it's good" buzz to pump up home video sales or even, as with Hobgoblins, finance a sequel.

[516] *Angels' Revenge*, a *Charlie's Angels* rip-off, has the same effect, not only humiliating TV sitcom legends like Alan Hale, Jr, Jim Backus and Pat Buttram, but also dragging in the declining Peter Lawford and even Jack Palance, pre-Batman and pre-Oscar™.

[517] In color, at least. *Radar Secret Service* (1950), with its washed out, grey print, grey men and grey clothing and vehicles, takes the black and white title, employing what MST3k calls "sleep-induction through hypno-helio-static-stasis" (Episode 620).

[518] The movie's base commander proudly says "it's even been called a rocket with a man in it," but in the real world it was known as "The Brick with Wings" and "The Widowmaker." Ten years later, Robert Calvert of Hawkwind would record a "satirical concept album" based on the Luftwaffe's experience with the plane: *Captain Lockheed and the Starfighters* (UA, 1974) Musicians who appeared on the album include members of Hawkwind, The Pink Fairies, Brian Eno, Arthur Brown, Jim Capaldi and Adrian Wagner; https://en.wikipedia.org/wiki/Captain_Lockheed_and_the_Starfighters.

combination of stock footage and non-actors[519] creates a cinematic black hole.

"It's like they forgot to have things happen."

"I really think there's more nothing in this movie than any we've ever seen."[520]

"Nothing," however, can only remind us of the final challenger to *Manos*, the first entry in the Coleman Francis Trilogy (the Godfather Saga of bad films), *The Beast of Yucca Flats*.

"About the most nothing film I've seen ... little more than a home movie someone might make." (Bob Burns, "film historian and erstwhile movie gorilla")

"An incredibly deadening experience." (Larry Blamire, B-movie director)

"Before this movie, there was no such thing as clinical depression." (Tom Servo, robot)[521]

And yet ... Bad as it is, *Beast* does edge out *Manos*, if only on points.

Beast's narration has its own Dadaist charms.[522] The cinematography is really rather good; although this was cameraman Lee Strosnider's first chance to film 16mm, he had just come form several years making industrial films, while Hal Warren came straight from industry — fertilizer, in fact — and was actually using little more than a home movie camera.[523] Larry Blamire comments on the "heartbreaking" quality of the shots of the Flannery O'Connor-esque mother wandering around looking

---

[519]   As the gang says about *The Skydivers,* Episode 609, rather than have the actors do their own flying, they had the flyers do their own acting.

[520]   MST3k, Episode 620.

[521]   All from the DVD extra "No Dialogue Necessary: The Making of an Off-Camera Masterpiece."

[522]   "I thought I was listening to *Spoon River Anthology* performed by atomic mutants." – Larry Blamire.

[523]   The MST DVD includes not only extensive contributions from Strosnider in the "making of" featurette — "No Dialogue Necessary: The Making of an Off-Camera Masterpiece" — he also gets his own interview segment, "Coleman Francis: The Cinematic Poet of Parking."

for her lost boys, and Frank Conniff ("TV's Frank") refers to the "dark kind of lyricism" seen in the next film, *The Skydivers* (although, as he admits, no one else agrees).

And that's the main reason: *Beast* is part of a trilogy, and needs to be judged as such.[524] Above all, it's only in the context of the three films together that the elements of repetition and futility emerge which make Francis's work the mythological masterpiece that it is.[525]

Repetition and masterpiece: that brings us to *Manos*. If you've read this far, you likely know the "plot," which has been summarized as:

> The peculiarly-paced story of a deeply uncharismatic man (director Warren) taking his wife Margaret (Diane Mahree) and daughter Debbie (Jackey Neyman) on a vacation that runs afoul of a cult led by the plurally-married Master (Tom Neyman) and his jittery, big-kneed manservant Torgo (John Reynolds).[526]

So why does anyone care about this cinematic turd, and why care about polishing it? Why any "bad" movie? Consider this:

> In attempting to explain the film's appeal, the *Los Angeles Times* hypothesized, "After screening *Manos* for probably the 10th time, I've concluded it has to do with intimacy. Because it is such a pure slice of Warren's brain — he wrote, directed, produced and starred, and brooked no collaboration — *Manos* amounts to the man's cinematically transfigured subconscious."[527]

---

[524]   Of a gunfight from ten feet away, after a careful, lovingly drawn out parking sequence, Crow remarks that "He's trying things here he'll perfect in *Red Zone Cuba*."

[525]   As in my review of the Coleman Francis Trilogy, above. *Starfighters* goes perhaps too far in the direction of entropy; the absence of "things happening" entails, of course, an inability to suggest the endless repetition of things. There is, however, the endless, repeated "refueling" stock footage, a lame practical joke that occurs twice (and actors so generic as to prompt the comment "Is that that one guy?") as well stock footage of take-offs/landings; the latter perhaps suggest the puppet theme as well, although, since the emphasis is on how gosh darn safe the F-104 is, there's only one bailout, and it's off camera. Francis's *Skydivers* (note the linguistic similarity) will by contrast be entire constructed of planes taking off and landing, and the eponymous skydivers diving, with the later a combination of stock footage and close-up shots of the actors hanging from harnesses in a warehouse.

[526]   "*Manos: The Hands of Fate* Restored – The So-Called "Worst Movie" Has Never Looked Better," by Sherilyn Connelly on *The Robot's Voice*, March 14, 2014, http://www.therobotsvoice.com/2014/03/manos_the_hands_of_fate_the_restoration_in_progres.php.

[527]   Wikipedia, quoting Dan Neil, "Why We Love Bad Movies," *Los Angeles Times*, August

But I, at least, am not interested in some pseudo-science like "psychoanalysis," but rather in the super-science of Traditional metaphysics.[528] As Luis Varady has recently pointed out, the ancient wise men may have lack our physics and astronomy, but since they had the ancient teaching that "As above, so below," the Microcosm is the Macrocosm ...

> All things mirror all things and to fully understand even a small fragment of reality gives an insight into reality as a whole – this is a common teaching in the mystical traditions of the world.[529]

... they could learn the deeper truths about reality by studying their own consciousness,[530] the results of which study they encoded in stories we call "myths."

Cosmological myths were used as a means to convey spiritual truths, and these spiritual truths pointed directly at the true nature of our psychology.

And so:

7, 2005.

[528] Let's get the "psychology" out of the way. Judging from the recollections of the actresses in the "making of" featurette, Hal Warren seems to have been the usual horndog/control freak typical of the males of the Mad Man era: suggesting an actress take off her blouse, then quickly retreating to "just joking" when she refuses; entering the same actress in the Miss Texas contest without her knowledge, a publicity stunt that backfires when tells the judges that she's an atheist, etc. This is clearly manifested in the film in three sequences: the infamous nightgown wrestling of the Master's wives (the MST crew suggest "this is why the film was made"); the scene where one of the wives sees the husband/director unconscious and tied to a tree, whereupon she begins to kiss him, lick his face, and then slap him (as Tom Neyman says on the commentary track, "Sure, it's what every woman wants"); and a scene cut from the MST version, in which the Master slaps his own tied up wife. Misogynistic, yes, but too amateurishly made to be either erotic or disturbing. Hal Warren though had nothing on the director of the above-mentioned *The Creeping Terror*, the Bob Crane-like Vic Savage, who "makes Ed Wood look like Ward Cleaver" according to the recent bioflick, *The Creep Behind the Camera* (Peter Scheurman, 2014).

[529] "To know and love one other human being is the root of all wisdom." – Evelyn Waugh, *Brideshead Revisited*.

[530] More recently, Bernardo Kastrup, in expounding his neuroscience-based "analytic idealism," has observed that if everything we perceive is a part of Mind, then "to understand the underlying nature of [the human] mind one has to turn inward, toward introspection and away from measurement [of a supposed 'outside' world]." See his *Why Materialism is Balone* (iff Books, 2014), p. 202.

It is not the reasonableness or likelihood of a myth that attracts human beings to it. Rather, a myth's attraction is its potential ability to convey spiritual or moral truths to every member of society, from the most intellectual to the illiterate.[531]

In the same way, it is not the "reasonableness or likelihood" of a movie — the myths of the 20th century — that explains their appeal, but their "potential ability to convey spiritual or moral truths to every member of society." And this potential is stronger in bad movies, which lack the pseudo-intellectual "sophistication" of the "quality production," which is usually just a big budget rehash of mainstream ideology, instead, most often accidentally, flying under the radar of both the director's consciousness and industry censorship.[532]

Furthermore, that "bad" movies should be the focus of attention makes sense, since humans have an odd relationship with truth, especially metaphysical truths about themselves and their situation: they crave it, yet fear and loathe it at the same time.

And this, I think, is the key to the "bad film": it sounds themes we suspect are true and important, but which we don't want to admit; hence, we mock it, as the Roman soldiers and crucified thief mocked Christ. "It's only a movie, and a bad one at that."

Regarding about the Gnostics, and why they lost out to the "orthodox" Christians, Michael Hoffman writes at his EgoDeath website:

Why did people embrace childish lower-level Christianity (i.e., literal interpretation of the myths)?

---

[531]   Luis Varady: *The Wisdom of the Serpent: The Gnostic Trinity of the Peratae* (Amazon Kindle, 2015). For more on Varady, see "Lords of the Visible World: A Modern Reconstruction of an Ancient Heresy," my review of his earlier essay *A Life Beyond Change: The Gnostic System of Carpocrates* (Amazon Kindle, 2015), reprinted in my *Mysticism After Modernism: Crowley, Evola, Neville, Watts, Colin Wilson & Other Populist Gurus* (Melbourne, Australia: Manticore Press, 2020).

[532]   See my discussion of Robert Aldrich's *Kiss Me Deadly*, whose intentions were subverted precisely because the screenwriter "had contempt for the material" and "wrote it fast, on autopilot," thus allowing Traditional themes to emerge. "Mike Hammer, Occult Dick: *Kiss Me Deadly* as a Lovecraftian Tale," reprinted in *The Eldritch Evola ... & Others* (San Francisco: Counter-Currents, 2014).

People were starting to shy away from some of the painful truths revealed in the mysteries. They had mixed feelings about being mere puppets of gods/fates.[533]

The scriptures offered a choice between supernaturalist Literalism that takes pseudo-history as reality, and allegorical myth that reveals determinism – most people chose to stay in the supernaturalist reading.

If some Michael,[534] Captain of the Deterministic Angels, were to actually do as the New Testament prophecies and reveal the Christian mystery of God's kingdom, and this kingdom turns out to be entheogenic Christ-myth determinism, and "eternal" life is experienced only during this life, most people would plug their ears.

What use is a mere revelation of the metaphysical truth about moral agency, especially when such a revelation robs us of infinitely open possibilities and puts strict limitations on the types of freedom we can have? This is the already famous red pill versus blue pill choice from the movie *The Matrix*: would you rather slumber in often-comfortable fantasy or awaken to often-uncomfortable truth? Do you want the bliss of fantastic, uncritical, wishful thinking, or the sober intellectual satisfaction of high rational integrity?

If you could resolve your metaphysical intellectual discomfort by waking up to deterministic consistency, would you want to?

If God's kingdom is deterministic, we don't want it. It is no wonder the quantum physicists rejected (by fiat) finite, hidden-variables determinism and insisted on the endless magic of Copenhagenism instead. It is no wonder people chose the psychologically open-ended Literalist reading of Christianity rather than moving on to let the mystery of the deterministic kingdom of God be revealed.[535]

---

[533] How appropriate, then, that included with the Restored Edition as a special feature is *FELT: The Puppet Hands of Fate*, a retelling of the Manos story — one is tempted to say, the Manos myth — with puppets.

[534] Michael, of course, is our "protagonist," but apart from the aforementioned lack of charisma, I will soon suggest our "hero" is someone else.

[535] See "Motives for Literalization of Christianity" at http://www.egodeath.com/MotivesChristianLiteralization.htm.

And, on a not-unimportant related point, boredom induction conduces to transmission of spiritual truth and ultimately to enlightenment, or at least, cultic membership.

What is this mythological or metaphysical element that is feared by the masses? As already hinted, and as you might suspect from what you've heard about the movie, or seen yourself, it's repetition. Obviously, the movie is about Fate, but specifically, in the words of the title of one of the soundtrack cues, "The Futility of Fate."[536] Life here in the material world, on the samsaric plane, is an endless, horizontal round, a Circle, of the same, karma-induced events over and over; liberation/salvation/enlightenment is a matter of tossing aside karma (what I've called "passing the buck" and ascending vertically, via a Spiral (a *Turn of the Screw*), to a new level.[537]

The cyclical nature of Manos's plot is actually fairly common, even as a screenwriting technique. What raises Manos to its unique status are the ways in which Manos, deliberately or not, takes it up to eleven.

The most notable, and perhaps the one "feature" that most everyone focuses on to explain the Manos Experience, is the extreme level of repetition in the dialogue, thus making it of a piece with the cyclical nature of the plot.

Torgo: There is no way out of here. It will be dark soon. There is no way out of here.

Torgo: He has left this world. But he is with us always. No matter where he goes, he is with us.

Torgo: There is nothing to fear, Madam. The Master likes you. Nothing will happen to you. He likes you.

---

[536] Oh, and the soundtrack, the kind of laid-back jazz noodling that older guys like Warren still thought was "cool" back in the early sixties, and which I, growing increasingly fogey-ish, have lately grown fond of, calling to mind as it does long summer afternoons, light rain, and the soothing tones of Jessica Walter asking Clint Eastwood to play "Misty" for her. Although Coleman Francis mainly used free "library" music, *The Skydivers* has two interesting exceptions: a brief excerpt from Lionel Hampton's "Going Home" (prompting Tom Servo to whine "Dad, change the station!") and, by contrast, an appearance by then-famous surf guitarist Jimmy Bryant playing his then-hit, "Stratosphere Boogie."

[537] See the essays reprinted in *The Eldritch Evola*, as well as "Thanks for Watching: Awakening Through Repetition in *Groundhog Day, Point of Terror, & Manhunter*, Part 1"and "Phil & Will: Awakening Through Repetition in *Groundhog Day, Point of Terror, & Manhunter*, Part II."

Maggie: Likes me? I thought you said he was dead!

Torgo: Dead? No, Madam, not dead the way you know it. He is with us always. Not dead the way you know it. He is with us always.

And my personal favorite, Michael and Maggie's rather philosophical — or fatalistic — duet in response to his daughter's dog's disappearance:

Maggie: Pepe's gone. I just hope Debbie will understand.

Mike: She'll understand. She's my baby, she'll understand.

Maggie: I hope so, darling. I sure hope so.

Mike: She's my baby, she'll understand.

It's like listening to Charlie Parker jam with Lester Young!

Further increasing the echo-effect is the soundtrack, which, as mentioned before, is entirely post-production. For various reasons, only two men and one woman were available, so the characters' voices quickly become indistinguishable,[538] and the child's voice, clearly a woman's falsetto, achieves a Brechtian level of alienation.[539] This kind of "dubbing" leads to the "doubling" I've frequently pointed out in films with mythological subtexts.[540]

Most of the repetitive dialogue belongs to audience favorite Torgo, who also acquires the equally beloved and repetitive "Torgo's theme," [541] which sums up the movie rather like some big Hollywood themes like those of *Gone with the Wind* or *A Summer Place*.

And mentioning Torgo leads us to the second theme: who passes the buck? Certainly not Michael, who we see at the very end, has replaced Torgo, even (of course) repeating his lines:

---

[538] "Hey, that's just one guy!" mutters Joel in muted wonder.

[539] The poor child burst out in tears on hearing her "voice" during the premiere showing.

[540] For example, in Brian De Palma's *The Untouchables*; see my review reprinted in *The Homo & the Negro: Masculinist Meditations on Politics & Popular Culture*; Second, Embiggened Edition, edited by Greg Johnson (San Francisco: Counter-Currents, 2017).

[541] https://en.wikipedia.org/wiki/File:Haunting_Torgo_Suite.ogg.

Michael: "I am Michael. I take care[542] of the place[543] while the Master is away."

No, surprisingly enough, it is Torgo who passes the buck to Michael. Yet, how can this be?[544] Torgo, when last seen, was running away, his coat sleeve aflame, while The Master held his burning, amputated hand aloft, laughing like a Bond villain.

But that's just the point: Torgo gets away. The obvious fakery of the burning hand suggests that there has been some kind of magic trick, on one or both their parts.

First Wife: You are losing your control. Even Torgo defies you.

This also makes sense of the odd moment right before, where the Master commands his wives to kill Torgo (or rather, in the Manos idiom, "Kill! ... Kill!) and they proceed to enact a kind of "liturgical dance" (MST3k) that culminates in what looks like an attempt to kill through ... massage. It's all fake, a set-up.

And finally, one can see, as Torgo is rolfed to death, that his hat has a large hole in the crown, alluding to the Traditional symbol of the vertical path of escape, like smoke through the hole at the top of a *teepee*.[545]

Or perhaps the hand, the symbolism of which is surely a displacement for the phallus, is sacrificed to the god Manos? Or is it the equivalent of the eye, which Wotan sacrifices for wisdom?[546]

---

[542]   In the first act, Michael, typically, shouted "Where the hell is that caretaker?" This is the only time Torgo is referenced as "The Caretaker." Michael's transformation at the end recalls — or rather, predates – Jack Torrance's in *The Shining*. "You have always been the caretaker."

[543]   "In dwelling upon the nature of God and the universe, the mystics of the Talmudic period asserted, in contrast to the transcendentalism evident in some parts of the Bible, that "God is the dwelling-place of the universe; but the universe is not the dwelling-place of God". Possibly the designation ("place") for God, so frequently found in Talmudic-Midrashic literature, is due to this conception, just as Philo, in commenting on Genesis 28:11 says, "God is called *ha makom* (המקום "the place") because God encloses the universe, but is Himself not enclosed by anything" (De Somniis, i. 11)." – Wikipedia on the Kabbalah.

[544]   "How can this be? For he is the *Kwisatz Haderach*!" – *Dune*. If this were MST3k, I'd shout out here "Give a dog a bone!"

[545]   See the essays collected in *The Door in the Sky: Coomaraswamy on Myth and Meaning* by Ananda Kentish Coomaraswamy, ed. by Rama P Coomaraswamy (Princeton, 1999).

[546]   See my comments on the Wotan theme embodied in the suicide of Lane Pryce in my collection, *End of An Era: Mad Men and the Ordeal of Civility* (San Francisco:

No one knows, or more significantly, no one seems to be curious about, what seems to me to be the most curious aspect of the whole production, the bizarre and unique hand symbolism[547] that permeates the film, from the title onward.[548]

Presumably, our Freudian friends will suggest this is a phallic symbol. Actually, the "hands" in question, starting with Torgo's staff, are usually upright, at the ends of arm-like structures, suggesting not so much hands as fists.[549] In any event, the symbolism seems muddled here; the vertical staff should symbolize escape or "upright" in the sense of virile and "upstanding," as Evola says in *The Hermetic Tradition*;[550] yet both Michael and the First Wife are tied to upright poles or trees, and subsequently are vanquished, while Torgo is forced to lie on a horizontal slab during his tickle-torture, and triumphs.

The symbolism is much clearer with a related theme: As Jackey Neyman ("Debbie") points out with remarkable insight, her character is always falling asleep on the couch, and the family members are always falling down – i.e., falling horizontally into *samsara*. But, she adds, Torgo never falls down, despite his unforgettable stumbling walk.[551]

Even the MST3k crew intuits this, observing that "Torgo wobbles but he won't fall down." The wobble/hand symbolisms come together when the Master once more spreads his arms to disclose the giant hands

Counter-Currents, 2015).

[547] "*Manos*" as the vibrant and diversity conscious modern viewer must know, is simply the Spanish word meaning "hands," so the title is essentially *Hands: The Hands of Fate*, which already begins to enunciate the repetition theme we will begin exploring.

[548] Apparently, quite arbitrarily. The "making of" featurette reveals that Tom Neyman (The Master) was also the production designer; he just happened to have a whole load of hand sculptures, since, as restorer Solovey says, dead pan, he had entered an artistic phase in which he was exploring the essence of hands. It was he (Neyman says) who suggested one day "Why don't we just call this "*Manos: The Hands of Fate*." But is not the theme of *Manos* that there are no "accidents"?

[549] Did Warren anticipate the practice of "fisting," which Edmund White called "the only new sexual act invented in recorded history"?

[550] At least one hand is imbedded in a block of stone, thus literally "ithyphallic." See Julius Evola, *The Hermetic Tradition* (Rochester, Vt.: Inner Traditions, 1995), as well as my essay on *Psychomania*, above.

[551] "It's like having Joe Cocker as your bellhop" (MST3k). Apart from being constantly high, John Reynolds was literally saddled with some kind of wire contraptions on his lower legs; people have speculated that he's a satyr, or goat-man, but Tom Neyman, the production designer, again reveals that they, like the hands, were just some stuff he had lying around.

embroidered on the inside of his robe,[552] and the crew suggests "Push him over!" Ultimately, this is what happens; the "Master" returns to his suspended, samsaric state, while Torgo makes a break for it. Michael and his family, attempting to escape, ultimately decide to return to the house (I guess on the principle of "they'd never think to look for us there!"), a horizontal trek that leads us back to the beginning, again.[553]

The idea that Torgo is the hero, or at least the protagonist, is not that forced. The featurette notes that the original (and only) review of the film, in the *El Paso Daily Post*, already referred to Torgo as "the hero." The character of Torgo, along with his "haunting theme music" immediately piqued the imagination of the MST3k crew, who incorporated Torgo into their cast of recurring characters (played by head writer Mike Nelson, who would eventually replace Joel Hodgson as the human host). There's the, 2008 making-of documentary is entitled *Hotel Torgo*. And as recently as March of this year,

> The murderers on the Elementary episode "T-Bone And The Iceman" used the physical features of Torgo (portrayed by John Reynolds) to compose a fake facial composite to get the NYPD off their trail. It worked for a while before they were caught, due to the character of Dr. Joan Watson having recognized Torgo's features from the film.[554]

What, then, of this restored edition? What was the condition of the earliest cut of the film, the so-called "workprint"; was the film always this hard to watch? Apparently not, according to the restoration team.

The trick about the cost-efficient on 16mm Ektachrome reversal film on which *Manos* was shot is that there was never a negative: when the film from the camera was developed, what resulted was the actual picture, not a negative thereof. That developed film was then duplicated for editing, eventually being assembled into the workprint that Solovey now possessed.

---

[552] Neyman designed this himself, and his (real) wife sewed it, but he say that it was director Warren who insisted on his doing this over and over.

[553] Torgo presumably heads for "the crossroads" where it was previously said the nearest phone is; this explains Michael's curious initial idea of "hid[ing] out in the desert until someone comes to help." The crossroad symbolism is obvious (the warp and woof of material elements) and it is from here that Torgo, like the initiate who has become the Realized Man, will ascend. See "The Corner at the Center of the World" in *The Eldritch Evola*, op. cit.

[554] Wikipedia, "*Manos: The Hands of Fate*," note 45.

It's a minor miracle that the workprint survived not only standard disposal, but also the 1994 Northridge Earthquake which (according to the Emersons) destroyed all the other extant *Manos* materials. And it's pretty, too, thanks to the inherent hardiness of Ektachrome material.

The few audiences that saw *Manos* at the time certainly didn't get to see anything as spiffy as the workprint. Once editing was complete, a 35mm blowup was made — making the picture twice as grainy — and prints for theaters were copied from that blowup. Not a single fuck was given about framing or color by the people who made those prints, resulting in a badly cropped picture with much of the color drained out. When the film hit VHS decades later, it was based on the horrible theatrical prints, and of course VHS is not exactly an archival format, so it made the picture look that much worse.

Although the result is better than anything seen by audiences in 1966, Solovey, in the restoration featurette, is adamant that the idea was not to "upgrade" the film into contemporary quality, in sound or vision, but to strip away accumulated dust, fingerprints, splices, etc., and return it to what was originally on the editing bench.

What we have here, then, is rather like the "historically informed performance practice" movement (misleadingly mislabeled "authentic practice") that aims not at a metaphysically impossible and aesthetically irrelevant attempt to "hear what the music sounded like back then" but rather to strip away centuries of acquired interpretations so that we can form our own interpretation of the work itself.[555]

So, how does the "restored" version differ from the theatrical version (included, dubbed the "Grindhouse" cut, on the Blu-ray two-disc set only) which was used on MST3k, and is available on numerous cheap DVDs (it's in the public domain[556]) other than in presentation?

---

[555]   See Nicholas Harnoncourt's remarks quoted in the liner notes to Telefunken's *Bach 2000* anniversary sampler disc (Teldec, 1999).

[556]   Or not: "*Manos: The Hands of Fate* is generally believed to be in the public domain because director Hal Warren failed to include a copyright symbol in the film (in the US in the 1960s this was enough to disqualify a film for copyright). When news broke of Solovey's restoration, the son of Hal Warren, Joe Warren, started exploring the possibility that the film was in fact not in the public domain. Joe Warren discovered in 2013 that the script had been copyrighted, and he believes this means that the film is also copyrighted. However, no precedent exists for this case so the legal status of the film is uncertain. The release of the restored film is going ahead in spite of this." – https://en.wikipedia.org/wiki/Manos:_The_Hands_of_Fate#Copyright_dispute.

Most notably, the infamous opening, a long, infinitely boring sequence of the family just driving along the highway ("The slowest car chase ever" – MST3k). The story is that this was supposed to have the opening credits superimposed, but for whatever reason — money, competence, or patience — it was never done. The non-MST DVD's I've seen just lop it off, and start with a simple title shot.[557] The restoration keeps all this footage, but starts with some establishing shots (including an appropriate "Waste" container) of the Mordor-like surroundings of the director's native El Paso ("Welcome to lovely Ground Zero" Joel says of a later "scenic" background, eerily foreshadowing 9/11).[558]

There's also the aforementioned sequence in which the Master taunts, slaps, and smears blood on his tied-up first wife. Otherwise, individual shots seem to sometime be slightly longer. Some sequences, like the family's escape attempt, have more shots included, the voices better synced; I suppose over time the theatrical release was subject innumerable cuts and splices, either to speed it up [!] for TV viewing or due to accidental damage.

There's nothing in all this that comes close to in any way challenging the film's reputation, for good or bad.[559]

In the featurette "Restoring the Hands of Fate," although he likes to use the word "schmutz" a lot, restorationist Solovey presents as an almost aggressively Western type in appearance, modest and plain spoken. He is a very trustworthy and pleasant person to listen to, considering the types one runs across in the film world.[560] He takes obvious pride in in speaking of the fine German scanner he managed to obtain for the task, and the amateur viewer tends to believe what he says about the difficulties and decisions involved in the restoration process.

Solovey ultimately makes a very important point: movies, a 20th-century invention, must be preserved, since so much of our history is now in them.[561]

---

[557]   What with "*manos*" = hands, the title sequence subtly recalls the equally accidental doubling of the Larry Buchanan opus *Attack of the Eye Creatures*; as the MST crew says, "They just ... didn't ... care."

[558]   According to the commentary track, the road is, in fact, called Scenic Drive.

[559]   "Will I have a bad rep?" is a line suggested by Tom Servo as the teenage girl confronts the highway cops.

[560]   "Investigator Graham interests me. Very purposeful looking." – *Manhunter*. "I like you, Tony, there is no lying in you." – *Scarface*.

[561]   A sentiment echoed by Bob Burns in his *Beast* interview: "All films are interesting ...

Speaking of history: one tends to think of productions like *Manos* as being in some sense auteur productions, for better or worse,[562] and so most attention has been focused on writer/producer/director/star Hal Warren. One thing that emerges from the *"Hands: The Fate of Manos"* featurette is that Tom Nyman, who played The Master, may have had far more influence on the film, providing, as he says with ironic modesty, "everything": he contributed his own daughter as the daughter, his dog is the dog, his car as one of the two cars (he's not sure which at this point), and as "production designer" he designed all the costumes (which were sewn by his wife, except for Torgo's overalls, coat, and hat, which were Tom's own) and above all, the set decorations: all those hands. Turns out, he had already sculpted dozens of such things ("His art was going through a period of fascination with hands" says Solovey, deadpan). Indeed, "One day I suggested we just call it *Manos: The Hands of Fate.*"

Graciously, Tom adds that Warren "was involved in everything on the film," And on that note, the featurette ends with Neyman, still photographer Anselm Spring (a German soldier who was hiding out — I mean, living in — El Paso), and Solovey paying homage to Warren as the kind of DIY culture-creator I've lauded before; Neyman emphasizes that Warren knew he was making a B-picture (if only!) with local community theater talent, but thought it would serve as "the start of something big." Solovey even attributes to Warren the start of "the kind of independent, self-financed" filmmaking we've become familiar with since, say, *Easy Rider* (made around the time and place of *Manos*).

Funded by a Kickstarter campaign, the restoration process itself is an instance of the same kind of "hey, let's make a movie" American can-do-ism as the movie itself – although, one must add immediately, on a far more successful level.

Finally, the audio commentary track brings us the Neymans reminiscing about the production; rather than a couple of film nerds one-upping each other with trivia, it's more like eavesdropping on a father and

---

It was a film, it did get made ... I think there's a place for every movie that's been made ... It has a place. I'm not sure what that place is, but it has a place. I don't think it should be forgotten." And Larry Blamire concurs "Every movie is important to see, even the miserably bad ones."

[562]   "Our auteur, ladies and gentlemen!" exclaims Crow T. Robot as Coleman Francis sits down on the floor of a "Cuban" jail and spreads his legs wide in *Red Zone Cuba* (Episode 621).

daughter still closely knit after all these years. Who knew *Manos* could be heartwarming?[563]

So, buy or not buy? Neophytes[564] should start with the MST3k'd version; it was available as a single disc from Rhino back in the day, now out of print, and currently Shout! Factory has a two-disc release, with the theatrical release and MST3k-centric special features.

Once — if — you decide to experience it firsthand, this set is the way to go. It makes for a far more "pleasant" viewing experience, if that word can ever be used in the context of *Manos*, and, to paraphrase Tolkien, those who approve of courtesy (at least) to long dead Texas fertilizer salesman will purchase it, and no other.

---

[563] "Say, I knew sex was corny, but who knew corn could be so sexy?" Another painful bit of "humor" from *The Starfighters*, delivered by the future Congressman Bob "B-1" Dornan.

[564] "What's a neophyte?" (MST3k, *The Starfighters*).

233

Filmography

A Dandy in Aspic (1966); 107 minutes; Directed by Anthony Mann and Laurence Harvey (uncredited); Written by Derek Marlowe (from his novel); Stars: Laurence Harvey, Mia Farrow, Tom Courtenay, Lionel Stander, Calvin Lockhart.

Breaking Bad (AMC); Created and produced by Vince Gilligan; January 20, 2008 – September 29, 2013 (62 episodes).

Gilmore Girls (2000–2007); Created by Amy Sherman; Stars: Lauren Graham, Alexis Bledel, Edward Herrmann, Melissa McCarthy, Chris Eigeman; (154 episodes).

Groundhog Day (1993); 101 minutes; Director: Harold Ramis; Writers: Danny Rubin (screenplay), Harold Ramis (screenplay); Stars: Bill Murray, Andie MacDowell, Chris Elliott, Stephen Tobolowsky.

Le Mans (1971); 106 minutes. Director: Lee H. Katzin; Writer: Harry Kleiner; Stars: Steve McQueen, Siegfried Rauch, Elga Andersen.

Manhunter (1986); 119 minutes. Director: Michael Mann; Writers: Thomas Harris (novel), Michael Mann (screenplay); Stars: William Peterson, Kim Greist, Joan Allen, Brian Cox, Dennis Farina, Tom Noonan, Chris Elliot.

Manos: The Hands of Fate – Restored Edition; 70 minutes. Written and directed by Harold P. Warren; Restoration Producer: Ben Solovey; Stars: Tom Neyman, John Reynolds, Diane Adelson, Harold P. Warren.

Point of Terror (1973); 88 minutes. Director: Alex Nicol; Writers: Peter Carpenter (story), Ernest A. Charles (screenplay); Stars: Peter Carpenter, Dyanne Thorne, Lory Hansen.

Psychomania (a.k.a. *The Death Wheelers*) (2015, 1973); 85 minutes; Synapse Studios. Director: Don Sharp; Writers: Julian Zimet, Arnaud d'Usseau; Stars: Beryl Reid, George Sanders, Nicky Henson.

Steve McQueen: The Man & Le Mans (2015); 102 minutes; Directors: Gabriel Clarke, John McKenna; Stars: Steve McQueen, Chad McQueen, Neile Adams, John Sturges, Alan Trustman, Lee H. Katzin, Jonathan Williams, Peter Samuelson.

The Coleman Francis Trilogy:

- *The Beast of Yucca Flats* (1961); Written and directed by Coleman Francis; starring Tor Johnson as The Beast; co-stars: Douglas Mellor, Barbara Francis, Coleman Francis, Bing Stafford, Tony Cardoza.

- *The Skydivers* (1963); Written and directed by Coleman Francis; starring Kevin Casey, Eric Tomlin, Anthony Cardoza, Marcia Knight, Titus Moede, Coleman Francis.

- *Red Zone Cuba* (1966; aka *Night Train to Mundo Fine*); Written and directed by Coleman Francis; starring Coleman Francis, Anthony Cardoza, Harold Saunders, Tom Hanson, Lanell Cado; special guest star: John Carradine.

Sitting Pretty (1948); Director: Walter Lang; Writers: F. Hugh Herbert (screen play), Gwen Davenport (novel); Stars: Robert Young, Maureen O'Hara, Clifton Webb.

Touch of Evil (1958); Universal; Written, directed, and starring Orson Welles; "Preview" version (108 minutes, released on DVD 1993); Theatrical release, 1958 (93 minutes); "Restored" version, 1998 (112 minutes); Based on the *Badge of Evil* by Whit Masterson; Stars: Orson Welles, Charlton Heston, Janet Leigh, Joseph Calleia, Akim Tamiroff, Ray Collins, Dennis Weaver, Mort Mills, Marlene Dietrich.

Index